THE SCOTTISH HIGHLANDS

Also in the Series

Buenos Aires by Jason Wilson
Oxford by David Horan
Mexico City by Nick Caistor
Rome by Jonathan Boardman
Madrid by Elizabeth Nash
Venice by Martin Garrett
Lisbon by Paul Buck
Havana by Claudia Lightfoot
New York City by Eric Homberger
Brussels by André de Vries
Prague by Richard Burton
Calcutta by Krishna Dutta
Helsinki by Neil Kent
Edinburgh by Donald Campbell
San Francisco by Mick Sinclair
Cambridge by Martin Garrett
Kingston by David Howard
Athens by Michael Llewellyn Smith
Istanbul by Pater Clark
Hamburg by Matthew Jefferies
Lagos by Kaye Whiteman
Miami by Anthony P. Maingot
Brittany by Wendy Mewes
Sicily by Joseph Farrell

THE SCOTTISH HIGHLANDS

A Cultural History

ANDREW BEATTIE

An imprint of Interlink Publishing Group, Inc.
Northampton, Massachusetts

First published in 2015 by
INTERLINK BOOKS
An imprint of Interlink Publishing Group, Inc.
46 Crosby Street, Northampton, Massachusetts 01060
www.interlinkbooks.com

Library of Congress Cataloging-in-Publication Data
Beattie, Andrew.
The Scottish Highlands : a cultural history / by Andrew Beattie.
pages cm. -- (Cultural histories)
Includes bibliographical references and index.
ISBN 978-1-56656-741-1 (alk. paper)
1. Highlands (Scotland)--History. 2. Highlands (Scotland)--Civilization. I. Title.
DA880.H6B43 2014
941.1'5--dc23

2014032543

Production: Devdan Sen
Cover Images: Eilean Donan Castle near Kyle of Lochalsh, David Ryznar/Shutterstock; MacDonald of Keppoch, Wikimedia Commons; overlooking Diabaig and Loch Torridon, Kevin Eaves/Shutterstock
Half-title page: Sidney Richard Percy, *Carn Dearg and Ben Nevis from Achintee*, 1874 (Wikimedia Commons)

Printed and bound in the United States of America

To request our complete 48-page full-color catalog, please call us toll free at 1-800-238-LINK, visit our website at www.interlinkbooks.com, or write to Interlink Publishing, 46 Crosby Street, Northampton, MA 01060
e-mail: info@interlinkbooks.com

Contents

Introduction

AN "ELEMENTAL" LANDSCAPE

In 1983 the American travel writer Paul Theroux, then living in London, turned his back on journeying to far-flung destinations in Asia and Latin America and instead cast his gaze closer to home. His subsequent journey around the coastline of Great Britain was to result in the book *The Kingdom by the Sea.* Of all the places Theroux visited on his trip around his adopted homeland, the Scottish Highlands seem to have made the greatest impression. The landscape, he wrote, was "elemental": unlike the Alps, Paul Theroux's Scotland was wild, raw, and wholly un-prettified. Around Ballachulish in the West Highlands, for instance, the scenery resembled "an alpine valley that had been scoured of all its softness—the feathery trees and chalets and brown cows whirled off its slopes, and all the gentle angles swept away, until it lay bare and rugged, a naked landscape awaiting turf and forest."

This sense of a severe, untamed landscape that is rough and unrefined and even has an indefinable quality of the primeval about it has struck many other writers—so much so that it seems to be the defining quality of the Scottish Highlands. According to the great man of letters Samuel Johnson, who travelled through the region in 1773 in the company of his friend James Boswell, the landscape of the Highlands was formed of an almost primordial combination "of stone and water. There is indeed a little earth above the stone in some places; but a very little, and the stone is always appearing. [The scenery] is like a man in rags; the naked skin is still peeping out." Sixteen centuries earlier the Roman historian Tacitus had come to the same conclusion. The northwest of Scotland, he wrote, was "virtually another island," divorced from the lowlands of the British Isles and dominated by "woods, ravines, marshes, and trackless wilds".

The edge of the Highlands—where the mountains plunge into the sea along one of the most storm-lashed coastlines in the world—merely accentuates the austere drama of the interior. According to Tacitus, the Scottish coastline comprised cliffs "beaten by a wild and open sea." To Paul Theroux the same coast was "ferocious… with a size and texture that was surprisingly unfinished… in certain pale lights it seemed murderous." Traveling the west coast between Oban and Fort William, Theroux found himself gasping in awe at "so much water, so much steepness, such rocks." In the northeast the mountains that fringe the coast may not be as steep but the scenery, if anything, is even wilder: the population is even more scattered here, and the cold grayness of the North Sea seems to render the winters even longer, gloomier, and more severe. This is the "relentless coast" populated by cormorants and herring gulls that was depicted by Neil Gunn, Scotland's most noted writer of the twentieth century, in his classic 1937 novel *Highland River*. To Gunn this was "a wild coast of gaunt headland and echoing cliff... where even on fine summer days the green water broke in foam... occasionally, in front of a headland, a stack would rise sheer, like a sword out of the hand of the sea." And in the far northwest, where Cape Wrath points towards Greenland and the great Clo Mor cliffs face north towards the Arctic, Scotland's most isolated and inhospitable tracts of coastline are to be found: this is the true edge of Europe, a land of dark rock and angry skies and foaming sea, where the rawness of the scenery is almost tangible in every stone and the hills are so steep they seem as if they are about to slide into the vast ocean.

Defining Boundaries

It is the upland region bounded by the western and northern coasts of Scotland that this book is concerned with. Within the pages that follow are considered the novels that have been set here, the poems that have been inspired by the landscape and people, the travelers who have journeyed here, and the long and often bloody history whose echoes can still be sensed in the contemporary culture of the region. But a book such as this one has to be sure of its parameters. And while these western and northern edges of the Highlands are easy to define, the southern and southeastern boundaries of the region seem much harder to determine. Traditionally the land boundary of the Highlands has been defined by the line of the Highland Boundary Fault, a geological gash that cuts a diagonal line across southern and central Scotland and separates the lowlands from the mountains. Where the fault cuts through Perthshire and Aberdeenshire the landscape is altogether softer than that of the West or Northwest Highlands: a gentle swell of low hills, thick forests and wide rivers, and pretty waterside towns such as Kenmore and Dunkeld that sit amidst an instantly recognizable British landscape of busy farms and thatched villages. Yet the fact that in

Looking across the River Tay from Birnam, with Dunkeld Cathedral just visible through the trees (Andrew Beattie)

many places the edge of the Highlands is marked not by a sudden elevation of the landscape, but by ripples that grow steadily higher, does make defining the boundary of the region difficult.

So where should a book about the Highlands draw the boundaries of the region it purports to describe? Should Callander or Comrie, both situated right on the Boundary Fault, be considered Highland towns? And what about the southern shore of Loch Lomond, fronting Glasgow's commuter suburbs? Come to that, is Inverness a Highland settlement? That city has long considered itself the "capital of the Highlands"; yet although it is rimmed by high mountains, Inverness spreads itself across land as flat as the Cambridgeshire Fens. The writer and engineer Edmund Burt, an English resident of Inverness in the early eighteenth century, maintained that the inhabitants of the town did "not call themselves Highlanders, not so much on account of their low situation, as because they speak English." Yet to ignore Inverness in a book about the Highlands would seem perverse. So in the end the inclusion or exclusion in this book of certain places is due solely to whether or not they "feel" as if they are part of the region: so descriptions of Comrie and Callander and Inverness make their way into these pages, while places that clearly owe their cultural allegiance to lowland regions at the fringes of the Highlands do not. These include Nairn and the villages of the Black Isle, situated on the gentle roll of flat land that stretches east and northeast from Inverness; Wick and Thurso in the far northeast, separated from the Highlands by largely flat and unremarkable reaches of farmland; and Balloch and the southern shores of Loch Lomond, which essentially form the commuter spread of Glasgow despite their inclusion in the Trossachs National Park.

As for the islands that anchor themselves to the coast of the West Highlands, these have been included in this book only on the occasions where their literary, cultural or geological heritage is shared by the mountain regions of the mainland: inevitably the islands of the Inner Hebrides, principally Skye and Iona but also Arran, Mull, Jura, Lismore, Raasay, Seil, and Rum, feature more than Shetland, Orkney, and the Western Isles—and it is worth stating from the outset that coverage of these far-flung outer islands is not this book's objective. Such geographical limitations as presented here are wholly the design of the author. But they seem to fit a book whose remit is the cultural, social and political history of the Highlands, rather than the oft lumped-together "Highlands and Islands" or simply "Northern Scotland." Whether such a limitation is apposite or not is, of course, ultimately for the reader to decide.

Even within a limitation that some might consider narrow, the Highlands are a place of great scenic diversity. The rolling landscapes of Highland Perthshire are as thoroughly Highland as the raw, severe mountains further north. Both areas share the same history too, of pride and clannishness, of bitter struggles and few victories, of dawns glimpsed and shattered, and of collective resolve to confront the enemies that have blighted the region: poverty and a harsh climate and often savage political repression. Away from the thatched villages of Perthshire and Aberdeenshire, and the busy centers such as Inverness, Oban, and Fort William, the Highlands remain the last great wilderness of Britain. And the scenery is indeed elemental: in its raw and otherworldly appearance the landscape seems to bring those who gaze upon it closer to the time of creation than it is possible to imagine. It is a landscape that has been sculpted by ice and wind and water since before life emerged on earth: and before these forces of nature had even begun their work, it was created by fire.

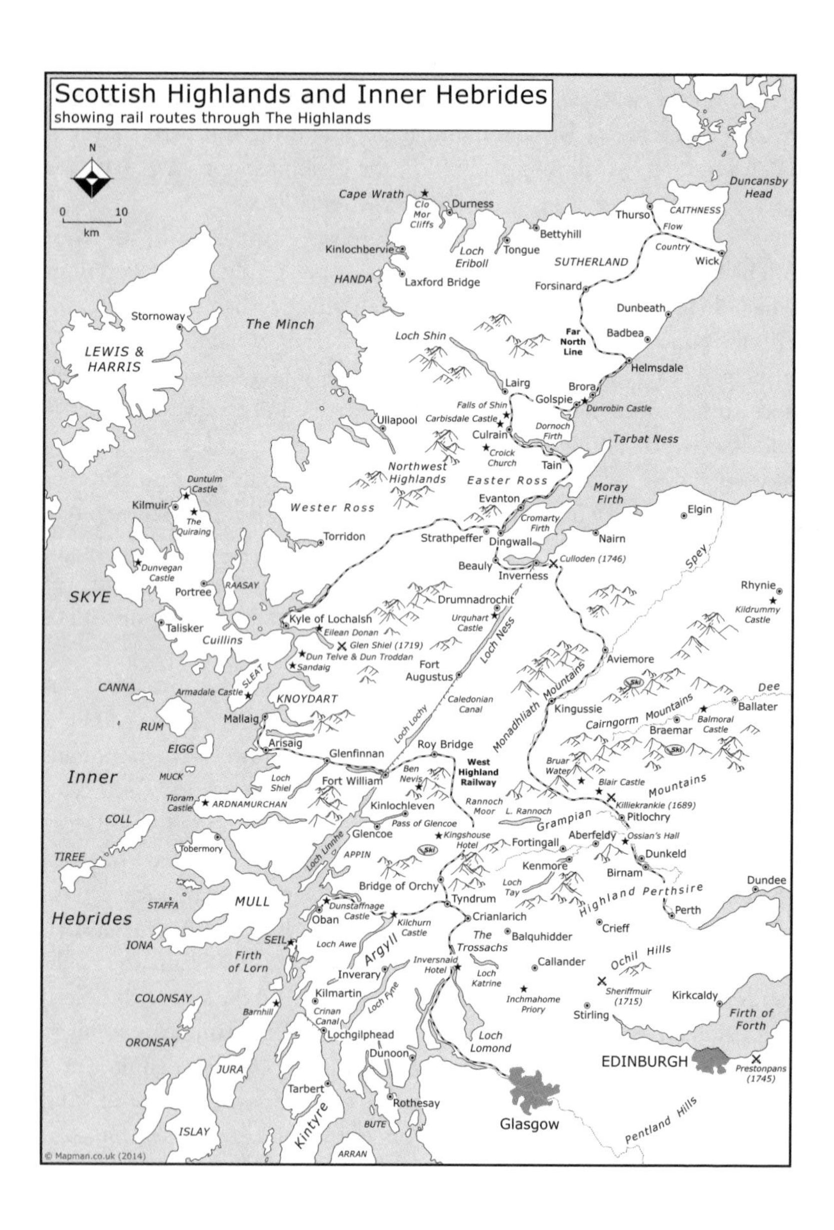

Scottish Highlands and Inner Hebrides
showing rail routes through The Highlands
N
0 10
km
Cape Wrath
Clo Mor Cliffs
Durness
Kinlochbervie
Loch Eriboll
Tongue
Bettyhill
Thurso
CAITHNESS
Flow Country
Duncansby Head
Wick
SUTHERLAND
HANDA
Laxford Bridge
Forsinard
Dunbeath
Badbea
Far North Line
Helmsdale
Stornoway
The Minch
LEWIS & HARRIS
Loch Shin
Lairg
Brora
Golspie
Dunrobin Castle
Falls of Shin
Carbisdale Castle
Ullapool
Culrain
Dornoch Firth
Tarbat Ness
Croick Church
Tain
Northwest Highlands
Easter Ross
Duntulm Castle
Kilmuir
The Quiraing
Wester Ross
Evanton
Moray Firth
Elgin
Cromarty Firth
Torridon
Strathpeffer
Dingwall
Nairn
Dunvegan Castle
Beauly
Culloden (1746)
Inverness
Spey
SKYE
Portree
RAASAY
Rhynie
Drumnadrochit
Kildrummy Castle
Talisker
Kyle of Lochalsh
Eilean Donan
Urquhart Castle
Cuillins
Glen Shiel (1719)
Loch Ness
Dun Telve & Dun Troddan
Sandaig
Fort Augustus
Aviemore
CANNA
SLEAT
Armadale Castle
KNOYDART
Caledonian Canal
Monadhliath Mountains
Kingussie
Dee
Ballater
RUM
Mallaig
Loch Lochy
Cairngorm Mountains
Balmoral Castle
Braemar
EIGG
Arisaig
Glenfinnan
Roy Bridge
West Highland Railway
Ski
Inner
MUCK
Loch Shiel
Ben Nevis
Fort William
Bruar Water
Blair Castle
Mountains
Tioram Castle
ARDNAMURCHAN
Kinlochleven
Rannoch Moor
L. Rannoch
Killiekrankie (1689)
COLL
Pass of Glencoe
Grampian
Pitlochry
Glencoe
Kingshouse Hotel
Fortingall
Aberfeldy
Ossian's Hall
Tobermory
TIREE
APPIN
Dunkeld
Loch Linnhe
Kenmore
Birnam
Bridge of Orchy
Loch Tay
Dundee
MULL
Tyndrum
Highland Perthshire
STAFFA
Dunstaffnage Castle
Perth
Hebrides
Oban
Kilchurn Castle
Crianlarich
Crieff
IONA
SEIL
Loch Awe
The Trossachs
Balquhidder
Argyll
Firth of Lorn
Inversnaid Hotel
Callander
Ochil Hills
Inverary
Loch Katrine
Kilmartin
Sheriffmuir (1715)
Kirkcaldy
COLONSAY
Inchmahome Priory
Barnhill
Crinan Canal
Loch Fyne
Stirling
Firth of Forth
ORONSAY
Lochgilphead
Loch Lomond
Dunoon
EDINBURGH
Prestonpans (1745)
JURA
Tarbert
Rothesay
Glasgow
Pentland Hills
Kintyre
ISLAY
BUTE
ARRAN
© Mapman.co.uk (2014)

Part One

LANDSCAPE

Suilven in the Inverpolly Nature Reserve, Sutherland
(Imladris/Shutterstock)

"The Grandeur Draws Back the Heart"

The Highlands of Scotland form some of the most awe-inspiringly ancient landscapes on earth. The geological newcomers—the Alps, the Himalayas, the Andes—are youthful in comparison. At the time of the extinction of the dinosaurs, some sixty-four million years ago, the Alps were still on the verge of rising: no diplodocus ever set foot on the slopes of the Matterhorn or Mont Blanc, for those creatures became extinct before any of those mountains were formed. Yet the Scottish Highlands were, even at the time of the dinosaurs' disappearance and the creation of the Alps, gnarled and venerable, the product of forces that had been active hundreds of millions of years before the first life forms had even emerged on earth.

Evidence of the incredible age of this landscape is everywhere the eye can see: every fog-shrouded summit, every rocky chasm, every bog (and there are many of them) has a story to tell that usually begins in what amounts to geological pre-history. For instance, the village of Rhynie, on the eastern fringes of the Cairngorms, is built on a rock known as Rhynie Chert, which contains fossils of plants and insects that are four hundred million years old—some of the oldest on earth. In northwestern Scotland, in the wilderness of Sutherland, the landscape is dominated by what is known as Lewisian gneiss, a heavy, gray, speckled rock whose color often mirrors that of the skies under which it occurs; geologists estimate that in some places this rock is up to three billion years old, making it well over half the age of the earth itself. Formidable cliffs are formed where this defiantly resistant rock meets the sea, creating a rugged coastline of sharp promontories and narrow inlets backed by monumental mountains. Inland the same rock can form scenery that is less dramatic but no less severe, characterized by deep pools of black water separated by dark hummocks speckled with moss and lichen. The ancient provenance of this Lewisian gneiss, formed at a time when the primeval earth bore no life, is palpable: walkers who stand on this rock can almost physically sense its incredible age through the soles of their boots.

These rocks—Rhynie Chert and Lewisian gneiss, along with many forms of granite—make up the three distinct ranges that form what we know as the Scottish Highlands: the Cairngorms in central Scotland, the Grampians to their south, and the great curving belt of the Northwest Highlands that occupies the "top left" corner of the country. In some

The Cairngorms
(Peter Mulligan/Wikimedia Commons)

places, particularly in the far northwest, there are no ranges, just isolated hills that rise like blisters from the surrounding countryside. The most famous of these peaks is Suilven, near Lochinver, whose sandstone slopes rise from an undulating sea of Lewisian gneiss and peat bog in one of the most remote areas of Europe—a "sandstone chord that holds up time in space," according to the poet Norman MacCaig. Few visitors get as far north as Suilven: settlements are sparse in the far northwest, and the winding roads are treacherous when the weather closes in (which it does, frequently).

Instead, most tourists tend to stick to well-beaten paths around the West Highlands (centered on Fort William), the Cairngorms (centered on Aviemore), or the softer scenery of the Trossachs, at whose heart lies the beautiful Loch Lomond. Beyond these ranges, though, are rugged and deserted landscapes that can prove hugely rewarding to those with the time and the patience to reach them (and a means of keeping dry). The poet Hugh MacDiarmid, for one, was keen to celebrate these far-flung reaches of his country. In his poem "The North Face of Liathach" he writes of the "spurs and pinnacles and jagged teeth" of the remote Liathach Massif near Torridon in the Northwest Highlands, whose "grandeur draws back the heart. Scotland is full of such places. Few (few Scots even) know them."

Volcanic Origins

The ranges that make up the Highlands have their origins in seismic shifts that occurred millennia ago. In many parts of the Highlands, and particularly in the Inner Hebrides, evidence of these momentous geological machinations can be read in the landscape and are obvious even to the geologically inexperienced. That is because the seismic shifts were accompanied by volcanic eruptions, and volcanic eruptions create features that remain stubbornly in the landscape. In western Scotland the best-known of these are the hexagonal basalt pillars known as the "colonnade" that fringe the island of Staffa. The pillars were formed by massive subterranean explosions sixty million years ago, and the subsequent slow cooling and solidifying of the erupted lava.

Not surprisingly the remarkable island of Staffa has drawn dozens of writers and travelers over the centuries. Among the first was the naturalist Joseph Banks, who gazed upon the island while on a journey north to Iceland in 1772 and wrote in the *Scots* magazine that "compared to this, what are the cathedrals or the places built by men? Mere models and play things." The regularity of the hexagonal columns astonished him: "Where is now the boast of the architect? Regularity, the only part in which he fancied himself to exceed his mistress, nature, is here sound in her possession." The following year James Boswell and Samuel Johnson sailed round the island on their tour of the Hebrides. Johnson thought Staffa the greatest natural curiosity he had ever seen, but according to Boswell the pair were unable to "land upon it [because] the surge was so high on its rocky coast." (The Atlantic swell plagues today's visitors too, and prevents many of the tourist launches that head out from the port of Fionnphort on Mull, or from the islands of Iona and Ulva, from actually landing on Staffa.) In 1814 Sir Walter Scott, the most prolific of all Scottish writers, sailed around Staffa and remarked on "the variety of tints" that characterized the basalt columns. (The colors—Scott noted yellow, cream, violet, and red—are the result of different species of algae and lichens growing on the columns.) The "grandeur of the scene," he enthused, was "unparalleled." Conversely the French novelist Jules Verne was struck by a different aspect of Staffa, namely its curiously hunched profile, which is clearly visible from Fionnphort and Iona, and which led Verne to liken Staffa in his 1882 novel *Le rayon vert*

(*The Green Ray*) to "an enormous tortoise shell, washed up in Hebridean waters."

Many more volcanic features can be seen up and down the west coast of Scotland. Basalt columns similar to those on Staffa can be seen above Talisker on Skye, at a place named Preshal Beg, where the eighteenth-century writer and traveler Thomas Pennant wondered whether the columns there were "the ruins of creation." On the neighboring island of Mull is Ben More, an extinct volcano, and on the same island is MacCulloch's Tree, a forty-foot conifer that was engulfed in a lava flow some fifty million years ago and which is now a petrified reminder of the violent volcanic activity that shaped this coastline. Eigg, another neighboring island, is also a former volcano, sporting a great stump of petrified lava known as An Sgurr at its center. In fact, a whole host of islands off the west coast of Scotland are actually nothing less than former volcanic summits protruding out of the gray seas: they include Rùm, Muck, and Canna, which make up the so-called "small isles" that sprinkle the sea south of Skye, as well as the remote and abandoned island of St. Kilda out in the Atlantic and the tiny islet of Rockall, marooned even further out beyond that, a lump of rock barely bigger than a small house that sits alone amidst hundreds of square miles of churning sea.

On Skye, the volcanic nature of the rock that forms the Cuillin range has rendered compasses unreliable, such are its crazy magnetic qualities: a further challenge, if one were needed, for walkers in this notoriously unforgiving environment. Compass Hill on neighboring Canna is so-named because it too sends magnetic needles haywire. On the east coast of Skye the heavy volcanic material has pressed down on the soft sandstone over which it flowed, squeezing the softer rock like cream in a cake and creating a unique landscape known as the Quiraing. Here the ground buckles and contorts like nowhere else in Scotland, forming an otherworldly landscape that feels primeval in its rawness and intensity and its sudden violence.

The volcanic activity that produced all these landforms (and the Giant's Causeway on the coast of Antrim—in popular imagination, at least, the most significant evidence of volcanic activity on the northwest coast of the British Isles) took place around sixty million years ago, when North America and Scotland split apart and seawater rushed to fill the gap between the drifting continents. The split widened and the sea became the

The Quiraing, Skye
(Paul Webster/Wikimedia Commons)

Atlantic Ocean; and it is still widening today, by as much as seven inches each year. What is now the Isle of Skye was once at the exploding, white-hot heart of the volcanic maelstrom. In Talisker Bay a trained geologist can recognize that the petrified lava flows on the beaches are identical to those that can be seen today on Iceland, which is not surprising since the volcanic activity on that mid-Atlantic island is the result of the processes that continue to prise the continents of North America and Europe apart.

The lava type that geologists look for specifically is known as pahoehoe: ropy waves in rock that are clearly indicative of flow and which can be seen in abundance on Iceland (and on Hawaii too: pahoehoe is a Hawaiian word). Pahoehoe lava characteristically cools to form a rocky surface that looks as if it has been distorted and melted; it is rare to find it on Skye, but it is there nonetheless, and it reveals the island's ancient volcanic origins. On Skye alone the splitting of the ancient continent known as Laurasia led to some five hundred cubic miles of lava being spilt, enough to cover the whole of France in a layer of volcanic debris ten feet thick. The Cuillins themselves, rising above the beaches where pahoehoe spreads like melted tarmac, are in fact remnants of an ancient lava chamber, exposed by erosion and then gnarled into their current shape by the movement of ice. Like Staffa these volcanic features have fired the imagination of writers and poets throughout the centuries: in *The Kingdom by the Sea* Paul Theroux called these spectacularly forbidding peaks "freakish… sharp-pointed, fantastic, and high, like peaks in dragon stories."

Yet the volcanic activity that has left its mark on Skye, Staffa and many other islands of the Inner Hebrides is a comparatively recent episode in the geological story of western Scotland. The eruptions might have produced the spectacular rock formations on those islands but they certainly did not produce the Scottish Highlands themselves. The ridges and summits of the land-based mountains ranges date from a much earlier era, some 425 million years ago, when northwestern Scotland was part of the North American continent, and central and southern Scotland, along with the rest of the British Isles, was part of the Eurasian continent. Separating the two landmasses was the Iapetus Ocean. When this great body of water closed, the resultant collision unleashed compression forces that were violent enough to thrust up mountains whose peaks reached higher than those of the Himalayas.

Reminders of the volcanic activity that accompanied the closing of the Iapetus Ocean can be seen today all over the Highlands. Ben Nevis, for instance, was an active volcano at this time, a pluton (or dome) of igneous rock intruded into the older rock that the mountain surrounds; the flat summit of the mountain on which walkers stand shivering in the mist is actually an ancient lava flow. And where the hot volcanic rocks came into contact with softer rocks such as river-deposited mudstone the heat and pressure was enough to set another profound geological transformation in motion as the mudstone metamorphosed into slate, which in recent times has been quarried at a number of sites on the west coast, including Ballachulish near Fort William and on the island of Seil near Oban. In a similar way limestone was squashed and heated into another very hard metamorphic rock, namely marble, which has been quarried on Skye.

Over time the compression forces caused by the closure of the Iapetus Ocean calmed and the mountains stopped rising. Their birth and adolescent growth spurt was over and now it was time for age to begin to wither them—and age takes its toll on mountain ranges in the form of wearing away by wind, water, and ice. Now those mountains formed from the closing of the Iapetus Ocean are gnarled and elderly versions of those original peaks. They are nothing like the fresh, sprightly summits of the Himalayas or the Alps, which are today being shaped by some of the same tectonic processes that formed the Highlands. But as the Highlands become worn down to dust, so it will be the turn of the Himalayas and the Alps to be ground down until they too begin to take on the same sort of contorted appearance as the Highlands: and so the cycle of mountain building and decay, which takes place over unimaginable eons of geological history, will continue unabated.

Geologists in the Highlands: "The Most Sublime Speculations Are Awakened"

One of the "joins"—the contact zones where the great collision of continents that threw up the Highlands actually took place—is clearly visible on any map of Scotland. It is the deep, narrow gash known as the Great Glen that cuts diagonally across the north of the country from Fort William in the southwest to Inverness in the northeast. The two principal settlements of the Highlands are thus linked by a long, straight valley, filled in part by the waters of Loch Ness and the smaller Loch Lochy. The gash cuts deep and long, splitting Scotland in a way that could have been caused by some sort of geological arrow fired towards the North Sea from Londonderry on the coast of Northern Ireland. Where the Great Glen meets the sea the line of the gash is simply extended, in the form of two estuaries that, like the gash, are oriented southwest-northeast: namely the Firth of Lorn in the southwest and the Moray Firth with its curiously straight-edged coastline in the northeast. Loch Ness, where the arrow wound cuts deepest, holds more water than all the lakes of England and Wales combined. Samuel Johnson was overwhelmed by it, calling it a "profundity scarcely credible" in his book *A Journey to the Western Isles of Scotland.* The shape of the loch is remarkable: the ribbon of deep water stretches twenty-three miles in length but is never more than a mile or so wide. On the northern shores the waters of the loch lap against ancient red sandstones identical in age and character to those that form the Catskill Mountains in upper New York State (it was stone quarried from the Catskills that was used for the construction of the venerable brownstone buildings characteristic of so much of central New York City). Once, these sandstones were separated from those rocks on the southern shore of Loch Ness by the Iapetus Ocean. The closure of that ocean, caused by the colliding continents, thrust up the mountains that rise on either side of the great gash in the earth's crust marking the collision point.

Yet this spectacular display of geological acrobatics is only one of many to have molded the landscape of Scotland in its current form. The rocks that form the Highlands have been subjected to more churning, stretching, folding, and compression than nougat in a sweet factory. Geologists estimate that some of the rock under the feet of today's tourists and walkers has in the distant geologic past been thrust fifty miles into the earth only to emerge eons later to create a new landscape—and that this cycle keeps on repeating itself over time.

These geological convulsions have created weird and wonderful anomalies. In the far northwest of Scotland the sandstone formed as a result of comparatively recent river deposition actually appears underneath layers of vastly more ancient Lewisian gneiss, a conundrum that confounded Victorian geologists, many of whom sought an explanation as to how a rock of such vintage could end up on top of far more recent deposits. They were used to new rocks being found on top of older rocks, yet here the earth presented them with a puzzle that turned everything they knew about geology on its head (just like the landscape itself). One of those geologists, Henry Cadell, realized that the anomaly was the result of compression forces that had actually folded layers of rock over themselves. To convince a sceptical scientific community of the veracity of his theory he built a piece of apparatus in his laboratory in Edinburgh to demonstrate how the compression might occur. His machine was an elaborate affair consisting of a long horizontal glass box and a screw mechanism that churned layers of colored sand into patterns. With it he demonstrated to his astonished audience how ancient rocks could be compressed and folded so that they spilled over younger layers, creating the geological anomaly in the northwest Highlands. But what Cadell lacked was an explanation as to how the folding actually occurred: a geological mechanism that could thrust and drag and fold layers of rock over the surface of the earth's crust as though they were little more than strips of warm lasagne.

That mechanism came to be understood a century after Cadell built his famous compression machine. The theory of plate tectonics was developed by a number of earth scientists over the course of the 1960s and

1970s to show how continents could shift around on the surface of the earth and how, when they collided, mountain ranges consisting of crumpled strata of crust were thrust towards the heavens. Alfred Wegener, a German meteorologist who developed an interest in earth sciences in the early twentieth century, suggested that continents moved around in his 1913 book *On the Origins of Continents and Oceans*, but he, like Cadell and the scientists who came before him, could only dream of discovering the actual mechanism by which great chunks of land appeared to float raft-like across the surface of the earth. The scientists who between them developed the theory of plate tectonics deduced that currents below the earth's crust, driven by heat from the nuclear reactions at its core, provided the great conveyor belt of continental movement. But this was unknown to nineteenth-century scientists in Scotland, for whom the notion that mountains were the result of colliding sections of the earth's crust would have been as outlandish as suggesting that the Highlands had been created by men from Mars.

Even more significant than Henry Cadell and his compression machine in the quest to discover the origin of the Highlands was the work of James Hutton, a farmer with a passion for geology who visited Arran in 1787 to conduct field research into the igneous rocks of the island. He was one of the earliest scientists to understand that landscapes were the result of unfathomably ancient processes, the appreciation of which was beyond human consciousness. Two years before the publication of his 1788 masterwork *A Theory of the Earth* Hutton wrote "we cannot estimate the duration of what we see at present, nor calculate the period at which it had begun." In short Hutton challenged the age of the earth that was offered in the Bible, and dared to suggest that the planet had been around longer than humanity. These radical theories soon gained currency: in 1805 the English scientist Humphry Davy wrote that "to the geological enquirer, every mountain chain offers striking monuments of the great alterations that the globe has undergone. The most sublime speculations are awakened, the present is disregarded, past ages crowd upon the fancy."

Hutton's fieldwork on Arran involved a close study of the landscape around Newton Point on the north coast of the island, where two rock types are set at right angles to one another in an arrangement that geologists know as Hutton's Unconformity. His work formed the basis for further investigations into folding and thrusting by a geologist named

Stac Pollaidh, near Ullapool
(Mehmet Karatay/Wikimedia Commons)

James Nicol, who in 1859 developed the theory of thrust faulting after studying geological structures just north of Ullapool on the west coast of the Highlands. By then the notion of mountain landscapes being the result of achingly slow but dramatic geological processes had seeped outside the realms of science and into public consciousness. The critic and mountain enthusiast Leslie Stephen, whose writings contributed hugely to the popularity of the Alps in the Victorian era, recognized this when he wrote in 1871 that "Our imaginations may be awed when we look at mountains as monuments of the slow working of stupendous forces of nature through countless millenniums."

The faulting that these early geologists discovered was, of course, the result of the stretching and compression of the earth's crust caused by tectonic processes. The Moyne thrust fault, which runs along the northwest coast of Scotland from Loch Eriboll to the Sleat peninsula on Skye, is a zone of faulting some six miles in width caused by the stresses associated with the closure of the Iapetus Ocean. It was discovered in 1907 and many theories concerning its formation were postulated until the theory of plate tectonics came to be accepted some sixty years later. Along this remarkable folding zone are mountains with extraordinarily complex geologies, such as Ben More Assynt, whose lower slopes consist of limestone, while the middle slopes are sandstone and the upper slopes are formed from quartzite. The folding associated with the Moyne thrust carried some material one hundred miles across Scotland—although "windows" in that material allow geologists to examine some of the rock beneath the more recent folds.

The Great Glen fault was formed at roughly the same time from roughly the same processes. That is why it is oriented, like most of the fault zones in Scotland, in a southwest-northeast direction. During the opening of the Atlantic the fault was reactivated and the whole of northwestern Scotland—that is, everything north of the Great Glen—moved about sixty miles to the northeast, creating the long, straight coastline of the Black Isle and the Tain peninsula, whose rocks would still be forming the northern coast of Loch Ness had they not been so comprehensively shifted towards the North Sea. And the Great Glen is a fault of global significance that transcends the modern arrangement of continents. The gash of the fault can be traced southwest from Fort William and Loch Linnhe through Lough Foyle and Donegal Bay in Ireland, where it is widened by the waters of the River Mourne. Over in Canada the same fault, separated from its European arm by the opening of the Atlantic Ocean, is known as the Cabot fault. When drawn on a map the fault line makes landfall at Baie Verte on Newfoundland. It then runs southwest, crossing under the Gulf of St. Lawrence, and from there it can be traced the length of the mountain ranges of eastern North America.

Just as significant as the Great Glen fault in geological terms is the Highland Boundary Fault, which crosses Scotland from the Isle of Bute in the Firth of Clyde to the mouth of the River Esk south of Aberdeen. It is this fault line—again oriented southwest-northeast—that marks the southern edge of the Highlands, so dividing Scotland into its clear Highland and lowland culture and landscape. The principal town on the Isle of Bute is Rothesay, and on its palm-fringed promenade the exact line of the fault is marked by an understated and easily missed wrought-iron archway, under which faulting enthusiasts can pose and have their photograph taken. "Welcome to the Highlands," it announces on one side of the arch, with a diorama of loch, mountain, and stag; "Welcome to the Lowlands" it says on the other, under a dairy cow and some ploughed fields.

The Highland Boundary Fault cuts Bute clean in half. Faults being long and narrow it also creates a long, narrow incision across the island, which is filled by the waters of Loch Fad. Heading northeast, the line of the fault is marked by the sprinkle of wooded islets in the southern part of Loch Lomond, and by Conic Hill, which rises on the loch's eastern shoreline; a fabulous view over the loch awaits those who slog their way up to its summit. The line of the fault then continues northeastwards, its progress marked by the preponderance in towns and villages of buildings constructed from the dark, lumpy red rock known as puddingstone created by movements along the fault. A number of puddingstone buildings can be seen in Callander, a popular tourist stop-over on the edge of the Highlands where few who patronize the town's tea houses and knitwear shops will be aware of the geological rumblings beneath their feat.

Comrie, further on along the line of the fault, is much smaller and quieter than Callander, but on the town's western edge is tangible evidence in gray stone that the fault runs through this gorgeous Perthshire landscape of woods and meadowland and distant, sombre hills. Marooned on a sloping field, surrounded by whitewashed, roses-around-the-front-door cottages, is the so-called "earthquake house," whose monitoring instruments, visible through the glass panel of the door, indicate that this is one of the most earthquake-prone areas in the British Isles. The squat, square hut with its pyramid roof has stood here since 1874 and is thought to be the oldest purpose-built earthquake observatory in the world. However, the original instrumentation, fashioned from boxwood cylinders embedded in sand, has long since been replaced by a modern seismograph whose data is regularly analyzed by the British Geological Survey.

THE ROLE OF ICE AND DARWIN'S "GREAT BLUNDER"

Neither the Highland Boundary Fault nor the Moyne Thrust makes as significant an impact on the landscape as the Great Glen fault. That is because the impressive depth of the cleft filled by the waters of Loch Ness, Loch Lochy, and Loch Linnhe is not just a result of plate movement. The valley of the Great Glen has been deepened over successive ice ages by glaciers, whose flow has been determined by the line of weakness in the landscape created by the fault. Those same glaciers—which disappeared from Scotland some ten thousand years ago, but which will make a re-appearance during the next, cyclical downturn of the earth's temperature—also smoothed and polished rock surfaces, created knife-edge ridges known as arêtes and carved out huge amphitheatre-shaped depressions in the mountains known as corries (or *coires* in Gaelic).

On slowing down when they reached the lowlands at the foot of the mountains the glaciers lost no time in relieving themselves of the load they had voraciously scraped from the higher ground. Drumlins are a landform made from some of this dumped material: much of Glasgow is built over these egg-shaped hills, the city's houses and streets resting on material that was scoured from what is now the deep scar filled by Loch Lomond. Drumlins commonly cluster in swarms, but singular examples of glacial deposition include so-called erratics, enormous boulders dropped onto the landscape by glaciers as they melted. One such is the Clach a'Choire or Ringing Stone on Tiree, which so caught the imagination of prehistoric humans that they decorated the enormous and immovable stone with runic markings.

Another erratic can be found at the summit of Ben Hogh on Coll, to where a giant was traditionally thought to have flung it in a fit of anger; James Boswell scrambled up to it in 1773 but was somewhat nonplussed, writing in his journal that seeing the great boulder "did not repay our trouble in getting to it."

When the ice melted at the end of the Ice Age yet more erosive features were formed, but these were scoured by torrents of meltwater rather than slow-moving ice. Such features include the extraordinary Black Rock Gorge in the east of the Highlands. Here, hidden in the woods behind the village of Evanton on the Cromarty Firth, a chasm so deep and so thin is carved into the hillside it is a wonder that it could have been caused by any force of nature. A wooden bridge crosses the gorge at its deepest part: the drop beneath the bridge is a hundred feet down, yet the chasm is so narrow that anyone who managed to reach the gorge's perilous base would easily be able to stretch out with their hands and touch both moss-covered walls at the same time. At the bottom of the chasm is the churning and seething River Glass. But the amount of water that flows in the chasm today is nothing like the tremendous torrent that crashed through here at the end of the Ice Age. For it was this rushing glacial meltwater that caused the gash: the torrent was possibly set in motion when the ice dam holding back a huge natural reservoir either burst or melted. On the other side of the Highlands a much wider torrent of glacial meltwater created the vastly contrasting Kilmartin Glen, north of Lochgilphead, a broad, smooth-based valley that is gentle rather than spectacular and which, a few thousand years after the melting of the ice, had become an important center of prehistoric settlement.

Ice has been responsible for many aspects of Scotland's history as well as its landscape. The deep glens gouged out by the ice, separated from neighboring valleys by unassailable ridges, meant that a fierce localism developed among the people who eventually inhabited them; in time each separate glen was occupied by a clan whose members would fight and quarrel with the clan who lived over the hill. Where those deep glens met the sea they created sea lochs that are similar to the fjords of Norway and New Zealand. The peninsulas between the fjords were shaped into remote and isolated fingers of land, where traditions could flourish and the Gaelic language could hang on tenaciously. Moreover the steep slopes cut by the ice supported only thin soils, leading to centuries of agricultural hardship and frequent famines. But exactly what the ice had done to the Highlands was a mystery until the middle of the nineteenth century. Just as the mechanisms of faulting and mountain-building had caused so much head-scratching among Victorian geologists, so those same researchers were confused by the evidence of glaciation that lay all around them in the Highlands. The notion that Scotland had once been covered in ice was seen as absurd by many scientists. Then the Swiss geologist Louis Agassiz, who had revolutionized the study of ice environments through his work in the Alps, visited Scotland and solved the problem of the Parallel Roads of Glen Roy—and as a result turned the understanding of the physical geography of the Highlands completely upside down.

Glen Roy is hidden in the folds of the Highlands to the east of Fort William. Its upper section, home to the "parallel roads," is reached by a single-track metalled road that winds up the valley from the small tourist village of Roy Bridge. The road passes through a scattering of farms and woodland before emerging into the austere landscape that provides the setting for the geological controversy. The "parallel roads," seen first on the valley's west side and then on its east, are not roads at all but flat, shelf-like indents that create pale scars in the steep, grassy profiles of the valley sides. The "roads" appear at three levels and in each instance run parallel with "roads" at exactly the same height on the opposite side of

View of Glen Roy and "parallel roads" (1823) by William Miller
(Wikimedia Commons)

the valley. It is clear from the *Guide to the Highlands and Islands of Scotland,* published by John Murray in 1834, that the origin of the parallel roads was something of a hot topic among scientists of that era. So keenly were the parallel roads debated that the book's authors maintained that the dispute had "given rise to a great deal of very violent and ridiculous discussion."

The primary purpose of Murray's *Guide* was to give practical advice to tourists venturing into the Highlands. But the "Parallel Roads of Glen Roy" were famous enough to form the subject of one of the book's long digressions into Highland geology. The authors of the guide explain that some anthropologists had reached the conclusion that the roads were man-made avenues through the forest cut for the "rapid passages of huntsmen." On the other side of the argument were geologists who had surmised that the roads were shorelines marking "the height at which some great body of water stood." Yet the precise nature of the "supposed barrier... of immense size" that had created the dam holding back all that water was a mystery—made all the more puzzling by the fact that the ancient dam was clearly no longer there. But at least with the guide to hand, visitors to the Highlands could travel to Glen Roy and see for themselves the site of the famous geological conundrum.

Three years after the publication of Murray's *Guide*, and possibly with that very volume packed in his luggage, Charles Darwin visited Glen Roy and in 1839 he published a paper in the *Journal of the Royal Society* in which he claimed to solve the mystery of the parallel roads: they were, he maintained, the shorelines of an ancient arm of the sea and hence, in effect, former beaches. But Louis Agassiz, who visited the area a few months later, knew better: he realized that the "roads" were indeed shorelines—but not marine shorelines. Instead, they marked the shores of an ancient lake that had risen and fallen to different levels at different times, so creating the distinctive parallel shelves on either side of the valley. Agassiz concluded that only one thing could dam up a lake of that kind, and that was a glacier. The immense block of ice would have closed the open end of Glen Roy, forming a natural dam, and water from melting ice would have filled the area behind the dam, creating the lake whose shorelines are still visible today. And Agassiz went on to conclude that if there had been a glacier in Glen Roy then there would have been glaciers all over Scotland during the last Ice Age.

He presented these revolutionary ideas to the British Geological Society in 1840, to the consternation of the scientific community of the day, and earning a firm rebuttal from Darwin. But over the ensuing years his ideas began to gain acceptance, and in 1861 Darwin asked the geologist Thomas Jamieson to visit Glen Roy and explore the veracity of the ice-dam theory. Jamieson did so, and reported back that Agassiz had been right. Darwin was devastated. "My paper is one long gigantic blunder," he later wrote to Jamieson. "I have been for years anxious to know what was the truth, and now I shall rest contented, though ashamed of myself." He also admitted to the geologist Charles Lyell that he was "smashed to atoms about Glen Roy." To this day Darwin's "great blunder" over the origins of the roads remains by far the most famous professional miscalculation of his career.

The Highland Coastline

Ice did something else to the Highlands too—specifically to its coastline. Ice is heavy, and in the depths of the Ice Age the ice sheets covering Scotland could be anything up to a mile thick. The weight of all that ice was enough to make sections of the earth's crust sink into the liquid mantle beneath, just as a boat does when its cargo is loaded. When the ice melted, the crust "sprang" back up again—but very slowly. In fact the "springing" back up of the formerly "squeezed" land has been going on for the last ten thousand years and is still active today. It was Darwin's trusted geologist Thomas Jamieson who first proposed that land rose in this way, back in 1865, but real progress in the understanding of what came to be known as the theory of "isostasy" did not come until a century later. Now it is reckoned that in some parts of the world, such as the Hudson Bay coast of Canada, land is rising by up to four feet per century because of isostatic rebound. On the west coast of Scotland the annual rise is vastly less, but the effects are still striking. At King's Cave on the Isle of Arran an abandoned cliff line can be seen behind the present beach, with ancient caves that today are never so much as splashed by the waves because they are set some thirteen feet above the high tide mark: the caves were formed when the cliffs were at the same level as the waves, but now they have been left high and dry by the rising of the land.

On the southern tip of the island of Kerrera in the Inner Hebrides there are similar abandoned caves. These were once used as dungeons and stores by the masters of Gylen Castle, which occupies a promontory of land cut right the way through by a former sea arch. Nearby, some abandoned sea stacks—columns of rock created by the erosion of waves—were used by preachers as pulpits. Like the caves and the arch, the stacks, once washed by the waves, now stand on land raised well above the present-day sea level. And as the west of Scotland rises, so the island of Britain tilts on an enormous pivot, sending the southeast of England slowly sinking into the waves; in time, the same processes that have resulted in raised beaches and abandoned sea stacks on the coast of Highland Scotland will create the opposite effect in London and Kent, drowning the marshlands abutting the Thames Estuary and rendering the Thames Barrier redundant.

It was ice that created the winding fjords and the raised beaches of Scotland's coast. But the other great agency of change along the coast—the sea itself—has been hard at work too. The highest cliffs in mainland Britain are at Clo Mor, east of Cape Wrath, where over thousands of years the land has been pounded into submission by waves thrown up by North Atlantic storms. Along the coastline to the east, at Durness, both the sea and a rushing river have gouged their way into the local limestone to create a monumentally impressive cavern (complete with cascading waterfall) known as Smoo Cave. Sir Walter Scott visited this cavern on his trip around Scotland, and wrote that it was "impossible for description to explain the impression made by so strange a place... a water kelpie or an evil spirit of aquatic propensities could not have chosen a fitter abode."

Vastly more celebrated by writers and artists, though, is Fingal's Cave, the deep cavern cut by the sea into the basalt columns of Staffa. In Gaelic the cave was originally known as *An Uaimh Bhinn*—the "melodious cave"—after the reverberating musical sounds created by the waves washing against the side of the opening. But this became mis-transcribed as *An Uaimh Finn* and this in turn led to the cave being associated with a mythical giant named Fingal. With its uniquely harmonious interior and its location on the fabulously exotic island of Staffa the cave has, just like the island into which it is carved, attracted the attention of many writers and artists. In a letter of 1818 to his brother Tom, the poet John Keats wrote that "for solemnity and grandeur [the cave] far surpasses the finest cathedral... the colour of the columns is a sort of black with a lurking gloom of purple therein, [suggesting that it was made by giants who] had

Fingal's Cave, Staffa (1774) by John Cleveley
(Wikimedia Commons)

taken a whole mass of black columns and bounded them together like bundles of matches, and then with immense axes had made a cavern in the body of these columns." In the years that followed, Turner painted the scene, while Mendelssohn was inspired to write his overture *Fingal's Cave* after his visit. Even Queen Victoria, lover of all things Scottish, stopped by in August 1847, on one of her Highland jaunts. She found the "effect [of entering the cave] splendid, like a great entrance into a vaulted hall: it looked almost awful as we entered, and the barge heaved up and down on the swell of the sea. The rocks, under water, were all colours—pink, blue, and green—which had a most beautiful and varied effect."

Jules Verne also visited the cave and gives a description of it in his novel *The Green Ray.* Inside the cave, he wrote, "a sort of sonorous silence reigned… only the wind carried its long chords into the cave... [the chords] seemed to be made from a melancholic series of reduced sevenths, rising and falling little by little. Under its powerful whistle, it almost seemed as if the prisms were resonating like the reeds of an enormous harmonica." Verne, like all of those who have visited the cave before and since, seems to have been utterly beguiled by sense of drama and mystery of Fingal's Cave: there are few places on earth where the churning sea and solidified lava have conspired together to produce such an extraordinary feature.

FOREST, MOORLAND, AND BOTANIC GARDENS: A BRIEF SURVEY OF HIGHLAND FLORA

At the time the North Atlantic Ocean began to open, some fifty-five million years ago, Scotland lay in equatorial latitudes and was covered in tropical vegetation. Before their extinction ten million years previously, dinosaurs had flourished in this environment; one of these creatures, believed to be a Megalosaurus, once took a walk across a beach in Staffin Bay on Skye, and we know this because its fossilized footprints were discovered in 1994 by an amateur geologist. As the Atlantic widened, tectonic plates also began shifting Scotland (and the rest of Europe) on a slow journey towards northern climes, and consequently the plant life also changed—and kept changing until Scotland reached its present position.

These changes occurred over millions of years; on a shorter time scale it was ice that was the primary influence on the plant life of the Highlands. During a succession of cold periods ice scoured away soils and freezing temperatures led to the extinction of hundreds of plant species. As the last ice receded around ten thousand years ago, the vegetation that gradually colonized Scotland was pine forest, which within a few hundred years had smothered the landscape from the lowland glens to the highest peaks. Although a certain amount of deforestation (to clear land for settlement and farming) occurred once the area was settled by humans, most of the country was still covered in thick forest in the first century CE when the Romans established their fortifications to the north of present-day cities such as Perth and Stirling. The invaders named their strange, cold, forested territory "Caledonia," derived from the Latin for "wooded heights."

Today, thanks to the voracious appetite of livestock and loggers and the clearing of large areas of woodland for game hunting, less than one percent of that indigenous woodland now remains. This wide-scale deforestation is not a recent phenomenon: it has been going on for centuries. In 1773, on his journey through the Highlands, Samuel Johnson noted that the area between Loch Ness and Glen Shiel was "totally denuded of its wood, but the stumps both of oaks and firs show that it has been once a forest of large timber." Yet more felling was to follow throughout the rest of the eighteenth century and into the Victorian era, when industrial needs and new transport links meant the demand for wood could only increase.

Today the few remnants of Caledonian forest are highly prized for their ecology. These forests are dominated by ancient oak trees, among which grow elm, ash, silver birch, and rowan. They can still be found in some lowland areas alongside lochs and rivers, and the best example is probably the thick woodland that thrives along the east bank of Loch Lomond, out of reach of car drivers but always busy with walkers (the West Highland Way passes right through this area of supreme ecological importance). On Speyside gnarled survivors of ancient forests still thrive in what the tourist authority likes to call "Big Tree Country," while the pretty thatched village of Fortingall, near Aberfeldy, is home to a yew tree that is supposedly five thousand years old, and is claimed by villagers to be the oldest living thing in Europe. This gnarled and stunted curiosity, an absurd tangle of knobbly branches that seems to have no trunk, was much revered by pagans, and when Christians came to Fortingall in the seventh century they built the village church beside the yew, where it still stands today. (Since the nineteenth century the yew has been partly enclosed behind a low wall, erected to stop village boys taking branches from it to light their fires for the festival of Beltane.)

Further up on the mountain slopes, however, the old forests of Caledonian pine trees have all but vanished. In the vast majority of the Highlands the grazing of sheep and deer (the latter find young saplings notoriously tasty) has prevented a natural forest cover from establishing itself except under highly controlled conditions. Woodland areas that do exist on the upper slopes of the Highlands largely comprise planted stands of conifers rather than Caledonian pine. These conifer plantations date from the 1920s and were created as a response to the realization that Britain lacked strategic reserves of timber during World War I.

The conifer of choice was the fast-growing Sitka spruce, a non-native tree whose coverage increased further in the 1970s when tax breaks allowed private investors a way of sheltering their assets by investing in forestry. The plantations can still be found everywhere. Most are fenced in (to deter deer) and are crisscrossed by vehicle tracks that also provide access to the hills for walkers. But the planted areas are ecologically sterile compared to the forests that once thrived here: little light can reach the forest floor, ensuring a lack of undergrowth, and soil is often damaged through the use of the heavy machinery.

The negative impact of this monocultural forestry is visual as well as ecological: Sitka spruce plantations rarely do anything to enhance a view. But in recent years there has been an attempt to rectify the aesthetic and ecological damage, with Sitka plantations gradually being replaced with a more diverse forest environment. One of the best examples of this policy is the six hundred square miles of Caledonian pine forest that has been planted by the charity Trees for Life in an area between Glen Carron and Glen Moriston, west of Inverness. On the eastern shores of Loch Lomond, the Ben Lomond National Memorial Park, opened in 1997 in memory of those Scots who fought and died for their country during World War II, has been the site of a forty-year project to develop an oak forest where conifer plantations once stood.

Moorland areas that characterize so much of the Highlands—the most celebrated stretch of which has to be desolate Rannoch Moor, famously traversed by the Fort William branch of the West Highland Railway—are typically smothered in heather, which brings explosions of purple blooms across the moors at the end of summer. Heather flowers in a diversity of forms: some varieties are more able to cope with boggy conditions, such as the cross-leaved heather found on Rannoch Moor, which thrives amidst bog myrtle and cotton grass, while drier areas are home to bell heather and heathland vegetation such as broom and gorse. Historically heather has been a versatile plant, harvested in commercial quantities by farmers and used as livestock fodder, fuel for fires, as the source of an orange dye, and as a material for bedding and basketwork. Bees are active in pollinating heather moorlands and their honey, characteristically a rich, dark amber color, is widely-acclaimed and sold in many parts of Scotland.

As the altitude increases, the heather gives way to hardy grass species that can cope with high winds and thin soils; at the summits of peaks in the Cairngorms and the West Highlands vegetation is subarctic in character and includes slow-growing species such as starry saxifrage and moss campion that can survive months of snow cover. And everywhere—or so it seems—there is peat, a black, spongy, super-saturated material that forms where cool temperatures and high rainfall prevent the complete decomposition of organic matter. As generations of farmers have discovered, it is useless for agriculture, but cut into slabs it provides valuable fuel for domestic cooking and heating.

The west coast of Scotland is blessed by comparatively mild temperatures—a point emphasized by the guardians of Scourie Lodge, in the far northwest, where (according to the lodge's own publicity) the most northerly palm trees in the world nestle in a walled garden. The benign temperatures are a result of the Gulf Stream, a warm current that flows across the Atlantic from the Gulf of Mexico. Taking advantage of this warmth are a number of botanic gardens, established in the nineteenth century by botanists who wanted to create formal gardens in which plants from all over the world were able to thrive. Typical among those of Scotland's west coast is Inverewe Garden in Wester Ross, where Osgood MacKenzie, who inherited the neighboring estate in 1862, used the area's famously temperate climate to establish a walled garden in which plants from Chile, Tasmania, and the Himalayas continue to thrive, as well as rhododendrons and azaleas—though pride of place goes to a eucalyptus tree that is the largest in the northern hemisphere. Astonishingly, some 180,000 visitors are attracted annually to this bleak and remote spot.

Numerous other gardens include Benmore Botanic Gardens, which spread across the Eachaig Valley seven miles north of the seaside town of Dunoon. The gardens here were established as a satellite of Edinburgh's Royal Botanic Garden and include a remarkable, arrow-straight avenue of giant redwoods that reach to heights of over a hundred feet. Beyond them the gardens climb up the slopes of Beinn Mhor, where winding paths lead past rainforest glades and clumps of rhododendron bushes to pavilions and look-outs hidden in the trees. Benmore was established in the nineteenth century, but there has also been a more recent tradition of establishing gardens: one of the most extraordinary was cultivated for ten years by two enterprising gardeners in the far north-west at Kerracher, and could only be accessed by boat (from the tiny port of Kylescu, thirty miles north of Ullapool); the plants here provided a riot of color and brightness in an otherwise bleak and ecologically monochrome area of the Highlands, but unfortunately in 2009 the owners decided that all the years of painstaking cultivation had taken their toll and they could no longer accept visitors to look round their extraordinary creation. Finally, in Pitlochry in the central Highlands a unique garden celebrating the work of Scottish plant hunters extends luxuriously over a hillside overlooking the River Tummel; here enthusiastic botanists wander through glades—planted with trees and flowers from the Himalayas, Japan, the Americas, and Australia—and contemplate the exotic foliage from purpose-built pavilions and terraces.

RED SQUIRRELS AND GOLDEN EAGLES: A BRIEF SURVEY OF HIGHLAND FAUNA

The wild animal most frequently associated with the Highlands is the red deer, often referred to as "the monarch of the glen" and found both in woodlands hugging the shores of lochs and also on higher, more open ground, where the animals move in summer to avoid the midges (see p.149). In late summer the open moor can resonate to the mating calls of these animals, during which males of the species famously lock horns with each other as they compete for females. Since wolves became extinct in the Highlands (the last was shot in 1743) deer have had no natural predator, and their numbers have been furthermore kept artificially high by estate managers so that stalkers have no shortage of targets. For these reasons they have multiplied spectacularly since the eighteenth century. However, deer have a voracious appetite and will clear ground of young saplings, and as forest management schemes become more widespread an increasing number of deer have been culled. The most common species seen in the hills are actually fallow deer and roe deer, smaller than the red deer but equally shy, and usually spotted bounding into thick woodland, away from walkers tramping along trails.

Equally shy, though apparently more welcome in the Highlands than deer, is the red squirrel, which thrives in this environment as it does nowhere else in the British Isles. These creatures can be seen particularly in the pine forests around foothills of the Cairngorms, where woodland is often deliberately managed to keep out competing gray squirrels. Rather less familiar are wildcats (*felis silvestris grampia*), which the naturalist Gavin Maxwell describes in his classic book *Ring of Bright Water* as "tawny lynx-like ferals [that] bear as much relation to the domestic cat as does a wolf to a terrier… [they] grow to an enormous size, at least double that of the very largest domestic cat." He encountered the animals feeding on rabbits and lambs near his remote cottage on the West Highland coast, noting that "where there has been a strong lamb at dusk, at dawn there are raw bones and a fleece like a blood-stained swab in a surgery." Other Highland

Red deer stag, Glen Torridon
(Mehmet Karatay/Wikimedia Commons)

mammals include mountain hares, which turn white in winter for camouflage, and, perhaps oddest of all, a community of feral goats that live in caves and woods on the rocky and remote eastern shores of Loch Lomond, descendants of goats that were simply let go from farmsteads during the Highland Clearances.

Birdlife in the Highlands is just as remarkable and attracts both hunters and conservationists from all around the world. Most magnificent of all are the golden eagles, the "monarch of the feathered tribe" according to one character in Walter Scott's *Waverley*, who then immediately aims his gun towards a particularly fine specimen. These birds often sport seven-foot wingspans and swoop from the high peaks to feed on the grouse that make their home on moorland. The creation of grouse moors has, of course, vastly increased the numbers of these birds, but elsewhere habitats have been removed and other species of bird have faced extinction. One species formerly believed to have been made extinct was the osprey, but in 1954 a pair of ospreys established a nest on the shores of Loch Garten near Aviemore, and their descendants still make their home in the Abernethy Forest Reserve on the lake shore—and in other sites across the mountains whose location is often kept secret. It is reckoned that today there are around 430 breeding pairs of ospreys living throughout the Highlands.

Just as magnificent are the peregrine falcons, whose numbers were reduced to extinction levels in the 1950s because of the use of pesticides in farming, but which have now been re-introduced thanks to the efforts of conservation bodies. Other birds of prey include kestrels, merlins, and buzzards, while seabirds attract birdwatchers from around the world to the coastline and to the islands of the Inner Hebrides. One island, Rùm, is maintained as a bird sanctuary by Scottish Natural Heritage to allow the community of white-tailed sea eagles to flourish. Neighboring islands such as Islay also teem with birdlife: here as many as 15,000 white-fronted geese nest between September and April, remaining until the first signs of summer when they head off to Greenland to breed.

Throughout Scotland many wild areas have been placed under strict conservation measures to allow their bird and animal life to thrive; preservation bodies include the RSPB and the John Muir Trust, which owns and manages around 50,000 acres of land in Skye and around Ben Nevis and is named after one of the great Scottish conservationists of the nineteenth century.

OTTERS, SALMON, AND DOLPHINS: AQUATIC LIFE

In terms of aquatic life, the most iconic fish to make its home in the rivers of the Scottish Highlands is the salmon. In traditional Celtic culture salmon were revered as being almost mythical creatures, emblematic of wisdom and knowledge. Neil Gunn explored this association in his 1937 novel *Highland River*, whose principal character is a young boy named Kenn (the Gaelic word for "knowledge") who longs to catch a salmon from the stream near his home. Kenn knows that the salmon make their first annual appearance in the stream in April, and for him this time was always marked by "a change that was felt rather than seen; a state of expectancy, of vague but disturbing excitement. Kenn knew that if he had been a salmon he would be cutting the water with his nose, exactly as he cut the air when he ran in a sudden burst of speed, letting out a shout at nothing."

In popular imagination salmon are most famous for leaping up waterfalls to reach their spawning grounds in the mountains. At the Falls of

Shin near Lairg, an hour or so north of Inverness by road, a number of viewing platforms have been built overlooking a churning waterfall to allow these feats to be observed. Late spring to late autumn, and particularly August, are the best times to see the fish leaping up the falls here. Salmon are thought to navigate their journey from the sea to the place where they were born—and where they in turn will spawn—by using the earth's electromagnetic field and the unique chemical signature of the waters of their own river. When at last they have reached their spawning grounds the female salmon dig nests, known as redds, in the banks of the river, and lay eggs for fertilization by males.

The fish face innumerable obstacles as they swim up to their spawning grounds: on some rivers in Scotland that have been dammed for hydro electricity generation salmon are caught in traps and then released upstream so that they do not need to navigate around the dams (although at the generating plant in Pitlochry a "salmon ladder," consisting of a series of ascending concrete pools, is provided for them, and allows 5,400 fish to pass up the River Tummel each year). Out at sea, salmon face threats from predators and commercial fishing fleets, while on land large-scale felling of trees can cause rivers to swell in volume, rendering the up-stream progress of fish an unwinnable struggle. Further threats come from damage to riverbanks by deer and from the planting of conifers which has increased the acidity of water. It is for these reasons that salmon numbers in Scottish rivers have halved in the last thirty years, and recreational fishing for salmon is carefully controlled. Still, anglers from all over the world wade into Highland rivers to catch the fish, as Paul Torday's novel *Salmon Fishing in the Yemen* makes clear. In the book an Arab sheikh's love for Highland fishing and his desire to create a breeding environment for salmon in the arid wastes of the Yemen form a somewhat fanciful backdrop to the romantic entanglements of a British government minister and the engineer recruited to build the desert water system that the sheikh requires. The book has fun playing with the incongruity of the sheikh's exotic living arrangements and their transposition to his Highland residence in Glen Tulloch: on one occasion the minister, Dr. Alfred Jones, encounters "a dozen or more Yemeni tribesmen in flowing white robes and bright emerald turbans" forming a welcome party outside the house, where the "soft green lawn" glistens in the Highland drizzle.

Bottlenose dolphins, Moray Firth
(Peter Asprey/Wikimedia Commons)

The seas off the coast of eastern and western Scotland are also rich in wildlife. Minke whales, killer whales, pilot whales, porpoises, and dolphins all thrive in the sheltered waters around the Inner Hebrides; in fact the island of Muck has gained its name from the Gaelic "Muc Mara" meaning "sea pig" or "porpoise." The naturalist Gavin Maxwell, whose raising of a colony of otters in a tiny house near Kyle of Lochalsh is discussed more fully in Part Three of this book, loved the porpoises and dolphins he encountered just off the coast of the West Highlands. In *Ring of Bright Water* he describes porpoises as "six-foot lengths of sturdy grace... at close quarters the wondering inquisitiveness of their eyes shows as plainly as it can in a human face, a child's face as yet uninhibited against the display of emotion. The face... appears good-humoured, even bonhomous. But they will not stay to be stared at, and after [a] quick gasp they dive steeply down into the twilight." Dolphins, by contrast, would seem almost to hang about waiting for the boat to come out and play with them. "When we were out among them with the outboard motor they would play their own rollicking and hilarious games of hide-and-seek with us... as long as I live, and whatever splendid sights I have yet to see, I shall remember the pure glory of the dolphins' leap as they shot up a clear ten feet out of the sea, one after the other, in high parabolas of flashing silver."

A community of almost one hundred bottlenosed dolphins nowadays makes its home in the Moray Firth, the wedge-shaped bay forming the eastern coastline of the Highlands, on the opposite side of Scotland to Maxwell's cottage. These thirteen-foot beasts are some of the largest dolphins in the world and can live to the age of fifty; gatherings of thirty or forty can often be seen in the Firth from spotting places on the coast such as Kessock Bridge, a mile north of Inverness, where zoologists from Aberdeen University have set up a field station to observe these beguiling creatures.

Haggis, Kippers, and "the water of life"

Not surprisingly, the harsh climate of the Highlands, and the animals and plants that thrive there, have influenced the native cuisine of the region. Historically potatoes, turnips, and onions have grown well in northern Scotland's cool, damp climate and have formed staple ingredients of the diets of Highlanders until relatively recently. Another root vegetable grown in Scotland is the purple-hued neep, which with potatoes ("tatties and neeps") provides the standard accompaniment to haggis at a Burns Supper (haggis itself consisting of the lung, livers, and heart of a sheep mixed with other ingredients such as onions and oatmeal).

Potatoes were introduced to the region in stages: in 1760 the traveler and writer Richard Pococke observed that around the far north coast they "are not yet come into the use of potatoes, but are making a very small beginning; in the middle and south of Scotland they are in plenty." Cultivation of the potato exapanded quickly after its introduction, though, and from time to time potato famines similar to those across the water in Ireland blighted the lives of many remote communities. In 1846, the year after the potato famine struck in Ireland, the Highlands were affected by a similar tragedy, spread by the same spores that had devastated the Irish crop. Though dreadful, a combination of charitable donations and relief work by the British government meant that this famine was not as catastrophic as the one in Ireland.

Another staple crop of the Highlands is, of course, barley, which again is suited to the damp, chilly climate and is malted, dried, fermented, and distilled to produce the most famous liquid product of the region, namely whisky (in Gaelic *uiske beatha*, or "the water of life"). The drink is produced all over the region, although the most famous areas of production remain Speyside and the Isle of Islay. On his trip around the Hebrides the usually abstemious Dr. Johnson only tried the drink once, in an inn at Inveraray, claiming his indulgence to be an "experiment"; the great man of letters found his dram of whisky to be "preferable to any English malt brandy… strong but not pungent." Today few travelers are as self-denying as Dr. Johnson, to the delight of both distillers and the tourist board: the drink draws thousands of visitors every year to distilleries and tasting sessions, and provides one of Scotland's most valuable exports.

Traditionally communities who lived near the sea would vary their diet with fish, and cullen skink, a Highland soup made from smoked haddock and potatoes, neatly blends ingredients derived from land and sea together. In 1769 the writer Thomas Pennant was told on his journey through Scotland that the superstitious Highlanders "abhorred eels" because of their resemblance to serpents. Nonetheless scallops, oysters, mussels, and crabs have been caught extensively around the coast for centuries—the *Annals of Ulster* mentioned that in the year 836 the West Highland port of Tarbert was home to a busy fleet of herring-fishers—and nearly twelve centuries later freshly-caught fish can be eaten in any Highland port, though it is deliciously fresh cod, rather than herring, that raises the fare available in the local "chippy" well above the standards seen in places not blessed with a fishing fleet.

In former times ports such as Mallaig and Oban were home to huge processing plants where the herrings were turned into kippers before being sent off to the major cities. In those ports the fish would be gutted in dockside warehouses by teams of migrant women workers before being loaded onto trains. The heavily-laden trains leaving Oban would then slip and slide as they tackled the Glencruitten bank just outside the town because of the saltwater that had drained onto the tracks from previous wagons. But herring never achieved the culinary status of salmon and trout, which, perhaps surprisingly, have also formed part of the traditional Highland diet. In his *Letters to a Gentleman* the writer Edmund Burt indicates that when he traveled extensively thought northern Scotland in the 1720s these fish were often consumed by the poor, a remarkable state of affairs given that in London Burt was used to these fish being "esteemed to be the greatest rarities." Today, of course, these fish are farmed extensively in commercial fisheries throughout the Highlands.

Kilchurn Castle
(Pics-xl/Shutterstock)

Part Two

History

A Romantic depiction of Highland clan chiefs, 1831
(Wikimedia Commons)

The history of the Highlands, and of Highlanders, is recounted in two distinct but parallel narratives. The first is a narrative of steely and often bloody resolve, of resistance and survival against the rigors of a bitter climate, challenging terrain, and geographical remoteness. The second narrative, which has its origins in the Victorian era, is the dreamy Celtic myth of bagpipes, kilts, and tartan, of lochs and castles lost in swirling mists, and feats of heroism played out amidst some of the most gloomily romantic scenery on earth. Occasionally, such as in the case of Bonnie Prince Charlie, the two narratives merge into a single story that is both historically valid and resonant in legend. But too often the two narratives coexist as uneasy parallels, with the work of Victorian and later Hollywood mythologizers smothering a history that, for the last five hundred years at least, has been characterized by a struggle against grinding poverty and savage political repression.

Urquhart Castle: from Pictish Fort to Tourist Magnet

Nowhere in the Highlands epitomizes both historical narratives quite like Urquhart Castle. This extraordinarily atmospheric ruin glowers over Loch Ness from a rocky promontory on the loch's northern shore, its crumbling towers and walls reflected in the dark waters of Britain's largest body of water. Often the castle's stone ramparts are shrouded in a thick mist that curls in from the loch, providing the perfect setting for a mystical story of heroic Celtic warriors or doomed medieval romance. The castle occupies an ancient site. It was probably first fortified by the Celts and was certainly fortified by the Picts, the peoples who populated northern and eastern Scotland when the Romans began to advance north from England. In 84 CE the Romans soundly defeated the Picts at Mons Graupius, the first battle ever recorded on Scottish soil. But the conquerors showed no desire to occupy the Highlands and Urquhart Castle—or, to be more accurate, the fort that stood then on this rocky promontory—probably remained under Pictish control throughout the Roman era.

By the early sixth century CE the Romans had left the British Isles and the Picts were at war with a new foe, the Kingdom of Dalriada, whose territory covered most of the West Highlands and Inner Hebrides. Dalriada was a Christian kingdom and soon after its foundation missionaries from

Ireland established a great monastic community on the island of Iona; from there zealous monks were soon busy spreading the Word of God to the heathen Picts.

In around the year 580 St. Columba himself, the founder of the Iona mission, probably stayed at the fort that was later to become Urquhart Castle during his travels through Pictish lands. But written records remain hazy. Was it here that Columba baptized a dying Pictish chieftain named Emchath? Or did the conversion take place at some other location in Emchath's realm? The events of subsequent centuries remain just as murky. Violence and lawlessness pervaded the Highlands, and rival kinship groups known as clans fought for control of Urquhart Castle.

In 1230 Alexander II, the King of the Scots, gave Urquhart to the loyal Durward family, to bolster royal authority along the shores of Loch Ness. It was the Durwards who constructed the earliest parts of the stone castle that still survive, albeit in skeletal form, to this day. In 1275 Alan Durward died without an heir and the king passed the castle into the hands of another loyal subject, John Comyn, Lord of Badenoch and Lochaber, who extended the fortress and constructed a Great Hall right beside the water, of which only the cellars now remain. The Great Hall had only been standing for a couple of decades when the English King Edward I invaded Scotland and captured the castle. But the English adventure in Scotland only lasted a few years, cut short by the Scottish hero-king Robert the Bruce, who retook Urquhart Castle and placed it once again under direct royal control.

Scottish kings found that royal authority was hard to maintain in the more distant parts of their realm. And in the lands to the west of Urquhart, a new power had emerged to challenge the Scottish monarch: the Kingdom of the Isles, led by the chieftain of Clan MacDonald. The MacDonald clansmen raided Urquhart for the first time in 1395 in search of plunder. They were the red-headed Highlanders of popular legend, and they swept up the Great Glen towards the castle from their strongholds in the West Highlands and Inner Hebrides, burning and killing as they went. Raid followed raid and Urquhart was eventually captured and then maintained as a stronghold of the Lords of the Isles. Finally, though, in 1493 the King of the Scots broke the power of the rebellious MacDonalds and once again brought Urquhart Castle under royal control, awarding its custody to Clan Grant. It was the Grants who built the castle's substantial remaining tower, a five-story structure on the water's edge that became the core of their family home. Even though the Kingdom of the Isles was no more, the MacDonald raids along the shores of Loch Ness continued; the most devastating, but also the last, came in 1545 when MacDonald clansmen dragged hundreds of sheep and cattle back to their lands on the west coast. Fierce though the raid was, there was nothing new to the violence: throughout the Middle Ages and beyond, the raid was typical of the bloody struggles fought by rival clans.

Clan Grant sided with Charles I during the Civil War. A Royalist garrison was stationed in the castle, and soon a force of Covenanters—Scottish Protestants allied with Oliver Cromwell—was lined up against them. The Covenanters raided the place, burned it, and left it empty. But in 1688 a company of soldiers returned, Protestants this time, loyal to King William III and his wife Mary, who just had ousted the Catholic James II from the English throne. The sworn enemies of William III and Mary were the Jacobites, who pledged support for the ousted James, and who, during a military campaign across Scotland in 1689, began a protracted siege of the Protestant-held fortress. However, the Jacobite commander, MacDonell of Glengarry, found the castle impossible to take, and eventually ordered his soldiers to withdraw. Yet despite their victory the Grants felt that the castle was too costly to upkeep and in 1692 they burned it to the ground to stop it falling into Jacobite hands. After that, the castle was abandoned to the encroachment of moss and weeds and it played no part in the cycle of religious and dynastic wars that were to culminate in 1746 in the Battle of Culloden and the defeat of the Jacobite pretender to the Scottish throne, Bonnie Prince Charlie. After Culloden the British government broke the power of the clans and in the centuries that followed society and economics became the dominant drivers of the historical narrative of the Highlands, rather than religion and politics. The most devastating economic change came in the early nineteenth century, when tenant farmers eking out a living in the mountains around Urquhart Castle—and all over the Highlands—were driven from their land during a process of occasionally brutal evictions that came to be known as the Clearances.

The Clearances continued until the 1870s. By that time a very different Highlands had started to emerge. Railways brought tourists from England to the north of Scotland, and although a railway line was never

Urquhart Castle, looking towards Loch Ness
(Nilfanion/Wikimedia Commons)

built along the shores of Loch Ness, an easy trip across the loch by boat from Inverness meant that Urquhart Castle became a popular tourist attraction. Robert Burns and Samuel Taylor Coleridge came here to admire the ruins and in 1878 John Everett Millais painted them: in typically Romantic fashion his brushstrokes portrayed the castle under assault from stormy gray waters of Loch Ness, the whole scene played out under a dirty and petulant sky. Another moody picture of the castle (again under a stormy sky) also appeared on the cover of *The Tourist's Rambles in the Highlands*, one of the first travel guides to the region. But the castle itself was crumbling. In 1715 a large part of the south wall collapsed into the loch and in 1913 the castle was bequeathed by the widow of the seventh Earl of Grant into the hands of the state, which, in the guise of Historic Scotland, remains the ultimate custodian of this and scores of other historic sites across the country.

Nowadays Urquhart Castle is the single most popular historic site in the Highlands. Every year nearly a third of a million visitors crawl over its tumbledown walls. An Olympic-sized parking lot, gift shop, and visitor center (where a short film about the castle is shown in a choice of six languages) have been built into the hillside above the ruins. Although undeniably atmospheric, particularly at night, when the castle is floodlit, the place is rather sanitized, with a cod-historical view of history defined by the presence of a trebuchet (an enormous catapult on wheels) that was built for a TV recording in 1998 and has been parked outside the walls ever since (despite the fact that there is no historical evidence that one was ever used here). The place becomes particularly busy when a cruise shop docks at Invergordon and discharges its cargo of tourists onto the A82 for a tour of the castle and then a visit to one or both of the Loch Ness monster exhibitions a couple of miles up the road in the village of Drumnadrochit (many of the supposed sightings of the Loch Ness monster have been made from Urquhart's ramparts).

In short, the history of this ancient castle—a Pictish fort, a much fought-over medieval stronghold, and an internationally famous magnet for tourists—is neatly emblematic of the last two thousand years of Highland history, which has seen a newly-Christianized country become a bloody battlefield before its transformation in the nineteenth century into one of the great tourist playgrounds of the world.

Standing Stones and Burial Cairns: Mesolithic and Neolithic Peoples

The ice that covered Scotland during the most recent ice age did not finally melt until around 8000 BCE. At that time communities were creating elaborate cave art in southern France and adventurous settlers were crossing the Bering Strait from Asia into America. But Scotland was for the most part uninhabited. During colder phases of the Ice Age there would have been no people living here at all. At other times, when the temperature warmed for a few hundred years, small communities might have established themselves on the coast. Inland, on the slopes of the mountains and at the foot of the glens, humans had barely ever set foot. But as the ice finally melted, so forests encroached on the barren land, and in time animals made their home among the trees; these animals, including reindeer, boars, wolves, and bears, all of them now extinct, were preyed on by the Mesolithic hunter-gatherers who slowly took to wandering along the west coast of Scotland, settling for a while and then moving on once the resources of a particular place had been exhausted.

One of these settlements was at the head of Loch Scresort on the island of Rùm. Here, in Scotland's oldest archaeological site, finds such as stone arrowheads and piles of hazelnut shells have been unearthed, with the date of 6500 BCE ascribed to the earliest finds. The remains here are scant, however, and much more extensive, though later, evidence of the Mesolithic era in the Highlands has been discovered in caves around Oban, where harpoons fashioned from deer antlers have been unearthed along with bone pins that probably fastened clothing made from animal hides. On the island of Oronsay, midway between Islay and Mull, middens—archaeological rubbish heaps comprising bones and shells—have also been discovered. Those excavated on the island in the 1970s suggest that Mesolithic-era islanders lived on a diet of crabs, oysters, mussels, seabirds, and seals.

From the first communities established along the coast, Mesolithic peoples spread to the islands of the Inner Hebrides rather than onto the high ground of the Highlands, which remained thickly forested and devoid of habitation for many centuries. During this time the climate was probably warmer than it is now, and population densities were sparse, so resources were bountiful; these early peoples had plenty of beasts to hunt in the forests, plenty of berries to pick from bushes and plenty of fish to catch in the rough seas off the coast or in the rapid torrents of freshwater that spilled down from the mountains. Yet their lifestyle was not as sustainable as we might imagine. Research on the island of Colonsay, where a midden of over 100,000 hazelnut shells has been discovered, suggests that the harvesting of so many nuts would have led to irredeemable ecosystem damage. And on at least one occasion during this time a natural disaster of unprecedented proportions was unleashed on the early communities. Around 5200 BCE a huge tsunami devastated settlements along the east coast such as the one established in a sheltered ravine over which Castle Street in Inverness now runs. This tidal wave was the result of a massive underwater landslide off Norway (known to geologists as the Storegga Slide); it must have killed hundreds if not thousands of people. Archaeologists in Inverness have dug out a layer of charcoal (from fires) and flints (from hunting spears) that provide evidence for the existence of communities that would have been wiped out here in a matter of seconds.

By 4000 BCE Mesolithic peoples had been living in Scotland for four thousand years. Settlement had at last spread away from the coasts to the interior of islands and to the mountains and glens. But societies were still semi-nomadic and had made few major advances in technology or organization. Now, however, this was about to change. New settlers from Europe began colonizing the region, bringing with them skills originating from the Middle East that allowed the cultivation of crops and the rearing of animals on farmsteads. These new settlers ushered in the Neolithic age. Gradually wheat and barley became dietary staples, replacing picked berries, and these cereals were supplemented with meat and milk from cattle, goats, and sheep. This meant that societies could at last become permanently settled rather than given to nomadic wandering; people cleared land and lived in stone houses rather than in caves or temporary camp grounds.

The most iconic reminders of Neolithic settlement in Scotland, namely the great stone circle at Callanish on the Isle of Lewis, and the extensive network of burial cairns on Orkney, lie outside the region covered by this book. Cases of single standing stones do exist in the Scottish mainland, however, such as the stone beside Loch Linnhe at Onich, a seven-foot-high monster that is famously bored through by two circular holes that were probably caused by erosion when the stone was lying flat (and which now make for an atmospheric photograph of the stone when taken at sunset).

In the Highlands some (comparatively unimpressive) stone circles remain, but it is burial cairns and isolated clusters of standing stones that provide the most immediate testimony to the civilization of this period. The best-preserved cairns can be seen in Kilmartin Glen in the southwest Highlands, to the north of the seaside town of Lochgilphead. Some eight hundred prehistoric sites have been catalogued around this glen, including twenty-five where there are standing stones: one can be seen in fields to the west of the main Oban to Lochgilphead road at Nether Largie, while two small stone circles slightly to the north of this at Temple Wood nestle under a glade of oak trees planted by the local laird at the end of the nineteenth century. Graves have been found among these stones, but like many burials in the Kilmartin region the bodies have dissolved to almost nothing in the acidic soil.

Close to the circles, laid out in a straight line along the floor of the valley, are six cairns whose interiors have been excavated to reveal stone-lined burial chambers known as cists. The oldest, South Cairn, dating from around 3000 BCE, comprises a just-accessible burial chamber roofed by giant slabs that lies at the center of a circular heap of rubble. Beakers, jewelry, and weapons found in these burial chambers are now on display at the excellent museum at Kilmartin, the picture-postcard village sitting on a ledge above the cairns. It is thought that the beakers, some of which are quite ornate, might have contained a drink for the deceased to consume in the afterlife.

Just as striking as the cairns of Kilmartin Glen are the Mesolithic-era grooves scoured on rock faces and on standing stones that are known as "cup and ring marks." The typical patterns formed by these grooves comprise a central cup-sized hollow surrounded by concentric rings, although more complex designs exist, some resembling wheels and even eyes. Over one hundred cup and ring mark sites have been catalogued around Kilmartin; some of the most surprising are at Ormaig, where a slope of rock in a forest clearing is smothered in symbols, while a more accessible collection can be seen at Achnabreck, a village just off the A816 just south of Kilmartin village. The purpose of these markings has long been debated by scholars: they could be religious symbols, or perhaps they were used to mark meeting places or territorial boundaries—and some archaeologists have even suggested that they were used as markers for copper prospectors.

THE BRONZE AGE AND THE IRON AGE—AND THE COMING OF THE CELTS

As the Neolithic Age gave way to the Bronze Age, the tradition of burying the dead in cairns continued. Some of the best examples of these later cairns lie east of Inverness, tucked under the northern slopes of Beinn Bhuidhe Mhor and known as the Clava Cairns. These four Bronze Age burial chambers date from between 2000 and 1000 BCE. Two of the cairns are "passage graves," their empty centers accessed by a passage cut through the mound of rubble that is open to the sky, their perimeters ringed with moss-smeared standing stones (one of which has similar "cup and ring" marks to stones at Kilmartin); the later "ring cairn" is merely an open enclosure formed by a circle of boulders. Traces of human remains have been found amidst these cairns, which were clearly vested with astronomical significance as the passageways are aligned in the direction of the setting sun at the midwinter solstice; these cairns once formed a lengthy and ex-

Reconstructed Bronze Age crannog at Kenmore on Loch Tay
(Andrew Beattie)

tensive linear cemetery, like the ones at Kilmartin, although most of the other cairns have disappeared over time.

In the Victorian era the local landowner romanticized the cairns by planting a grove of beech trees around them, and now they lie in a shady and peaceful spot, the only disturbance coming from the occasional rattle of trains crossing the impressive brick-built Nairn viaduct spanning the valley to the east. Like the Kilmartin cairns, which lie close to a Dark Age fort established during the early Christian era, the Clava Cairns are also situated in a historically resonant area, for the battlefield site of Culloden lies just over a mile away across the river.

The Bronze Age derives its name from the items, particularly weapons, manufactured using that metal; the era coincided with a cooling of the climate and a reduction in food resources, so these weapons were developed in part from the need for communities to defend their territories. This is reflected in a number of skeletons that have been unearthed across the Highlands: wounds associated with battle and conflict are rarely present on skeletons of those who lived prior to the Bronze Age.

Mindful of the need for security, Bronze Age settlers typically built their houses at the edge of lochs or rivers, on stilts or artificial islands fashioned from stones and tree trunks. These dwellings have come to be known as crannogs; accessed by canoe or causeway, their design was intended to dissuade both attackers and wolves. The frames of most crannogs were fashioned from trunks of alder trees, which are water-resistant as they typically grow right at the water's edge; this meant that the crannog's wooden frame would withstand immersion in water. The circular structures were then capped with a conical roof and covered in thatch.

One such crannog has been reconstructed by archaeologists on the edge of Loch Tay, close to the pretty waterside town of Kenmore in the Perthshire Highlands, in a reconstruction inspired by the remains of crannogs excavated elsewhere around the loch's shore. The dim interior of the crannog is complete with sheepskin rugs and wooden bowls for eating and drinking. There is no hole for smoke from the fire to escape: it simply filtered out through the reeds that covered the roof. It is reckoned that an extended family of fifteen would live in such dwellings, which lined lochs all over Scotland, their former presence often marked by small, circular islands just offshore that are the remnants of the waste that would have fallen through the structure's floor. (One of these islands in Loch Tay, Spry Island, was enlarged in 1842 by the Marquis of Breadalbane so that Queen Victoria could take a picnic on it.) Crannogs survived into Roman times and beyond: one, excavated in 1933 on Eaderloch near Fort William, was used by a local chieftain in medieval times for council meetings, and was known as the *Tigh nam Fleadh* or House of the Feasts. This crannog, like its Bronze Age and Iron Age forebears, was built partly to express prestige and influence. Poorer members of Bronze Age communities lived not in the comfort of a crannog but in the damp gloom of a weem, an underground dwelling that was accessed via a passageway, which could at least be kept warm in winter.

The new Bronze Age technologies of metal working required the use of tin. This metal came from Cornwall, resulting in Highland communities forming links with the Celtic tribes that had already settled there. Trade gave way to migration and settlement, and by 400 BCE Celtic peoples had colonized the Highlands and had introduced iron working, relegating bronze to use only in jewelry; so these settlers ushered in the Iron Age. Celts lived in tribes and had developed economies based on animal husbandry and growing crops; well-organized legal, administrative, and educational systems stood alongside a religion that was overseen by druids and frequently involved human sacrifice.

As the Celts established their settlements along the coast of the West Highlands, so Roman ships were drawn to the area in search of slaves and plunder. To counter the threat Celtic chieftains ordered the construction of fortified stone towers known as brochs, some of which can still be seen today: the most extant can be found in a lushly forested, secretive valley south of Kyle of Lochalsh named Gleann Beag, where two circular towers named Dun Telve and Dun Troddan still stand. Brochs were built with double walls for protection and it is these that are the most striking in Dun Telve, the first broch the road along Gleann Beag passes. The central area these walls enclosed was fifteen feet in diameter, yet the walls were constructed from rough stone with no lime or mortar to act as cement. The walls tapered towards the top and from outside the windowless structure looks not unlike an ancient cooling tower. A little way along the valley, Dun Troddan sits on a ledge overlooking a farm, and is in a slightly less well preserved state, though the double walls and the tightly-packed stones are again clearly discernible. It is thought that brochs such as these served as both defensive forts and domestic dwellings (their interiors consisted of a number of stories separated by wooden floors); and that they were built by specialist, itinerant broch-builders, which is why they are all of pretty similar design.

Contemporaneous with the brochs were the hill forts that Iron Age communities constructed around the fringes of the Highlands. One of these, Craig Phadrig, can be found on a thickly forested hill that rises above the mushrooming suburbs of Inverness. Only a ring of raised earthworks remains, and the woodland trails and the views over the Moray Firth are the main draws today to this ancient site. Hill forts such as Craig Phadrig probably served as the military and administrative headquarters of a particular Celtic tribe; in the lowlands at the foot of the fortified hills farming communities would grow crops and raise animals. In Celtic, these hill forts were known as *duns*, which explains the prevalence of that word in the names of places on the fringes of the Highlands, such as Dunkeld, Dunfermline, and Dunsinane, the latter the famous hill that features in the last act of Shakespeare's play *Macbeth*.

One of the most famous archaeological finds from the very early

Celtic era in the Highlands is the so-called Ballachulish Goddess. This is a life-size image of a female, carved from dark alder wood, which was discovered in 1880 under four feet of peat on the shores of Loch Leven near the village of Ballachulish. The statue was fashioned around 600 BCE; how it ended up in the mud of Loch Leven is unknown, but the oxygen-denying properties of peat, as well as the water-resistant properties of alder wood, have ensured the remarkable state of its preservation. The figure can be seen in the National Museum of Scotland in Edinburgh, and there is an authentically realistic copy in the eccentric volunteer-run folk museum in Glencoe, just up the road from Ballachulish.

The goddess has no feet, just stumpy legs that end in a block into which is carved a niche, which possibly served as a receptacle for prayer offerings. With its strangely elongated torso and its eyes made from pebbles, the goddess is an otherworldly figure, strange and indecipherable; two and a half millennia after it was fashioned, it seems unwilling to divulge its secrets to those visitors to the museum who peer at it today through the glass panels of its display case.

THE PICTS AND THE ROMANS

Less is known about the Picts than any other of the original peoples of Scotland. It is thought that Pictish peoples formed a loose agglomeration of tribes that might have been in existence in Scotland since before the arrival of the Celts. The first written mention of them dates from the year 297 CE and comes from the pen of the historian Eumenius, who described how Pictish tribes would venture south and launch raids on Roman towns in northern England. But by then the Picts had clearly been living in Scotland for a number of centuries. They were an agrarian people, rearing sheep and goats and cultivating oats and barley. At their most expansive and powerful, Pictish kings ruled much of eastern and northern Scotland, and they played a vital part in defending these regions from the Romans. To Eumenius the Picts were the "painted peoples" on account of their body tattoos, which is a possible origin of their name, although "Pict" could also be a corruption of the Latin term *Priteni* used to describe the inhabitants of Britain in the fourth century BCE, the word later morphing into *Britanni*. In Sir Walter Scott's novel *Rob Roy* a tradition is recounted that Picts were "half-goblin half-human beings, distinguished… for cunning, courage, ferocity, and the length of their arms, and the squareness of their shoulders." This is in part fanciful legend, of course. But the Picts were clearly fierce and tenacious fighters, for the Romans never engaged them militarily after securing victory at the battle of Mons Graupius.

The reason why much about the Picts is derived from legend is that they left no written culture behind. We do not even have an idea as to the language they spoke. Their name survives in place names such as Pitlochry, in the central Highlands, and archaeological evidence survives too, in the form of intricately decorated stones that can be seen in many museums throughout the north and east of Scotland. These stones are decorated in designs that can vary from clear representations of birds and animals to more abstract geometrical shapes and squiggles; all are carved with bold, simple strokes to convey effective messages that in many cases still speak clearly to the onlooker, so many centuries after they were fashioned. Many of these stones were unearthed on the fringes of the Highlands rather than in glens or beside lochs. The decorated stone named Rhynie Man, for instance, was found in the village of Rhynie in Aberdeenshire in 1978, at a place where the rolling woods and cultivated fields of that county finally give way to more substantial uplands; the stone depicts, with almost cartoon-like simplicity, a figure in profile clad in a tunic and carrying a ceremonial axe. It is a highly unusual Pictish stone in that it depicts a figure rather than animals or symbols and is displayed in an unusual place too, at Woodhill House, the offices of Aberdeenshire Council, situated on the outskirts of Aberdeen. As to who the figure is, theories abound: it could be a Pictish king, or the Celtic God Esus, or even St. Matthew.

Rhynie itself is overlooked from the northwest by a steeply conical, heather-clad hill that rises to a height of 1,851 feet. On its flat summit are the remains of one of the best-preserved Pictish hill forts, Tap o'Noth, where Rhynie Man may originally have been carved. Nothing remains of the fort save a ring of stones that surrounds the leveled-off summit. These stones show clear evidence of having been vitrified, a process that deliberately fused stones by burning them at temperatures of up to 2012°F (1100°C) and which was a hallmark of Pictish military architecture. More engaging, though, than the stone fortifications at Tap o'Noth is the stupendously panoramic view from the summit, surely one of the best in Scotland and encompassing both Highland and lowland scenery (the stiff walk up to the summit takes

Remains of the Pictish hill fort at Tap o'Noth
(Andrew Beattie)

an hour and begins at a signposted car park on the A941). When the Picts took over the former Iron Age fort at Craig Phadrig above Inverness they also vitrified the stones there—some of which are on display in the history museum in the center of Inverness, their blackened and melted edges clearly visible to this day.

Political ties between Rome and the Pictish kings were forged well before the invasion of Britain in 43 CE. In fact according to oral tradition the Pictish king Metallanus had allowed the Romans to establish an iron ore mine and an associated military encampment near the hill fort of Dun Gael, in the southern Highlands, some time after the expedition of Julius Caesar to Britain in 55 BCE. It was at the military camp, according to legend, that Pontius Pilate had been born some twenty-five years later, the son of a Roman officer who was an emissary of Caesar Augustus. This legend is still adhered to in the village of Fortingall, close to the site of Dun Gael and situated in soft Highland countryside between Loch Tay and the foot of Schiehallion. But firm evidence that Pontius Pilate was born in the Highlands is actually non-existent. The legend has persisted, though, due to discovery of the "Pilate Stone" in the Mediterranean port of Caesarea in present-day Israel. This is a pale slab of limestone on which is carved the inscription "iberieum Pontius Pilate." Most scholars are of the opinion that the first word (with its first letter missing) refers to a building known as the Tiberieum. Those seeking evidence for the legend that Pilate was born in Scotland have suggested rather fancifully that the first word on the slab is Hiberieum and refers to Hibernia, the Roman name for Scotland—and that the full inscription reads, in translation, "Pontius Pilate, Scot." It is, it has to be said, an extremely tenuous piece of evidence for what has always been a rather fanciful legend.

It was under the rule of Gnaeus Julius Agricola, the Roman Governor of Britain from 78 CE to 85, that the Romans began their occupation of southern Scotland. Their advance north was recorded in detail by Agricola's biographer, the historian Cornelius Tacitus. In 83 CE, having dealt with resistance in southwest Scotland, Agricola's military units pressed north towards the Highlands, with supply ships plying the east coast to ensure that soldiers were adequately fed and armed. The decisive military clash came the following year when Roman forces defeated a Pictish army at the Battle of Mons Graupius, which was fought near Bennachie to the northwest of Aberdeen. The Picts proved themselves to be rather undisciplined fighters; during the battle their soldiers abandoned their positions on high ground—where according to Tacitus they had been "posted… in a manner calculated to impress and intimidate"—to rush headlong at the enemy, only to be met by Roman cavalry held in reserve. As a result ten thousand Pictish lives were lost as opposed to only 360 on the Roman side.

The Romans celebrated their victory by burning settlements, plundering farms, and taking slaves; Tacitus maintained that the Caledonian commander Calgacus—whose name is a Latinized adaptation of the Celtic "sword-wielder"—dubbed the Romans "a people who create a desert and call it peace." But once victory was theirs the Romans did not press their advantage. A fleet was sent north and landed on Orkney, but Agricola was recalled to Rome by the Emperor Domitian and the half-built fortress he had established at Inchtuthil, on the banks of the Tay as it flows from the Highlands towards Perth, was quickly abandoned (all that remains of the camp today are a series of bumps and ridges in a field). Calgacus must have regarded the withdrawal as a victory. "We, the most distant dwellers on earth, [are] the last of the free," is the sentiment ascribed to him by Tacitus. The Picts, Calgacus maintained, had been "shielded by our very remoteness and by the obscurity in which it has shrouded our name."

Tacitus claims that the reason for Agricola's recall to Rome was that Domitian was jealous of his spectacular achievements in Scotland. But this judgement is clouded by a fair degree of bias (Tacitus was married to Agricola's daughter) and the probable reason why the Romans never occupied the Highlands beyond their southern fringes was that they believed a line of control drawn deep into Scotland would be too challenging to maintain. So Roman policy towards the Picts became one of containment. This reached its fullest expression in the construction of Hadrian's Wall across northern England between 122 and 128 and then in the Antonine Wall, constructed between the Forth and Clyde and completed in 144. Caledonian tribes often proved difficult to contain behind these walls, and along with tribes from northern England they participated in a number of raids on Roman Britain, such as the sack of York perpetrated by the Brigantes in 197. Throughout their time in Britain the Romans regarded Scots, and Highlanders in particular, with fear and contempt. Tacitus records that Highland men could often be observed dancing around swords laid on the ground, a practice that is a clear forebear of more contemporary Highland dances.

THE GAELS AND CHRISTIANITY

The last serious breach of Hadrian's Wall came in 367, when the Picts, in alliance with a number of other tribes, pillaged and fought their way south, pushing deep into Roman territory. By then it was clear that Roman rule in Britain was over and that the Empire was facing severe challenges throughout continental Europe. The last Roman troops finally withdrew from Britain in 410, never having occupied Scotland north of the Tay. Their exodus meant that the way was clear for settlement by new arrivals. Just as the Saxons settled in southeastern England, so a people known Gaels (or Scotii to the Romans) crossed the narrow sea channel between Antrim and Argyll to settle in the western parts of Scotland. Throughout the fifth century CE Gaelic settlements were founded along the coastline of the Kintyre peninsula and the West Highlands, and on the islands of the Inner and Outer Hebrides. Previously members of the same tribe had settled in Pembrokeshire and other parts of coastal Wales; but their settlements in Argyll were to prove the most enduring.

The settlers in Scotland founded a new kingdom and named it Dalriada, after the original Scotii Kingdom of Dalriada in Antrim. Its first ruler, Fergus Mor, established his seat of rule at Dunadd, near modern-day Lochgilphead on the Highland coast south of Oban. Dunadd is only a couple of miles to the south of the prehistoric sites of Kilmartin Glen, making this one of the most historically resonant areas in the Highlands. The knobbly hill on which the fort was established had been a fortified farmstead before the days of Fergus, and it is not difficult to see why: the surrounding flat land is fertile and the natural hillock makes for a prime defensive site.

In Fergus Mor's time Dunadd became the center of trade in slaves, fur, and leather, and the largest-ever hoard of European pottery ever unearthed in Britain has been found here, indicating that this was a major trading port. Archaeologists investigating the site have also found hundreds of molds which would have been used to make brooches that were then given by the king to his followers. But today there is little to see of the place where Dalriada's finest warriors once feasted and their bards told the epic sagas of their Ulster homeland. The few visitors who make their way up to the former fortress (a stroll of only five minutes or so from a car park off the main Oban to Lochgilphead road) encounter only the indistinct foundations of walls, although an ancient well is also discernible. More arresting is the impression of a footprint on a flat sheet of exposed rock right at the summit. According to legend this had been left by the mythical warrior Ossian as he leapt across the valley to Dunadd, and it was believed that a king, by placing his foot in the impression, signalled his domination over those who lived on his land. The first king to do this was Fergus Mor, in or around the year 500 CE.

A period of aggressive expansion followed the establishment of Fergus Mor's kingdom. First Galloway in southwestern Scotland was invaded and occupied, and then after 574, under their ruler Aeden MacGraban, the Scotii pushed eastwards, threatening the Picts, whose territory was becoming a central, unified kingdom that encompassed much of northern and eastern Scotland. Links with the Kingdom of Dalriada in Antrim remained strong during the early decades of the new kingdom, and Aeden MacGraban and those who followed him could always count on help from across the Irish Sea in their entanglements with the Picts. As their kingdom expanded, so the name of the Scotii was ascribed to the whole of the north of Britain—although the creation of Scotland as a nation was still some centuries away.

Unlike the heathen Picts the Scotii were a Christian people and Dalriada was destined to become Scotland's first Christian kingdom. A hanging bowl found at Tioram Castle in the Ardnamurchan peninsula, and now displayed in the West Highland Museum in Fort William, provides a valuable insight into this era: the bronze bowl, of which only the greenish, oxidized, saucer-sized rim remains, was probably used to mix water and wine during Christian rituals (though how it ended up in the castle, built several centuries later, is something of a mystery). Among those early Gaelic settlers in this part of the West Highlands, who quite possibly worshipped at Dunadd and used the Tioram bowl in services, were monks with a zealous mission to spread the new faith across Scotland.

One of the first, named Lorn, settled with his brothers Fergus and Oengus near Oban in around the year 500, and the Firth of Lorn, the narrow gulf between Oban and the Isle of Mull, is named after him. Around four decades later, in the year 542, the well-traveled monk Brendan the Navigator (who probably had already brought Christianity to the Faroe Islands) founded a Christian community on a small island in the now uninhabited Garvellach chain south of Oban; the island became known as Holy Isle and to this day the remains of monastic cells can be seen on the island (though they are from a later community of monks who built them three centuries after Brendan's first community settled here).

These early Gaelic monks also proselytized among Picts in the wild territory of the northern Highlands. One of the most tangible pieces of evidence of the spread of Christianity into Pictish lands is the so-called Ballachly Stone, a pale-colored slab of rock dating from the seventh century on which Christian carvings can be faintly discerned. The stone was unearthed in 1996 in Dunbeath on the northeast coast of Scotland—deep into Pictish territory—and is now on display in the heritage center there. On the stone are depicted the upper section of a Celtic cross—complete with florid twists and curls—together with a fish, an early symbol of Christianity. The stone's discovery has led some to suggest that Dunbeath

The Farr Stone with its Pictish inscriptions, outside the Bettyhill Museum (Andrew Beattie)

emerged as a high-status center of Pictish Christianity soon after the first monks came here.

Slightly later in execution, though rather more complete in its current state, is the so-called Farr Stone, a substantial slab of rock that can be seen in the graveyard surrounding the deconsecrated church now housing the Bettyhill Museum on the north coast of Scotland. This stone depicts a familiar Celtic "ringed" cross alongside the animal symbols that the Picts were so keen on: the two animals depicted on the stone may be swans, which mate for life and so are suggestive of faithfulness.

Lorn, Fergus, and Brendan were by no means the only monks spreading Christianity around Pictland. Tales and traditions surrounding dozens of other missionary monks abound. One of those was a Briton named Ninian, whose exploits in fifth-century Scotland were chronicled extensively by the Venerable Bede, who praised him as "a most reverend bishop." A monk called Angus introduced the new religion along the lonely shores of Loch Voil, in the southern part of the Highlands, and when he died he was buried in the village of Balquhidder under a slab etched with his effigy; today that burial slab, which may date from as far back as the seventh century, can be seen in Balquhidder's nineteenth-century church, which lies just a few yards away from the crumbling ruins of an older church where the body of St. Angus is still thought to lie. In Wester Ross the new religion was spread by a monk named Maelrhuba, and a thousand years later people here were still sacrificing bulls on his feast day in his honor—a clear indication that for centuries paganism infused the rituals of the new religion. A Pictish slab known as the "Red Priest's Stone," on which can be discerned the faint carving of a Christian cross, is the traditional marking place of Maelrhuba's burial, and can be found in the remote countryside between Bettyhill and Altnahara in the far north of Scotland, some three hundred yards from the nearest road. In 580 Bishop Donan was active in the Knoydart peninsula and possibly founded a community on the island just along the coast from Kyle of Lochalsh that bears his name, Eilean Donan, now home to one of Scotland's most visited castles. A century or so later, Donan's fellow countryman Fillan began preaching in Dochart near Killin in the heart of the West Highlands. Fillan's famed "healing stones" are held to this day by a folklore center in the village, and in Strathfillan, between Tyndrum and Crianlarich, a couple of tumbledown stone walls beside a farm house are all that are left of a priory that he supposedly founded. In the centuries that followed his death his cult grew in Scotland, and Robert the Bruce was recorded as taking a holy relic of Fillan into battle with him at Bannockburn in 1314. Needless to say, Lorn, Ninian, Fillan, and a host of other missionary monks all achieved sainthood in the early Catholic Church, though their precise exploits (and in some cases their actual existence) is a matter of some debate, so deep in the Dark Ages were their lives and missions.

ST. COLUMBA AND THE CHRISTIAN MISSION IN IONA

None of those early missionaries, not even Fillan, achieved the lasting fame of their most famous brother, a monk named Columba. Little is known of Columba's early life but it seems clear that in 563 he fled Ireland after a quarrel with King Diarmait that had escalated into a full-scale battle, fought at a place named Cuildremne. On his arrival in Scotland Columba probably traveled to Inverness where he converted Brude, the King of the Picts, to Christianity—at least, that is the story told by the Venerable Bede three centuries later in his *Ecclesiastical History*; the few contemporary accounts are vague over this, and Brude, or Bridei, might already have been a Christian when Columba first met with him. The probable site for the conversion (if it took place at all) was Craig Phadrig, the great Pictish hill fort that lies on the outskirts of Inverness. Bede then goes on to recount that Columba was looked on favorably by Brude and was granted the Hebridean island of Iona in recognition of his missionary work. This, however, is unlikely, as at the time Iona (along with the other islands of the Inner Hebrides and much of the mainland of the west of Scotland) was ruled by one of the tribes (or *tuath*) into which Dalriada was divided, and it is far more likely—and indeed attested to in annals compiled in an Irish monastery—that Iona was gifted to Columba by the leader of the *tuath* that ruled that part of Dalriada.

However the island of Iona came into his hands, the monastery that Columba established on the island as penance for his misdeeds in Ireland soon became home to a monastic community whose members were instrumental in spreading Christianity across Scotland and northern England. That we know so much about Columba's life is due to one of his successors at the monastery of Iona, Adamnan, who assumed the role of Columba's biographer. One story Adamnan recounted about Columba concerned his dispute with another missionary, Moluag, over which of them would claim Lismore island in Loch Linnhe as a missionary base: Moluag allegedly cut off his finger as the two monks raced towards it, and threw the severed digit ashore ahead of him, thus claiming the island for himself.

Columba had more success in Inverness, where he founded the High Church, which occupies another possible site of his supposed conversion; no trace of Columba's church remains today (the current church dates from the 1770s) but it seems certain that the site's religious significance, overlooking the banks of the River Ness just a short walk from the city center, dates back to the very early Christian era. The most enduring of the religious houses founded by Columba's monks was the distant monastery on the island of Lindisfarne off the coast of Northumberland, whose king, Oswald, had spent time on Iona as a young man. One Iona monk, however, named Dorbbene, got even further than the founder of Lindisfarne and traveled as far as modern-day Switzerland. It was he who gave the name Stäfa to a village on the shores of Lake Zurich, naming the place after the island of Staffa, which can clearly be seen from the shores of Iona. Dorbbene also brought to Switzerland a copy of Adamnan's biography of Columba, dating from the year 704 and copied out by the monks of Iona. It is now preserved in the Stadtbibliothek in the Swiss city of Schaffhausen and is the oldest extant version of Adamnan's work.

Columba's monastic foundation on Iona quickly became one of the richest in Scotland. Over the decades and centuries that followed the monastery developed into the center of a Celtic Church that came to rival that of Rome. Manuscripts and other documents of faith flowed from the scribes here, including (possibly) an illuminated edition of the gospels that came to be known as the Book of Kells, which some scholars maintain was fashioned in Iona in around the year 790 (although other monasteries across Ireland and northern Britain also claim to be the origin of the famed manuscript, which now resides in the library of Trinity College, Dublin). Monks and nuns remained on the island for the next seven centuries. By the late Middle Ages the site of Columba's original wood-built monastery had long been abandoned (the spot is marked today by the remains of earthworks) and a new monastery had been built, the kernel of today's religious complex. Then came the Protestant Reformation: Abbot MacKinnon, who once lived in a cell on Staffa—a chair-like feature on the island's coast is supposed to be his altar—was the last of Iona's great abbots before the monastery was closed by the Church commissioners. After the monks left the old buildings were simply left to sink slowly into Iona's peat.

Yet enough of the ruined monastery remained for literary travelers Dr. Samuel Johnson and his friend James Boswell to gain satisfaction from a visit in 1773. After landing on the island the pair spent the night in a barn and, according to Boswell, were shown round the ruins the next morning by "an illiterate fellow... who called himself a descendant of a cousin of Saint Columba." Although Iona did not quite reach Boswell's high expectations his companion was much more impressed. Boswell remarked that "to have seen it, even alone, would have given me great satisfaction; but the venerable scene was rendered much more pleasing by the company of my great and pious friend... who had described the impressions it should make on the mind with such strength of thought, and

Iona Abbey
(Andrew Beattie)

energy of language, that I shall quote his words... 'that man is little to be envied, whose piety would not grow warmer among the ruins of Iona.'" Further travelers followed in their wake. The poet John Keats visited Iona on his epic walk through Scotland in 1818, and wrote to his brother Tom that he had been shown around by a local schoolmaster, barely "four foot tall and an ignorant little man but reckoned very clever… it is rich in the most interesting antiquities. Who would expect to find the ruins of a fine cathedral church, of cloisters, colleges, monasteries, and nunneries in so remote an island?" The novelist Jules Verne, whose travels in Scotland inspired his novel *The Green Ray,* indicates in that book that there was nothing but "ruins" and "debris" on the island, although tourists of the day seemed quite happy visiting them: the old chapel, "heavy, severe, and silent, exuded the poetry of past eras."

This was before Iona's modern renaissance. In the early twentieth century the medieval abbey church underwent a wholesale reconstruction and the island was established as a place of Christian retreat. Today the abbey church and its cloister come as something of a surprise to visitors to Iona, a bright, contemporary, and airy space where visiting Christians who step through the front door are invited to "pick a Bible in their own language" from the dozens available. Now thousands of Christians come here in search of peace and solace every year, and the abbey, among whose ruins James Boswell once "indulged in solitude and devout meditation," stands amidst a clutch of other heavily restored buildings.

The oldest structure here is a simple, sturdy chapel dedicated to St. Oran whose origins date to the year 1080. Surrounding the chapel is a cemetery where Scots Kings Duncan and Macbeth, as well as a number of kings of France, Scotland, and Norway, are supposed to have been buried, though their headstones have long been lost to Iona's blistering winds. Those who are buried here under identifiable slabs include John Smith, the former Labour Party leader who suffered an untimely death in 1994, and who was born in the West Highland hamlet of Dalmally, between Tyndrum and Oban.

THE BIRTH OF SCOTLAND

In 685 the Picts met the Angles of Northumberland, one of the two tribes that had settled in the south of what is now Scotland, on the battlefield at Nechtansmere near Forfar. The Angle chieftain Egfrith was slain and the Angles were soundly defeated. Emboldened by their victory, the Picts turned their attention westwards to the Scotii of Dalriada. In 736 the great Scotii hill fort at Dunadd fell to King Oengus (or Angus) of the Picts, forcing the Scotii to recognize their eastern neighbors as their political overlords. At the same time as the ascendancy of the Picts the Celtic Church went into decline. Its fate was sealed in 664 at the Synod of Whitby, where clerics accepted Augustine's Canterbury-forged variant of Christianity over that of Columba. In 717 the Pictish King Nechtan expelled all the Irish monks from his kingdom, further reducing the strength of the Celtic Church in northern Britain.

But the ascendancy of the Picts over the Scotii was to be reversed in the middle of the following century. Pictish succession rules were complex, weakening the state by allowing multiple claimants to the throne whenever a king died, and the Picts were suffering grievously at the hands of the Danes, who fought and defeated them in 839. The political and military weakness of the Picts was exploited by Kenneth MacAlpin, the King of Dalriada, who absorbed the Pictish kingdom into his own in 843 to create a kingdom known to the Gaels as Alba and to Latin-speaking clerics as Scotia (later, of course, Scotland).

MacAlpin was a ruthless and ambitious leader—the most famous story surrounding him was that he invited some Pictish chieftains to a banquet and promptly slaughtered them—but his new kingdom covered a large area, incorporating much of the southern and central Highlands. Never before had so much of Scotland been united under one ruler. MacAlpin chose the village of Scone, just north of Perth, as the capital of the new kingdom. Scone had formerly been the seat of the Pictish kings and MacAlpin ceremonially confirmed the place as the capital of his new united kingdom by moving the famous Stone of Destiny there from Dalriada. This stone is of obscure provenance and almost mythical significance. There is a legend that formerly it had resided in Dunstaffnage Castle near Oban, to where it had originally been brought from Ireland by the first Scotii settlers. Dunstaffnage has no known connection with Dalriada or its monarchs, however, and this legend is based on a single document from the sixteenth century written in rather vague terms. Later on, of course, the stone was moved from Scone to London by Edward I to symbolize his overlordship of Scotland, and it formed part of the Coronation Chair in Westminster Abbey until its return to Scotland in 1996.

The rules of royal succession adopted by the Scots dictated that the throne of Scotia should pass to a monarch's cousin or brother after his death in preference to a son or daughter. The intention in setting these rules was that minority rule (by children or infants) would be avoided. However, the rules also meant that changes in kingship were comparatively frequent and were often accompanied by violent power struggles. The flow of blood was increased by the feudal nature of Scotia: power was exercised locally by vassal kings who were in theory subservient to the King of Scotia but who could, if ambition drove them, turn against their overlords. The most powerful of these kings ruled the Kingdom of Moray, which stretched from Inverness west across the northwest Highlands to Knoydart and Lochalsh; and the most famous ruler of Moray was a man known to history as Macbeth.

Scotland's most infamous king was probably born in Dingwall, a market town to the west of Inverness, situated at the place where the mountains begin to rise from the flat lands of the Moray Firth. Just off the town's main shopping street, nestling incongruously amidst suburban front gardens, is a squat octagonal tower complete with windows and arrow slits, which is all that remains of the hereditary seat of Macbeth's family. Little is known about Macbeth's life before he became king, apart from the fact that he grew up amidst political turmoil that frequently expressed itself in murder and revenge. In 1040 Macbeth murdered Duncan, the King of Scotia, and assumed the crown for himself; but in 1054 Macbeth was in turn murdered by Duncan's son Malcolm III at Lumphanan in the eastern foothills of the Highlands.

Shakespeare used a fair amount of dramatic licence when retelling these events five centuries later in his play *Macbeth*, but the kernel of his story was real enough. The main drama of *Macbeth* takes place over a hundred miles to the south of Dingwall, around the Tayside village of Birnam, situated at the foot of a wooded gorge that forms the southern gateway to the Highlands from Perth. Above the gorge on the slopes of Birnam Hill are the scant remains of a fort known locally as Duncan's Camp, supposedly the former stronghold of King Duncan. On the wooded banks of the Tay as it flows past the village a gnarled tree, its thick branches curling away stiffly from a massively-girthed hollow trunk and its bark rough and pitted with age, is supposedly the sole remainder of the mobile forest that features so memorably in the final parts of the play (one of the witches prophesizes that Macbeth "shall never vanquish'd be/until Great Birnam Wood to high Dunsinane Hill/shall come against him").

Dunsinane Hill itself lies well to the southeast of Birnam, part of a spine of high ground divorced from the Highlands proper. Dramatic though this landscape is, this is not the moor-and-mountain Highlands of popular imagination, and the scenic environment is softer here than the violence and bloodletting portrayed by Shakespeare might suggest. According to local tradition the playwright actually came to this part of Scotland prior to writing the play, so he knew the local geography; records show that a company of English strolling players did indeed stage a play in nearby Perth in 1589, but unfortunately the names of the actors were never recorded.

During much of the twelfth and thirteenth centuries the thrones of England and Scotland remained very close. Many princes of Scotland were brought up in the English court or were apprenticed to the English army, and a number married English noblewomen. One very anglophile King of Scotland at this time was David I (1124–53), who was created Earl of Huntingdon and became a brother-in-law to Henry I. David introduced a number of French-speaking families into Scotland to create a new Scottish aristocracy that echoed the creation of a Norman aristocracy in England. In theory these nobles would shore up loyalty to the Scottish crown in areas prone to rebellion, such as Moray. One of these nobles was Robert de Brix (or Bruis) from the Normandy town of Brix, whose descendant Robert the Bruce was to be the most famous of all Scotland's medieval monarchs. By the time of Bruce's rule the closeness of the two thrones was a thing of the past; but in the high Middle Ages the two crowns remained strongly allied, largely because both countries faced a common enemy, which lay across the sea to the east and wrought havoc on the coastlines of both England and Scotland for centuries.

The Vikings in Scotland: A "violent and cursed host"

That common enemy was the Vikings, whose exploits in Scotland are gorily recounted in Norwegian and Icelandic sagas. According to the writers of these sagas, Viking raids on a community were often foreshadowed by the visit of spirits known as the Valkyries, the hand-maidens of the god Odin, who would use a weaving loom to foretell which of their masters' enemies would die on the field of battle. The grisly machine required men's heads to be used as weights, intestines as thread, and a sword as a beater. If the sagas are to be believed such blood-crazed apparitions would have been a frequent sight around the coast of Scotland from around 750 onwards. And the viciousness of the raiders seeped into popular tradition of the day. "The Northmen," it was remarked in Neil Gunn's novel *Sun Circle,* set amidst a community of Christianized Picts in ninth-century northeastern Scotland, "were such experts with their sharp iron axes that in one blow they could split a man in two from the crown in his head to the place between his legs." No wonder the fictional community in Gunn's novel awaits the arrival of the men from across the water in abject terror: and when the Northmen finally arrive the violence unleashed is predictably blood-soaked.

One place where the blood ran copiously, and from which the Viking longships departed laden with booty and slaves, was the monastery on

Iona. After one of the earliest raids, in 795, some of the monks took flight across the sea and sought refuge in Kells, north of Dublin, possibly bringing with them the famed illuminated manuscript destined to be known as the Book of Kells. In 806 sixty-eight monks were slaughtered during a raid. Then in 825 Viking longships made landfall on the beaches of Iona yet again. This time the raiders murdered the abbot, Blathmac, after he refused to reveal the precise whereabouts of the burial shrine of St. Columba, which would have provided a rich source of plunder. Walafrid Strabo, a fellow monk of Iona and witness of the slaying, later told how Blathmac stood his ground against the raiders "with unshaken purpose of mind" before being "torn limb from limb" by the Nordic terrorizers whom he damned as a "violent, cursed host."

The Vikings who came to Scotland tended to hail from Norway, leaving the rich pickings of the east coast of England to their Danish cousins. During the early Middle Ages significant Viking fortresses were established along the northern and western coasts of Scotland by men who rejoiced in names such as Olaf the White, Thorstein the Red, and Ketil Flatnose, whose daughter was Aud the Deep-Minded. Some of these castles, such as Varrich on the north coast of Scotland near Tongue, and Duntulm on the northwest coast of Skye, still remain. Castle Varrich is now nothing more than an empty square shell, but its situation, on a precipitous spur of land overlooking the Kyle of Tongue, is one of the most awe-inspiringly dramatic in Scotland (it is surprisingly accessible too, via an easy walk of less than thirty minutes from the village of Tongue).

Varrich is thought to be "Beruvik" of the sagas, where the Viking Thorfinn fought a great sea battle, although in truth the castle's origins are as mist-enshrouded as the north coast of Scotland that it overlooks. Duntulm, on the cliffs below which are scars caused by the dragging of a longship, has fared a little better, though even here only a few tumbledown walls survive. The castle ruins occupy a blustery promontory close to the road rounding the northern tip of Skye, and it is the exhilarating setting of this castle, on the edge of sheer cliffs and with a great fine-weather view across to the Western Isles, which is the real draw. Despite their holding of Varrich, Duntulm and other coastal fortresses, the Vikings met their match on occasion. When forty longships sailed up Loch Leven under the command of Erragon of Lochlann the raiders were met with unexpectedly valiant and furious resistance by the people of Glencoe.

The ruins of Duntulm Castle on Skye
(Andrew Beattie)

Erragon suggested that both sides picked 140 of their most courageous warriors for a fight to the death. In the ensuing battle, fought nearby at Achnacon, Erragon was killed and the people of Glencoe duly kept their lands.

The Viking fortresses at Duntulm, Varrich and elsewhere were mostly founded as a result of a series of successful military campaigns waged in the ninth century by Sigurd the Powerful, the Earl of Orkney, and his ally Thorstein the Red. The source of our knowledge of these campaigns is principally the great Norse saga the *Orkneyinga*, whose account is, of course, somewhat biased. Nonetheless it would seem that by the year 900 all of Scotland north of a line from Dingwall to Ullapool was under the control of the powerful Orcadian earls, as were many of the islands of the Hebrides. Later on the great Viking earldom would be extended to include much of Ireland and southwestern Scotland, and in 1098 all of the islands off western Scotland came under Viking control when the Scots king Edgar ceded them to Magnus Bareleg, King of Norway. (Magnus attempted, and failed, to add the Kintyre peninsula to his possessions by dragging his longship across the narrow isthmus at Tarbert and declaring that, because he had rounded the peninsula by boat, it should in fact be categorized as an island.)

Magnus and his fellow Viking warriors would have launched their military campaigns against Scotland using longships. These were long, easily maneuverable vessels that the writers of sagas often compared to serpents: the vessels were versatile enough to transport up to eighty men across hundreds of miles of open sea, but they could also navigate the narrow sea lochs (similar to Norway's fjords) that punctuated the coast of Highland Scotland, and they could be powered just as successfully by oar as by sail. Later, when Vikings came as settlers rather than raiders, they used a different vessel known as a *hafskip* or *knorr*, which was deeper and broader and could transport the populations of entire settlements to their new homes. In some respects the Viking civilization brought from Norway on these ships was an advanced one, with a well-established legal system; but some scholars suspect that the Vikings practiced human sacrifice, and they certainly had a diverse panoply of gods to worship, at whose head stood Odin, the patron of warriors, and Thor, his son, feared as the strongest of all the gods.

By 1000 CE Viking settlement stretched from Ireland to Russia and from Greenland to Byzantium. The need for settlement resulted not so much from the urge to conquer than as a result of the pressure posed by population growth in Scandinavia. Norway, in particular, was difficult to farm, and successive generations of Viking rulers sought new land to settle across the sea to the west—hence the Viking settlement of Iceland and Greenland as well as Scotland. These later generations of Vikings adopted Christianity, partly so that they could assimilate themselves with the populations of the regions in which they settled. But they continued to meet fierce resistance from the Scottish kings. The fortress of Eilean Donan on Loch Duich near Kyle of Lochalsh was one of a number of castles established by the Scots to counter the Viking threat; that threat is now long gone but the much-rebuilt castle's formidable keep still stands guard on the water's edge, the sheer mountainsides all around forming a dramatic backdrop to one of the most photographed castles in the country.

Other castles confronting the Viking threat along the west coast include the one at Rothesay, the capital of the Isle of Bute, which is barely a minute's walk inland from the seaside town's Victorian promenade. The castle was built in the twelfth century by the powerful Stewart family, who later spawned a dynasty of Scottish monarchs, possibly on a site that had already been fortified by the Vikings and then abandoned or retaken. The Vikings launched raids on the castle in 1230 and 1263 and the strong gatehouse and the solid curtain wall were architectural embellishments that it was hoped would protect the castle from similar onslaughts. Today the ruins that remain are both substantial and accessible—and Rothesay is highly unusual among castles of the Highlands and Islands in that instead of standing on a rocky spur it is positioned on flat land, its defense provided by a moat that, like the high curtain wall that encircles the ruined interior, remains resolutely intact.

Norse ambitions did not end in Scotland. In 1066 Harald Hardrada died trying to seize the English throne at the Battle of Stamford Bridge in Lincolnshire. His body was brought back to Skye—probably to Duntulm—and from there was taken on to Norway. A memento of Harald's exploits remains to this day in Skye's Dunvegan Castle, in the form of a silk banner that is set in a frame and hangs on the wall in the castle's opulent drawing room. The ancient banner, now somewhat torn and faded, is thought to have been Harald's battle standard. Its tattiness is understandable: the silk from which the flag is fashioned was manufactured in Rhodes as far back as the fourth century. The banner was brought to Scotland by Harald from Constantinople, where he had once served as commander of the Imperial Guard to the Byzantine Emperor, whose guards were traditionally Viking warriors of the most hardened kind.

The End of Norse Rule and the Rise and Fall of the Kingdom of the Isles

Scotland's Norse heritage is felt most keenly in Shetland and Orkney, which remained in Norwegian hands until 1468. Norwegian possessions in mainland Scotland were ceded to the Scottish kings much earlier, after William the Lion waged a successful campaign in Sutherland against the Earls of Orkney in 1197. In Orkney and Shetland the names of most villages and towns are derived from Norse, but on the mainland a melting pot of place names derived from Norse, Gaelic, Celtic, and Pictish reflects a more complex history of settlement. Neil Gunn highlighted this in his novel *Highland River*, which is set in Dunbeath, a small fishing village on the east coast of Sutherland. "On one side of the harbour mouth the place name was Gaelic, on the other side it was Norse," Gunn writes. "Where the lower valley broadened out to flat, fertile land the name was Norse, but the braes behind it were Gaelic."

This juxtaposition of place names of different origins can also be seen on the West Highland coast. The name of the seaside town of Arisaig, for instance, is derived from the Norse meaning "river mouth bay" but the adjacent village of Morar takes its name from the Celtic for "Great Water." Other Norse-derived place names across northern Scotland include the two-house hamlet of Laxford Bridge, derived from the Norse *lax* meaning "salmon" ("ford" simply being a corruption of the Norwegian *fjord*); and Dingwall, whose name is derived from the Norse *thing*, meaning "parliament," and *vollr*, meaning "field"—so making the town's name essentially the same as Thingvellir in Iceland, the legendary site of the world's first parliament. Cape Wrath, the northwestern tip of Scotland famed for its foaming and violent seas, takes its name from the Norse word *hvarf*, meaning "turning place," as it was there that Viking ships had to turn south towards the west coast of Scotland after their westward journey from Norway. In an odd twist of linguistic convenience, however, "Wrath" is an entirely appropriate moniker for this remote headland, as the sea conditions around this treacherous area of coast can indeed be vengeful, as generations of mariners have discovered through the centuries, often to their cost.

Although in theory the Vikings ruled over the Hebrides as well as much of mainland Scotland, the situation here was more complex than this simple statement suggests. For by 1050 a powerful Gaelic chieftain named Somerled held sway over Mull, Skye, Jura and the mountainous West Highland mainland between the Kintyre and Ardnamurchan peninsulas. In theory Somerled was a vassal of the Earls of Orkney, but in practice he was his own man, a ruler with the strength and charisma of the semi-mythical Irish warrior chieftain, Conn of the Hundred Battles, from whom he claimed descent. Somerled's fierce spirit of independence was passed on to his descendants and was expressed in stone in castles such as Dunollie, the ruins of which continue to watch over the strategic approach to Oban from the sea. In 1249 the Scottish King Alexander II mustered a fleet in the shadow of this fortress to persuade Eòghan MacDhùghaill (or MacDougall), Somerled's great grandson, to submit to his rule; but Alexander contracted a fever during the campaign and died on the island of Kerrera, which, like Dunollie, stands guard over Oban's sheltered bay, and to this day the spot on the east of the island where he died is known as *Dail Righ*, the King's Field.

With Alexander's death it seemed that, for a while at least, the former kingdom of Somerled was safe from invasion. But now it was Norway's turn to try to bring the wayward fiefdom back under its control. The most remarkable military feat accomplished by King Hakon during his 1263 invasion of western Scotland came when he ordered his boats to be dragged over land to Loch Lomond in the manner of his Viking forebears. From these boats devastating raids against lochside settlements were launched. Farmhouses burned and blood flowed in Highland streams just as it had during the Viking raids of five centuries before. But Hakon's campaign ended in defeat, at the Battle of Largs, and the king shuffled back to Orkney, to expire in his palace in Kirkwall, the last bastion of Norse rule in Scotland. In 1266 his son Magnus officially gave up Norwegian claims to the Hebrides and the west of Scotland, and outside Orkney and Shetland Scandinavian rule in Scotland was now over. The Kingdom of the Isles had survived once again as an independent fiefdom.

The wayward kingdom was to remain a powerful threat to Scottish monarchs through the course of the Middle Ages. Somerled had sired two fiercely ambitious clans, the MacDougalls and the MacDonalds, and when the latter proved triumphant they were to rule Somerled's kingdom as Lords of the Isles, their power emanating from their palatial stronghold at Finlaggan, on the Isle of Islay. This was a place that echoed with the Gaelic ceremonies and traditions handed down from the Kingdom of Dalriada, of which the Kingdom of the Isles was the natural successor; nowadays the old palace is little more than an indecipherable clutter of nettle-covered stones nestling beside a loch at the island's center.

To counter the threat posed by the Lords of the Isles, who also controlled castles such as Eilean Donan, the Scottish monarchs constructed castles of their own, such as Tioram Castle on the Ardnamurchan peninsula, built by Ranald of Clanranald at the behest of King Robert II (and now in ruins). The MacDonalds launched raids on Tioram and other Royal strongholds from square-sailed, clinker-built galleys known as "birlinns" that were a close relative of Viking longships and could spread as much terror around the coast of the West Highlands and Inner Hebrides as the Norse ships had in previous centuries. But in 1493, shortly after he had brought Orkney and Shetland into the Scottish fold, James III set his sights on the rebels in Finlaggan, and commanded his parliament in Edinburgh to have the title of Lord of the Isles relinquished to the Scottish crown (Prince Charles is the current holder).

Six armed conflicts erupted over the next half century as the MacDonalds tried to reclaim their title. All ended in failure, including the last and most daring, in 1545, when 180 birlinns and 8,000 men were gathered together by a charismatic leader named Donald Dubh, who had managed to forge an alliance against the King of Scotland with England's ailing monarch Henry VIII. But the alliance faltered, Dubh became ill and died, and the engagements fought by his scattered navy were inconclusive. With the collapse of the Kingdom of the Isles the Scottish kings now had control—or at least nominal control—over the whole of Scotland.

HEROES AND REBELS: ROBERT THE BRUCE AND WILLIAM WALLACE

But this unity took a long time in forging, and fast-forwarding this narrative to take in the demise of the Kingdom of the Isles has meant that vital parts of Scotland's history have been skipped over. So we must return to the high Middle Ages, when the country's politics entered a period of crisis that culminated in an English invasion and a subsequent war of independence. However, most of the political and military engagements of the wars of 1297–1314 were played out amidst the towns and countryside of the lowlands, well away from the forests and glens of the Highlands. The crisis began in 1286 when King Alexander III died following a fall from his horse. The accident happened when he was riding by the Firth of Forth during a storm. The king's advisers had famously tried to persuade him from riding out on an evening that was not only astrologically inauspicious but also stormy; but the king ignored their advice and his body was found the next morning at the foot of some cliffs. Alexander had achieved much during his reign, defeating the Norwegians at Largs and marrying off his daughter to the King of Norway. On his death the throne passed to his granddaughter Margaret, the "Maid of Norway," who was an infant of three years and was living across the North Sea with her mother. Arguments raged as to whom should govern Scotland during her minority, and when the young girl died four years later in Orkney during the voyage to her new realm, arguments turned as to whom should succeed her.

Civil war threatened and the Scottish nobility asked Edward I of England to adjudicate over the succession crisis, largely because the nobles wanted a ruler who would keep Edward and England happy. Edward had thirteen candidates, including a Norwegian king and a Dutch count, to choose from (although the latter had his claim rejected when he failed to produce some required paperwork). In 1292 at Berwick Edward chose John Balliol, Lord of Galloway, as the new ruler of Scotland, in preference to his chief rival, Robert Bruce; both men were descended from David, Earl of Huntingdon, the younger brother of Kings Malcolm IV and William I of Scotland, and both had a good claim to the throne.

Edward's choice of John Balliol as king created a fearsome foe in the Bruce clan. The thwarted Bruce died in 1296 but his claim was taken up by his grandson, also called Robert—popularly known as Robert the Bruce—who was destined to carve a reputation as one of Scotland's greatest heroes. Bruce's enemy had, by then, proved himself a weak king. The first indication of this came in 1297, when Balliol was persuaded by Scottish nobles to forge an alliance with King Philip IV of France, the arch enemy of Edward I, who immediately retaliated by launching an invasion of Scotland. Edward's victory, at Dunbar, was decisive, and after his triumphant return to England he left Scotland in the charge of one of his trusted lieutenants, the Earl of Surrey.

It was inevitable that English dominance over Scotland would meet with opposition. It coalesced at first not around Robert the Bruce but around an outlaw and brigand named William Wallace, who raised an army in the lowlands while his follower Andrew Murray supported him in the Highlands, launching assaults on Urquhart Castle and Inverness. Wallace won a decisive victory at Stirling and was briefly made "guardian" of Scotland, but his army subsequently lost at a battle fought near Falkirk and Wallace was eventually captured and tried for treason in London. His fate was the bloodily brutal one of being hung, drawn, and quartered.

With William Wallace dead the way was at last open for Robert the Bruce to lay claim to the throne that he believed was rightly his. After launching a number of onslaughts against Highland castles held by the English or their supporters, the final showdown was fought at Bannockburn near Stirling in 1314, when the English, now under King Edward II, were finally and decisively routed by an army that included many

Robert the Bruce at Bannockburn by Edmund Blair Leighton, 1909
(Wikimedia Commons)

Highlanders; as they retreated south across the border the victorious shouts of the army of Robert the Bruce must have still been ringing loudly in their ears. Fourteen years later, in 1328, the English finally acknowledged Bruce as King of Scotland in a treaty signed at Edinburgh; his descendants were to rule Scotland until 1371, when the throne fell into the hands of the Stuart family.

During this long period of instability the Highlands remained lawless and clannish and largely isolated from the events determining Scotland's political destiny. The antics of Robert the Bruce and the English invaders really formed a sideshow to the endless and often bloody conflicts that erupted between the various clans. From time to time, however, the campaign waged by Robert the Bruce led to military engagements that were fought amidst the glens of the Highlands. In 1297 a brief naval skirmish erupted in Loch Linnhe between the MacDonald clan, supporters of Bruce, and those of Balliol, during which two warships were lost to the loch's dark waters. In the summer of 1306, when Robert the Bruce had gone to ground in the West Highlands, his army clashed with the Balliol-supporting MacDougalls at Dalry near Tyndrum; Bruce's army had recently been defeated by English forces at Methven near Perth and his demoralized and exhausted troops were soundly defeated in a battle fought in remote and uncompromising terrain. Two years later, in 1308, the MacDougall clan struck again in the Highlands, and this time Bruce was ready for them. The MacDougall clansmen attempted to ambush Bruce and his soldiers as they passed through the Pass of Brander, a narrow defile west of Loch Awe with precipitous slopes through which the main road and railway line to Oban now pass. But James Douglas, Bruce's loyal commander, led a bold rush from the heights of the pass into the army of John MacDougall and the ambush was foiled. (It was James Douglas who was later entrusted by Bruce to rip his heart from his body on his death, and carry it in a silver casket to Jerusalem.) A strangely-curved stone shaped like a chair, now situated across the road from the Dalmally Hotel a short distance east of the pass, has traditionally been considered Bruce's resting place after his victory.

The engagements at Dalry and the Pass of Brander were, however, unusual episodes of the war and it seems that for the most part Bruce viewed the Highlands as a haven of peace as conflict raged in the east and south of Scotland. During the war he even sent his family to live in the comparative safety of Kildrummy Castle, situated beside the River Don on the eastern fringes of the Highlands, thinking that they would be out of the way of the slaughter. But this only swung the ravages of the conflict towards Kildrummy, albeit briefly. The castle blacksmith, bribed by the English with as much gold as he could carry, set fire to the place so allowing it to fall into their hands. The unfortunate turncoat was later punished by Bruce's men for his duplicity by having molten gold poured down his throat, while the entire garrison of the castle was hanged, drawn, and quartered.

Dunkeld Abbey and the Medieval Highland Monasteries

The later Middle Ages might have been a time of battles and bloodletting in Scotland; but it was also during this time that the country's kirk flourished to an extent not seen since the days of St. Columba and the missionary monks. In the year 850 Kenneth MacAlpin had made Dunkeld, a small town some twelve miles north of Perth, the country's ecclesiastical capital, for the simple reason that it was situated at the meeting point of highland and lowland cultures. In 1100 work was begun on a cathedral in Dunkeld that would express in stone the power and wealth of the kirk. But delays set in and work was abandoned, only to resume again a century or so later on the original site. By the time of the high Middle Ages Dunkeld had a glorious cathedral that could rival any across the border in England—a fitting place to house the shrine where St. Columba was buried. But this renders the cathedral's current state even more surprising: for Dunkeld Abbey now lies in ruins, its roof open to the sky, its nave a grass lawn, its windows simply openings for birds to flit through. The church has been in this state since the Scottish Reformation of the 1560s, when the church was abandoned and St. Columba's remains were taken across the Irish Sea to be reburied in Downpatrick in County Down. The choir of the cathedral, however, was rebuilt in the eighteenth century and now serves as the parish church for Dunkeld.

Nowhere in Scotland are there ecclesiastical ruins as tranquil as those that sit beside the Tay in Dunkeld. But similarly ruined shells can be seen in a number of other Highland locations, broken echoes of an era when the Catholic Church held sway throughout the British Isles. One is the ruined priory of Inchmahome, which is situated on an island in the Lake of Menteith in the foothills of the Highlands west of Stirling. The first Augustinian monks took up residence here in 1238 at the behest of the Earl of Menteith, the monastery's founder, who maintained his family seat on a neighboring island in the lake. In 1547 the infant Mary Queen of Scots sought shelter on the island with her mother after the English rout of the Scots at the Battle of Pinkie forced the pair to leave the royal residence at Stirling Castle. A couple of decades later the Protestant Reformation took hold in Scotland and the priory on Inchmahome was closed; the buildings were then abandoned to the encroaching hazel, willow, and alder trees that the monks had planted on the island to supply them with timber. Now the ruins, like those of Dunkeld, are open to the sky, and are cared for by Historic Scotland. Visitors can cross to the island to look round them by means of a small ferry that operates from the village of Port of Menteith, tracing the same route across the still water as Mary and her mother did nearly five centuries ago.

The whispers of medieval monks are almost audible among the gray stones of Inchmahome—perhaps because the ruins are on an island, where the only sounds are birdsong and the ripple of the wind across the water. Those echoes are harder to discern in the town of Beauly, just west of Inverness. Like Dunkeld and Inchmahome this is a place at the edge of the Highlands, where the ripples in the countryside begin to rise to more substantial, heather-clad summits. At one end of the town's handsomely expansive market square are the sandstone ruins of Beauly Priory, a ghostly skeleton of stone overlooked by trees and surrounded by a substantial graveyard. Once again, the walls of the former abbey remain intact but the interior, complete with moss-covered medieval tombs, is open to the sky. And here too there is a connection with Mary, Queen of Scots. It was she who conferred on the town the name Beauly—*beau lieu* or "beautiful place"—after her visit here in 1564, at about the time when, as at Inchmahome, the Reformation was claiming the livelihood and position of monks across Scotland, and they were abandoning their monastic houses to the weeds and brambles. A hundred years after Beauly's demise the builders of Oliver Cromwell's new fort in Inverness, of which no trace now survives, pilfered much of their building stone from the ruins at Beauly. Nowadays the ruins seem a little lost amidst this expanding Inverness commuter town.

Rather more atmospheric are the ruins of a former nunnery on the island of Iona, fashioned from pink and gray stones and, thanks to the Reformation, in a similar state to the abbeys at Inchmahome and Beauly. The ruins are just up the hill from Iona's ferry terminal, set amidst the cottages of the island's main settlement, and are separate to the buildings of the completely rebuilt abbey, which is a five minute walk away. Ranald, the son of Somerled, the Lord of the Isles, had founded the Benedictine monastery on Iona in 1200, and it was from the ruins of the former abbey that the modern structure arose. That the Benedictine monastery on Iona was a creation of the Lords of the Isles was a conscious bid by the Lords to confirm their supposed descent from the Kings of Dalriada; for it had been under the patronage of Dalriadan kings that Columba had founded the original monastery on Iona, though Columba's original monastery had been located in a different part of the island to Ranald's later medieval foundation.

Ecclesiastical ruins of a different sort can be seen in Tain, a town on the eastern fringe of the Highlands whose sandstone buildings spread themselves handsomely over the lower slopes of a chain of mountains that rise between the Dornoch and Moray firths. In the Middle Ages Tain was one of the most important pilgrimage centers in Scotland. Its holiness stemmed from its being the birthplace of St. Duthus (or Duthac), an early Christian monk who achieved cult status in Orkney and eastern Scotland; a small and not particularly picturesque ruined chapel, surrounded by a cemetery and situated on the flat land overlooking the Dornoch Firth, marks the supposed place of his birth. No traces remain of his relics or his shrine, which vanished in the Reformation; the much-restored Collegiate Church in the center of Tain, where the relics were once housed, now hosts an exhibition relating to the saint and the pilgrimages he inspired.

THE CLANS: "EVERY PROVOCATION WAS REVENGED WITH BLOOD"

When James VI, who had ruled Scotland from the age of one, became King of "Great Britain, France, and England" (as he styled himself) on the death of Elizabeth I in 1603, he resolved to govern Scotland through his Privy Council based in Edinburgh, and he visited the country only once after acceding to the English throne. His rule over much of Scotland was tenuous at best: the Highlands, along with the Western Isles, Orkney, Shetland, and parts of the Borders, were viewed by James and his predecessors as remote, even alien territory, lawless and difficult to govern, and given to frequent rebellions that had to be put down by armed force. James' accession to the English throne coincided with a particularly vicious raid along the shores of Loch Lomond by Macgregor clansmen, in response to which the king promptly ordered the arrest and execution of the clan's chieftain. His Privy Council in Edinburgh, also perturbed by the raid, devised an order that every Highland clansman who owned sixty head of cattle or more must in future send his children to England to be educated, in an attempt to break the culture of violence and banditry that councillors maintained was handed down through the generations. This was ignored and neither new legislation nor the executions made any difference to the endemic lawlessness of the Highlands.

In fact for centuries it was lawlessness—and little else—for which the Highlands were best known, at least in the imagination of lowlanders and the English. Sir Walter Scott played on this in his classic novel *Waverley*, set just over a century after the accession of James VI. In the novel the hero Edward Waverley, who travels to the Highlands from southern England, is told of the "diverse thefts" of the Highlanders, who maintained "a wholesome terror among their lowland neighbours," and is astonished that "these deeds of violence [should be] within the common order of things, and happening daily in the immediate vicinity… in the otherwise well-ordered island of Great Britain." But Evan Dhu Maccombich, a proud Highlander, has to explain to Edward that thieving is part of the culture of Highlanders: "to take a tree from the forest, a salmon from the river, a deer from the hill, or a cow from a lowland Strath, is what no Highlander need ever think shame upon," he tells Edward.

By the time James acceded to the English throne Highland clans had been around for centuries, dominating the politics of the west and north of Scotland but having little influence on the country's broader affairs. The clans themselves were quasi-tribal groupings of families who claimed a single common ancestor; the word "clan" is derived from the Gaelic word *clann* meaning "children"—thereby highlighting the paternalistic relationship between the clan chieftain and his clansmen. At the root of the clan system was the Gaelic notion of kinship that also embraced the concept of *duthchas*, an untranslatable Gaelic term that suggests a sense of belonging and identity, both to an extended family unit and to the land secured for clansmen by the clan chieftain.

The clan system was wholly Gaelic in origin and was introduced to Scotland by the Irish settlers who came to Dalriada in the sixth century. Yet some clans, such as the Sinclairs and the Stuarts, actually had Anglo-Norman heritage, while the heritage of the clan MacAulay (whose name is derived from Olaf) was Viking. Often, too, the common ancestor of clansmen was mythical rather than actual. On several documented occasions families actually changed their surnames and became part of a rival clan if it suited them.

Many scholars have remarked that the clan system emerged as a response to the geography of the Highlands: such kinship groups were the best way of organizing farming and settlement in a region of steep terrain, harsh weather and difficult farming conditions. This challenging environment gave rise to a symbiotic relationship between chieftain, clansman, and the land. The men sought protection from their clan chieftain, whose land they were entitled to farm as his tenants; in return, when their chieftain demanded it, the clansmen would take up arms in support of him. Chieftains rarely took much interest in the day-to-day management of the clan farms and the organization of clansmen into fighting units: those were the responsibility of the tacksman, the chieftain's trusted factor and administrator. Often a tacksman was a chief's blood relative, and sometimes the tacksman would be so trusted that the chief would hand over his sons to be raised in the tacksman's household. But the chieftain was always the most powerful figure in any clan: just some of his powers included passing the death sentence in the courts over which he presided, claiming the prime bull of a recently-deceased tenant, and the right to claim one child to be raised as his own when a clanswoman bore twins.

Today the most instantly recognizable emblem of clan identity is the style of tartan worn by different clans. But when James VI came to the throne there was no real tradition of using different tartans to distinguish clans. That came later on in the seventeenth century and was not formally set down (by the Highland Society of London) until the Victorian era—when the Society bowed to pressure from weaving companies anxious to make money by manufacturing tartan. By that time the clan system had been dismantled and any adherence to a particular tartan was largely a romantic one.

Many clans nurtured long-standing rivalry with their neighbors. Such feuds had often festered for generations, their origins long forgotten over the passage of time. In his *A Journey to the Western Isles of Scotland* Samuel Johnson maintained that an ancient feud between the Macdonald and Macleod clans on Skye was the result of a Macdonald clansman divorcing his wife, who was a Macleod, as she had borne him no children. He went on to attribute the causes of clan rivalry to the terrain of Highland Scotland: any area, he maintained,

> intersected by many ridges of mountains naturally divides its inhabitants into petty nations, which are made by a thousand causes enemies to each other. Each will exalt its own chiefs, each will boast the valour of its men, or the beauty of its women, and every claim of superiority irritates competition; injuries will sometimes be done, and be more injuriously defended.

Sometimes these rivalries would "burn on for ages sullenly glowing in secret mischief" and on occasions they would "openly blaze into public violence... every provocation was revenged with blood." True to tradition, this violence would sometimes culminate in the piling up of severed heads or the burning alive of the vanquished to the sound of bagpipes, and the exploits of both victors and vanquished would be told and retold by bards around firesides during the long winter nights for generations to come. On occasion the violent settling of these feuds would be officially ordained: the Privy Council in Edinburgh could issue Letters of Fire and Sword against a particular clan and could command a rival clan to perform the killings. After one of these commands was served by the Stewart clan against the Macdonalds the severed heads were sent back to Edinburgh in a barrel. The most famous of the Fire and Sword letters was that issued in 1603 against Clan Gregor, which drove members of that clan to a life of banditry on Rannoch Moor. Writing in 1769, Thomas Pennant maintained that the Gregor clansmen were "hunted down like wild beasts" but that they had since inveigled themselves into other clans, distinguished "not only by the redness of their hair, but by their still retaining the mischievous disposition of their ancestors."

Occasionally a more formal way of settling feuds would be invoked. Typical among these was the pitched battle fought on the North Inch at Perth in September 1396 between the Chattan and Kay clans, staged on a specially erected enclosure in front of an audience that included King Robert III and an invited assembly of English and French knights. The battle was fought by thirty men from each clan, and the bloodletting did not let up until the king, exasperated by the violence, threw down his baton and announced Clan Chattan the winners. The showdown forms the climax to Sir Walter Scott's novel *The Fair Maid of Perth* and was fought, according to Scott, on a "beautiful and level plain... the feud of a hundred years, with all its acts of aggression and retaliation, was concentrated in the bosom of each combatant. Their countenances seemed fiercely written into the wildest expression of pride, hate, and a desperate purpose of fighting to the very last." The battle itself was a "scene of tumultuous chaos, over which huge swords rose and sunk, some still glittering, others streaming with blood [which] flowed fast, and the groans of those who fell began to mingle with the cries of those who fought... the wild notes of the pipers were still heard above the tumult, and stimulated to further exertions the fury of the combatants." When the first bout of fighting was over "about twenty of both sides lay on the field dead or dying... arms and legs lopped off, heads cleft to the chin, slashes deep through the shoulder." But still the clashes resounded, and as the fighting raged the king demanded of a nobleman watching with him why "these wretched rags and remnants of humanity be suffered to complete their butchery"; as he brought the proceedings to a close the king mourned "that so many brave Scottish men lie here slain, whose brands might have decided a pitched field in their country's cause."

Staged events such as these did little to quell the state of lawlessness that pervaded the Highlands. Contemporary reports to the government in Edinburgh indicated that in the late Middle Ages the whole region was suffering from a "great and horrible destruction... justice, as if outlawed, [lay] in exile outside the boundaries of the realm." Periodically Kings of Scotland would try to quell the ungovernable situation by force. We have already seen that on his accession to the English throne James VI arrested

Duart Castle, Mull
(Andrew Beattie)

the chieftain of the Macgregor clans after the Loch Lomond raid. But for the most part Highland clans were just left to get on with things in their own way, ignored by and ignoring the government in Edinburgh (which became Scotland's capital in 1437).

And so the litany of violence and blood-letting continued throughout the Stewart era. In 1646 thirty-six men of the Lamont clan were murdered by their Campbell rivals, hanged from a tree in Dunoon that later, according to legend, gushed blood from its roots when it was cut down. The Campbell men were busy again in 1691, torching the hereditary seat of Clan MacLean, Duart Castle on Mull, whose shell now makes for a spectacular view for those on ferries plying the popular route from Oban to Mull.

Clashes between clans grew more venomous as the century progressed, when clans who had taken up arms in support of the Catholic Stuart line of succession through James II regularly clashed with those clans who supported the Protestant William of Orange. The latter included the Clan Cameron, who burned the town of Dunkeld to the ground in 1689 because a cohort of troops loyal to James II was stationed there. The region was still seething three years later when, in Glencoe, the tension was to boil over into the most notoriously violent episode in the history of the Highlands.

The Civil War and the Rise of the Jacobites

The roots of the Glencoe massacre and the subsequent Jacobite rebellions run surprisingly deep. As deep, in fact, as the Protestant Reformation of the early sixteenth century and the subsequent conflicts over how Britain should be governed. In Scotland the Protestant Reformation had seen firebrand priests such John Knox do much to challenge the Catholic Church in cities such as Glasgow, Edinburgh, and Perth, and in 1560 the authority of the Catholic Church in Scotland was formally abolished in favor of a uniquely home-grown brand of Protestantism known as Presbyterianism. Seven years later the Protestant hegemony in Scotland was cemented by the abdication of the Catholic Mary Queen of Scots and the accession of her son James.

But the rise of the new Church made little headway outside the towns and cities of the lowlands. This meant that in 1638, when James I's son

Charles I attempted to impose a new and dangerously Anglo-Catholic prayer book on the Presbyterian Scots, the opposition of radical Protestants known as Covenanters drew little interest or support from Highlanders. Quite the converse, in fact, for during the Civil War that raged through England from 1642 to 1648 the Highlands emerged as a seedbed of royalist support.

Skirmishes erupted in many parts of Scotland during those years. One of the most vicious took place on the island of Kerrera, off Oban, when Cromwell's General Leslie discovered a small force of Royalist soldiers sheltering in Gylen Castle, on the island's southern tip. Leslie promptly slaughtered all those inside the castle, even though the Royalists had by then surrendered; only the child John MacDougall, the nineteenth chief of Clan MacDougall by dint of his father's early death, was allowed to go free. Then Leslie's troops torched the castle, which has lain in ruins ever since. Today Gylen is one of the most stunningly situated ruined castles in Scotland, the lack of easy road access ensuring that only the hardiest of visitors

Gylen Castle

get here. The castle's box-shaped keep is the only surviving part of the fortress. It forms a stone appendage to the steep cliffs that drop down to the frothing sea on three sides of the promontory—but it is within this ruined keep that the most tangible evidence of the destructiveness of the Civil War in the Highlands and Islands can be sensed, in every broken flagstone and through each draughty window opening.

The skirmish at Gylen Castle was, however, just that—a skirmish. Elsewhere armies clashed and battlefields ran with blood. Charles' principal ally in Scotland was the Marquis of Montrose, who raised an army in support of the king and placed it under the command of a fierce Highland chieftain, Alasdair MacDonald of Colonsay. MacDonald's soldiers fought Cromwell's army on two occasions, at Inverlochy near Fort William in February 1645 and at Alford on the eastern fringes of the Highlands in July of the same year. Both engagements resulted in victory for the Royalist cause. This was perhaps surprising at Inverlochy, where a freezing night camped out on the slopes of Ben Nevis must have sapped the spirits of MacDonald's already depleted army. But the next morning the Covenanter forces under the Duke of Argyll were taken wholly by surprise by the presence of the Highlanders, whom they had thought were in a completely different location. Fifteen hundred Covenanters were slaughtered in the ensuing violence, which contrasted with Royalist losses of just two hundred and fifty.

One reason for the liberal shedding of blood was the weapons employed by the Highlanders. They had no firearms, but they did have claymores, fearsome Highland swords on which, in the words of one Gaelic bard, a "cleaving, sharp, blue edge of steel" would glint in the sunlight. (A splendid example of one of these formidable weapons can be seen in Dunvegan Castle on Skye, fashioned in 1528 by the hereditary armorers to the Clan MacLeod. Samuel Johnson was not impressed with this claymore when he saw it on his visit in 1773—calling it "ill-contrived"—but he declined an invitation to defend himself with it against a man wielding a traditional clansman's dagger, known as a dirk.) At Inverlochy, and again at Alford, Highlanders hacked their way through the ranks of Covenanter troops with their claymores as the Covenanters struggled to reload their cumbersome muskets. Yet in the end both battles were more feud-settling brawls between clans than serious contributions to either the Royalist or the Parliamentarian causes. In fact throughout the war Highland soldiers rarely strayed from the mountains and seemed more interested in plunder than in championing the Stuart cause. Montrose, for his part, was eventually captured and executed in 1650, the year after Charles I lost his head in London.

In 1688 Charles's avowedly Catholic successor James (ruling as James II of England and James VII of Scotland) was chased out of England and sent into exile, to be succeeded by his Protestant daughter Mary who ruled with her husband, William of Orange. This decisive change in the fortunes of the Stuart dynasty (and English Protestantism) came to be known as the "Glorious Revolution"—a peaceful resolution to the question of the kingdom's religious destiny that was vastly preferable to the violence and bloodshed of another civil war. The exiled James, seething with fury at the manner in which he had been deposed, knew that he had supporters in Highland Scotland and commanded James Graham of Claverhouse, the Viscount Dundee (not a Highlander, but a lowlander from Angus) to raise an army in his support. This Claverhouse did, successfully uniting a number of Highland clans against William. In response William sent an army to Scotland under General Hugh Mackay (ironically, a Highlander from Sutherland) who was later to write loftily that he considered Highlanders to be lacking "a true sense of the deliverance which God had sent them."

On July 27 MacKay marched north from Dunkeld with the intention of seizing Blair Castle, the ancestral home of the Dukes of Atholl, which had fallen into Dundee's hands. His route took him through the Pass of Killiecrankie, a narrow, forested defile near Pitlochry that today provides a route through the mountains of Perthshire for the main road and railway from Perth to Inverness. As Mackay's troops emerged from the pass they found Dundee's forces on the slopes above them, ready to charge down the hill. "Nothing was heard for some few moments but the sullen and hollow clashes of the broadswords, with the dismal groans and cries of dying and wounded men," was how Dundee's second-in-command, Ewen Cameron of Lochshiel, described the few violent minutes of the bloody encounter. Afterwards, "the enemy lay in heaps… so disfigured with wounds, and so hashed and mangled, that even the victors could not look upon the amazing proofs of their own agility and strength without surprise and horror." Those victors were the Highlanders. Their battle tactic once again was to launch a furious charge into the startled ranks of English soldiers, the clansmen wielding their fearsome claymores and their faces contorted into a terrifying battle cry.

Today there is nothing to see of the Killiecrankie battle site. The busy A9 road cuts right through it, and traffic thunders past the place where so many English troops were slaughtered. The site is marked by a memorial cairn accessible on a minor road leading away from the B8079 (which follows the route of General Wade's old military road through the pass), northwest of Killiecrankie village. But in the pass itself paths lead down through the woods from the Killiecrankie visitors' center towards the River Garry, where two reminders of the battle can be found. A flat rock marks the spot where a fleeing government soldier, Donald MacBean, leapt an astonishing eighteen feet across the water to escape a band of pursuing Highlanders, while further down the valley along the riverside path, a flat stone lying right across the path supposedly marks the grave of Barthold Balfour, the Dutch commander of the left wing of Mackay's army, who was killed beside the river here by a Jacobite soldier.

Viscount Dundee was also killed—in the battle that his troops won. To the northwest of Killiecrankie village, in a field beside the B8079, is a slightly crooked prehistoric standing stone against which he was supposedly lying when he died of his injuries. His body was carried away from the battlefield by respectful clansmen, who buried him in the church at Old Blair, which today can be reached by a brief stroll through woodland from Blair Castle; the church is now in ruins, roofless and with a grassy floor, though a memorial plaque (installed in 1889 to commemorate the two hundredth anniversary of the battle) records that Dundee's body lies within the vault of the church. As befitted a soldier he was buried in his armor. (In the 1790s his tomb was opened and the armor removed, and his blackened breastplate and helmet can now be seen in one of the downstairs rooms in Blair Castle.)

After the battle, with "Bonnie Dundee" no longer standing at the head of the Highland army as its charismatic leader, the clansmen drifted away, and continued to do so even when their new commander, Colonel Cannon, arrived in the Highlands from Ireland with reinforcements. Not surprisingly the putative rebellion finally ran out of steam the following year, when the Jacobites, as supporters of James were becoming known, were defeated at Dunkeld, only a short distance downstream from Killiecrankie.

After Dunkeld the clansmen headed back home with the shame of defeat weighing heavily on their shoulders. But the region remained restless, and the British government was quick to stamp on any trouble. In 1690 a British frigate bombarded Armadale Castle on the coast of Skye when the chief of Clan MacDonald refused to pledge his support for William; the castle was wrecked and one of the cannon balls fired from the ship was unearthed when a heritage center for the MacDonald clan was being constructed on the site in 2001.

In the 1650s Oliver Cromwell had ordered the construction of a number of forts across the region to bring the Catholic Highlanders to heel—"civilizing [Highlanders] by conquest, and introducing by useful violence the arts of peace" according to Samuel Johnson—and one of these, at Inverlochy, was rebuilt by William in the 1690s and named Fort William in his honor. A name was also needed for the cluster of dwellings that began to surround the walls of the fort, and Maryburgh was chosen, to honor the queen who ruled by William's side. That name has long fallen into disuse, but the name of the fort was later adopted by the town, which is now the largest in the West Highlands.

Fort William provided a useful base for English forces in the Highlands, even if the soldiers and commanders posted there detested the place for its remoteness and foul winter weather. (Nothing remains of the fort bar some paltry remains next to the roundabout outside Fort William's railway station.) But then a shift in international politics meant that England found itself at war with France. That was sure to lead to more trouble in the Highlands, as the French habitually supported the Jacobite cause in the hope of destabilizing the crown in London. Not even the spread of new forts could adequately ensure that the Highlands would remain peaceful. William knew that as the war raged in Europe he had to show the Highlanders that his government was determined to quell all demonstrations of Jacobite sympathy, using brute force if necessary. And he also knew that he could use the natural enmity between the clans to his own advantage.

THE MASSACRE AT GLENCOE

The conflict with Louis XIV of France—the Nine Years War, as it was later dubbed—was to last until 1697. It was ignited by William's determination

Glencoe
(Ad Meskens/Wikimedia Commons)

to thwart French territorial ambitions in the Low Countries. To raise the stakes higher Louis had pledged support for James II, exiled in the sumptuous palace at Saint-Germain-en-Laye near Paris, and had sent French warships to patrol off the Hebrides, fueling English concerns that France was offering material support to Highland Jacobites. William had no wish to become embroiled in a military entanglement in Scotland that would take troops away from the main campaigning theater in continental Europe. Securing the loyalty of the clans to his cause became his top priority, and the massacre of the MacDonald clan in Glencoe in February 1692 turned out to be the bloody manifestation of William's political will.

But the causes of the massacre run considerably deeper than William's war in Europe. John Prebble, in his classic 1966 book *Glencoe: The Story of the Massacre*, has maintained that the destruction of Clan MacDonald stemmed directly from the lowlanders' hatred of the Highlanders, the *Mirum mor nan Gall*, which was expressed in later centuries at Culloden and then in the brutality of the Highland Clearances. Prebble credits Sir John Dalrymple, the First Earl of Stair and Secretary of State for Scotland, as harboring such a loathing: the "Master of Stair," as the minister was known, was a passionate advocate for the formal union of England and Scotland, and saw it as his duty to bring to heel by force those Jacobite clans who opposed him.

The topography of Glencoe renders the place both a fortress and a trap. There are only two natural entrances to the cavernous valley: from Loch Leven in the west, where the village of Glencoe hunkers down in the lower slopes of the glen, and from Rannoch Moor in the east, where the widening glen is overlooked by the bulks of Buachaille Etive Mor and Buachaille Etive Beag, the Great and Little Herdsmen of Etive, so-named for the rich grazing land that lies in the shadow of these mountains. In his novel *Kidnapped* Robert Louis Stevenson described Glencoe as "a prodigious valley, strewn with rocks, and where ran a foaming river. Wild mountains stood around it; there grew there neither grass nor trees."

In 1691 the cattle that grazed this land were herded by men of the MacDonald clan, who had been granted Glencoe three centuries before by Robert the Bruce. The MacDonalds prided themselves on an ancient lineage and a proud tradition, claiming descent from Fergus Mor, the leader of the Gaels who had brought Irish settlers to the Highlands in the fifth century. Like all clans the MacDonalds had often clashed with their neighbors. But disputes with their old adversaries, the Stewarts, had often been resolved in a surprisingly unconventional manner. Instead of violence, formally sanctioned or otherwise, the two clans would settle their differences by get-togethers on the "Isle of Discussion" in the Inner Hebrides where indulgent sessions of partying and feasting took place while arguments were resolved over the conference table. But then the Campbell clan of Argyll began to encroach from the south and it was clear that this clan would not be pacified by a few days of raucous merry-making on a Hebridean island. The seat of the Campbells was at Inveraray, at the time the only town of any size in the West Highlands. After William granted land and titles to the chief of Clan Campbell, ensuring the chief's unwavering loyalty to the cause of the Protestant Stuarts, it was from Inveraray that royal authority in the Highlands emanated.

In the spring of 1691 William ordered that every chieftain in the Highlands should swear an oath of allegiance to him. By swearing the oath the clan chieftains would be pledging their loyalty to the Protestant crown, rejecting the Catholic claim to the throne through James II. On August 27 the first notice announcing the order was posted on the Mercat Cross in Edinburgh. Soon similar notices were appearing all over the Highlands. According to the terms arranged by the Master of Stair, Highland chieftains had to swear their oath in front of the sheriff of their shire, and were obliged to do so by January 1 of the following year or face severe consequences. Yet despite the clear pressure from London the clan chieftains prevaricated. No chieftain wanted to be the first to swear the oath; and while not wishing to express outward disloyalty to William they were also wary of demonstrating disloyalty to James II. Eventually the exiled James discharged the clansmen from their bond to him and gave them permission to take the oath. But his letter releasing the clansmen from their bond did not arrive in Edinburgh until December 21. James' procrastination was to prove fatal. In the depths of a Highland winter it would be more or less impossible for chieftains to travel from their seats to take the oath in front of the sheriff of their shire. Roads were impassable and the weather was treacherous. In the end Cameron of Locheil was the first to appear before his local sheriff, taking the oath three days before the end of the year. His example was gradually followed by his fellow chieftains across the Highlands.

The MacDonalds of Glencoe were led at that time by their chieftain Alasdair MacIain. Despite his long-standing Jacobite sympathies MacIain resolved to swear the oath to William, and twenty-four hours before the deadline he appeared at the gates of Fort William offering to do so in front of the fort's commander, John Hill. But Hill turned him away, back into the fierce December blizzard: the oath, Hill maintained, could only be taken in front of a sheriff, and he was no sheriff. MacIain's local sheriff was in Inveraray, and was a Campbell, and the proud chieftain was loath to take the oath in front of his sworn enemy. But Hill told him he had no choice. And so MacIain took to his horse and rode from Fort William across the snowy glens to Inveraray, where he discovered that the sheriff was making merry at his private residence some distance away, celebrating the dawning of the new year with his friends from Clan Campbell. When MacIain finally appeared in front of the sheriff he was again turned away, on the grounds that the deadline for the swearing of the oath had passed. MacIain pleaded that he might be given a fair hearing. Eventually he took the oath in a courthouse in Inveraray, some three days into the New Year. But he was too late; the Privy Council in Edinburgh, stuffed with men loyal to the Campbell clan, refused to accept that MacIain had sworn the oath on time. In London, the Master of Stair had the excuse he needed to make an example out of Clan MacDonald.

Only Stair and a few of his closest associates appreciated the full horror of the plan. In his correspondence Stair maintained that he intended that the massacre would be "secret and sudden." The Campbell commander, Robert Campbell of Glenlyon, certainly did not know what Stair had planned when, in late January, he received his instructions to billet his men in Glencoe with those of the MacDonald clan. The Argyll men were billeted two or three to a house and for two weeks men of the rival clans feasted and fought together in the mid-winter chill. Highland games, including tossing the caber, were played, as were violent matches of a hockey-like game known as shinty, in which as a matter of course players' limbs would often be broken (in Glencoe the shinty balls were often made from a fungus found growing on birch trees, which was then covered in wool and placed inside a leather bag). There was piping and sword dancing, and after the milky winter sun had set behind the western hills, bards from both clans would tell stories of clansmen past in the flickering light cast by the peat fires in the dwellings.

So Robert Campbell was understandably startled by the letter he received on February 12 from Robert Duncanson, a major in the Argyll regiment, commanding him that the Campbells were "hereby ordered to fall upon the rebels, the MacDonalds of Glencoe, and to put all to the sword under seventy… this you are to put in execution at five of the clock precisely; and by that time, or very shortly after it, I'll strive to be at you with a stronger party… this is by the King's special command, for the good and safety of the country, that these miscreants be cut off root and branch." It is likely that Duncanson knew his forces would not arrive in the glen until seven that morning, some two hours after Campbell's men had unleashed the bloody show of violence, so leaving Campbell with the sole responsibility for the execution of the massacre.

Campbell spent the evening before the massacre drinking and gambling with Alasdair MacIain, knowing that before the night was out his host would be dead, killed in cold blood by Campbell's own soldiers. As the appointed hour drew near a snowstorm began swirling through Glencoe; when dawn broke the driven snow was drenched with the blood of the murdered MacDonalds. Thirty-eight clansmen were butchered by the Argyll men. MacIain himself was killed while he was dressing, under the impression that his hosts were leaving their cottage and he had to bid them goodbye. One cottage was torched as fourteen people cowered inside it. Forty women and children died as they fled into the frozen hills. As first light came the Campbells looted property from the houses in which the bodies of the MacDonald men lay, and took their cattle too, ready to lead the beasts over the hills to their farms in Argyll. By then around one-tenth of MacIain's people were dead: that the massacre had not caused more deaths was due to the blizzard, which made it difficult to hunt down those who had taken refuge outside, and the professional incompetence of Robert Campbell. But what was to linger in the folk memory of the Highlands was, of course, that the murderers of the MacDonald men had been welcomed by their intended victims as guests: an abuse of the proud tradition of hospitality in the Highlands that transcended the squabbles between the clans. "The hand that mingled in the meal/At midnight drew the felon steel," wrote Sir Walter Scott in his 1814 poem "On the Massacre of Glencoe." "The friendly hearth which warm'd that hand/At Midnight arm'd it with the brand."

The viciousness of the massacre and the duplicity of the Campbells shocked the political establishments in both London and Edinburgh. The king was persuaded to establish a commission of enquiry into the affair, which sat in special session in Holyrood House in the summer of 1695. The enquiry exonerated William but blamed Stair for the "barbarous murder" of Glencoe and pointed the finger at him as the "original cause of this unhappy business." But William in turn exonerated Stair and, in a circular game of passing the buck, laid the blame for the massacre at the feet of the soldiers and officers who had been quartered in Glencoe. Resigning his position as Secretary of State, Stair nonetheless found favor under William's successor Queen Anne. Through the early years of her reign he continued to forge the formal union between England and Scotland, dying just before his life's work could be fully realized.

The massacre itself, of course, lives on in the folk memory of the Highlands, an act of brutality and savagery as severe and as unforgiving as Glencoe itself. To this day, every February 13, the Clan Donald Society of Edinburgh stages a wreath-laying ceremony at the memorial to the massacre, which consists of a soaring Celtic cross atop a rugged cairn and is situated at the eastern end of Glencoe village. The ceremony is attended by local people and by members of Clan Donald from all over the world.

THE "OLD PRETENDER" AND THE 1715 AND 1719 JACOBITE REBELLIONS

With the accession to the English throne of Mary's sister Queen Anne in 1703 the Protestant Stuart line continued into the eighteenth century. During Anne's reign the Act of Union was passed, formally uniting England with Scotland, though leaving the Scottish legal and religious systems intact. But despite the massacre at Glencoe the belief in a Catholic Stuart succession hung on tenaciously in the Highlands.

Anne had no surviving children and no immediate heirs, so on her death in 1714 the Stuart dynasty came to an end and the English throne passed to George, the Protestant Elector of Hanover. George's claim to the throne came by virtue of his descent from James I and VI, but he could barely speak a word of English. A rival Jacobite claimant to the throne quickly emerged in the form of James Francis, the son of the exiled James II and known as the "Old Pretender," On September 6, 1715, John Erskine, the Earl of Mar, raised the Stuart standard in support of James at

Braemar in the eastern part of the Highlands. With his assembled army of six thousand, largely drawn from the Mackintosh and MacDonald clans, Erskine quickly captured Perth and Inverness. Yet Erskine's commander William Mackintosh fared less well in an attack on northwestern England, which ended in military disaster at Preston. Soon Erskine was also in trouble, waging an equally disappointing campaign that ended in an inconclusive battle fought at Sheriffmuir, near Stirling, where the earl found himself up against superior forces of the Duke of Argyll, the head of the Campbell clan and a key supporter of the Hanoverian succession.

It was in the wake of this indecisive battle that the Old Pretender himself decided to rally his supporters in Scotland, making a landing at Peterhead (after original plans to land at Dunstaffnage Castle near Oban were abandoned). But James failed to establish himself among Highlanders: his health suffered in the icy Scottish winter and few emerged from the warmth of their turf dwellings to support him. Meanwhile further skirmishes between Jacobite and Hanoverian forces broke out all over Scotland and particularly in the Highlands. Most of these ended badly for Jacobite supporters. One of the most unfortunate Jacobites turned out to be Allan, the fourteenth Chief of the MacDonald Clan of Clanranald, who chose to blow up Tioram Castle, his hereditary seat, to ensure that it did not fall into the hands of a company of Hanoverian soldiers. (Today this castle, situated on a remote neck of land jutting into Loch Moidart on the Ardnamurchan peninsula, looks solid enough from the outside; but the irregular curtain of windowless grey walls hides an interior that is largely full of rubble, and it is a pity that the current owner of the castle, a descendant of a local Jacobite family who lives in California, keeps the iron entrance gate securely locked and bolted.) In the end the destruction of Tioram and other fortresses, and the trouncing of a number of armies raised by clan chieftains, meant that the Old Pretender had no option but to admit to the futility of his scheme and slink off back to exile in France.

Despite the failure of the 1715 rebellion the new British government was taking no chances with the Jacobites. Support for the Jacobite cause was strongest in the West Highlands, and George I ordered a major new fort to be constructed at the southwestern tip of Loch Ness that was later named Fort Augustus. It was a substantial facility, described in 1760 by the traveler Richard Pococke as a "very handsome regular building consisting of four bastions." Although the village of Fort Augustus remains, the fort itself has long gone, its site occupied by an apartment building that once served as a Benedictine monastery. However, two other barracks from this time remain. Along the coast from Kyle of Lochalsh, in the hamlet of Glenelg, are the crumbling ruins of the three-story Bernera Barracks, fenced off nowadays for safety reasons, while at Kingussie in the central Highlands unhindered access is allowed to the better-preserved Ruthven Barracks, situated on a hillock near the town. The growing British military presence, expressed in stone in these and other army bases across Scotland, did nothing to quell the political unrest in the West Highlands, however, and Britain's rivalry with Spain elsewhere in the world heightened the tension still further.

The rivalry was most intense in the Mediterranean, where Philip V of Spain and his chief minister, the Italian Cardinal Giulio Alberoni, were itching for a showdown. It was Alberoni's suggestion that this could be done by destabilizing the British government. A Jacobite on the British throne, Alberoni reasoned, would surely be more sympathetic to Spanish expansionist policies than the German Protestant George I. Soon Philip and his advisers were drawing up an ambitious plan to land a sizeable army in Wales, under the command of James Butler, the second Duke of Ormonde, whose Jacobite sympathies had led to his exile in Spain; at the same time a secondary force under George Keith, the Scottish-born Earl Marischal who also had Jacobite leanings, would land on the west coast of Scotland and rouse the sympathy of Jacobite clan leaders. But in the end the main invasion fleet was scuppered Armada-style by a severe storm, while Keith's forces found they had little support among the Highland clans after they had established their headquarters in Eilean Donan castle near Kyle of Lochalsh. The response of the government in London to the Spanish occupation of the castle was to despatch three Royal Naval frigates—HMS *Worcester*, HMS *Flamborough*, and HMS *Enterprise*—to Loch Duich, the narrow sea loch over which the fortress stands guard. When one of the Spanish soldiers billeted in the castle opened fire on the ships the response was devastating: an hour's bombardment by the frigates was followed by a swift surrender from the Spanish forces. The British then used twenty-seven barrels of gunpowder to demolish the castle; today some of the cannon balls fired during the bombardment can be seen in the Billeting Room of the much-rebuilt fortress.

Although it was clear by now that Spain's military designs on Britain were doomed, the Spanish commanders in the Highlands gathered Jacobite-supporting clansmen together for a final showdown. This came on the evening of June 10 amidst the dramatic surrounding of Glen Shiel, at the head of Loch Duich, where remnants of the stone barricades built by Spanish forces can still be seen on the slopes above the glen. By 9PM, with the light at last beginning to fade at the end of a long northern summer's day, the victor was clear. The Jacobite and Spanish forces were poorly equipped and were no match for the Hanoverian army that had marched from Inverness to meet them. Among the many wounded on the Jacobite side were the famed Scottish outlaw, Rob Roy MacGregor, the hero of Sir Walter Scott's novel *Rob Roy,* who had commanded a unit of his own clansmen; fighting alongside those MacGregors were men from the Mackenzie and Murray clans. But, just as four years previously, a Jacobite victory was not to be. Despite the defeat the Jacobites were grateful to the Spanish for their support, and to this day one of the peaks that rise above the site of the battle is named Sgurr nan Spainteach, the Peak of the Spaniards. The battle of Glen Shiel also claims an important place in British history in that it was the last to be fought on British soil against a substantial force of foreign soldiers.

Despite the failure of both the 1715 and 1719 rebellions the British government still felt the need to increase their military presence in the Highlands. In the 1730s a leading figure in the British Army, General Wade, was put in charge of keeping peace in the region. The force of troops he gathered together for that purpose became known as the Black Watch regiment, and Wade's soldiers, drawn from the Highlands, became some of the first to wear Highland uniform. Wade moved his new regiments swiftly around the Highlands by a new network of roads that were constructed on his orders. One of those roads is now the route of the B862, which skirts the shores of Loch Ness beyond Fort Augustus; but the most famous legacy of Wade's road building is the handsome stone bridge on the edge of the town of Aberfeldy that still carries traffic across the River Tay to this day—indeed the volume and weight of vehicles that cross this bridge is vastly greater than Wade intended. Opened in 1735, this sturdy bridge with its handsome central arch topped by distinctive square columns was intended as a showpiece. It is overlooked by a nineteenth-century monument commemorating the Black Watch regiment, from

Wade's handsome bridge over the River Tay at Aberfeldy
(Andrew Beattie)

where a kilted and armed Highland soldier keeps watch from atop a high stone plinth.

The bridge at Aberfeldy was just one of forty stone bridges that Wade constructed across torrents that previously lacked any fixed crossings. The writer Thomas Pennant, who travelled through the Highlands in 1769 along some of the new roads, was hugely impressed by Wade's achievements: "Like another Hannibal, he forced his way through rocks supposed to have been unconquerable," he wrote in his *Tour of Scotland.* "Many of these rocks were too hard to yield to the pickaxe," Pennant went on, so their "obstinacy" had to be "subdued with gunpowder" with workers often "suspended from above by ropes on the face of the horrible precipice." Pennant also noticed that the names of the regiments the builders belonged to had been carved on rocks beside the roads, echoing the habits of Roman road builders.

Another writer who had much to say about these new roads was Edmund Burt, who worked as a surveyor for General Wade and who wrote a number of letters about his impressions of Scotland to a friend in London that were later published as a book. At one point, Burt says, the builders of the Glenalmond to Crieff road discovered a Roman burial urn and reburied it with military honors, including a gunfire salute. He also explains how on slopes the new roads were built with drainage systems to stop them being washed away, and recounts how one of the bridges over the Tay was adorned with a Latin inscription specifically written by "Dr Friend, Master of Westminster School."

It was not just soldiers who used the new roads. Locals used them too, and the network hugely improved the economy of the Highlands, replacing as it did numerous fords and muddy tracks. "Had you seen these roads before they were made," went a popular rhyme of the day, "you would lift up your hands and bless General Wade." No wonder anti-British feeling was very slowly, but perceptibly, on the wane.

The 1745 Rebellion and the Battle of Culloden

Inevitably it was in the West Highlands (specifically around Loch Linnhe, Loch Shiel and Loch Sunart) and in the islands of the Inner Hebrides that the last and most famous of the Stuart pretenders sought support. James Francis' son Charles Edward Stewart, "Bonnie" Prince Charlie, the "Young Pretender," had grown up in exile in France and had little grasp of English and none of Gaelic when he landed on the island of Eriskay in the Outer Hebrides in July 1745. His father was still alive, in exile in Rome, and had no knowledge of his son's bid to reclaim the English crown for the Stuarts. It was a mission that seemed doomed to failure: in March of the previous year Charles had set sail with a French invasion fleet that was then scuppered by storms, and when he finally landed on Eriskay he was told to "go home" by the locals—a command that was met with the reply "I have come home… my faithful Highlanders will stand by me." Charles had no supporting fleet when he landed. But England was at war with France and Charles' supporters hoped that enough English troops would be tied up in a continental campaign to allow this new bid to succeed. And their hopes also rested on the prince's legendary charismatic charm: "If the prince once sets his eyes on you," Donald Cameron of Locheil had once commented to his brother, "he will make you do what he pleases."

From Eriskay Charles made his way to the mainland, landing at

Borrodale on Loch nan Uamh (the Loch of Caves) southeast of Mallaig. Accompanying him were just seven loyal companions. Their memory is celebrated today by a row of seven now rather storm-ravaged beech trees that line the shores of Loch Moidart and can be seen from the road at the hamlet of Kinlochmoidart, which was Charles's next stop. From Kinlochmoidart Charles and his men headed over a shoulder of land to Dalelia on Loch Shiel, from where a hastily purloined rowing boat took them to Glenfinnan, situated at the head of Loch Shiel some nineteen miles west of Fort William. Here Charles raised his military standard. The sound of the Jacobite pipers quickly drew clansmen to the lochside: the first chieftain to join Charles was Cameron of Loch Shiel, and soon numbers were swelling as more followed his example. A few days after the raising of the Stuart standard a force of eight hundred men was looking on as the prince proclaimed his father the rightful ruler of Britain, as James III of England and IX of Scotland. "Long live King James the Eighth and Charles, Prince of Wales!" was the toast delivered by the chieftains. "Prosperity to Scotland and no union!" Yet some already realized that the campaign was doomed: the chief of the MacDonalds of Clanranald wrote that Charles' mission was "a sheer act of madness and doomed from the outset to certain ruin"—although even he hedged his bets on the outcome by sending his son to the ceremony.

Despite promises of support from Jacobite supporters in both England and France failing to materialize, the prince and his followers pressed on with their planned military campaign. Perth was easily captured and other cities were threatened. Shocked by the rapidity of the Jacobite advance, a force hastily brought up from London under Sir John Cope secured the strategically important center of Inverness for the Hanoverians. Cope then dithered, eventually sending his forces south towards Edinburgh by sea to secure the Scottish capital, while the Jacobites won a decisive victory at Prestonpans on the east coast before launching an invasion force into England.

Carlisle was quickly in Jacobite hands and Charles' army, fired with the euphoria of their unprecedented success, pressed on south. Many Jacobite soldiers were drovers who had experience of driving cattle south from the Highlands as far as Derby, where there was a great livestock market. The drovers knew the inns, byways, and shortcuts, and guided the Jacobite soldiers along them, evading local militas. But George I, angered by the poor performance of Cope's forces, had already sent his son William Augustus, the Duke of Cumberland, north to meet the Jacobites. Cumberland commanded a powerful force and it soon became clear to the Jacobites that their campaign was doomed.

At Derby, where the drovers' intimate knowledge of routeways dried up, the Jacobites acknowledged the weakness of their position and began to retreat, Cumberland's army in hot pursuit as the Jacobites headed back to Scotland. Although defeat by then seemed inevitable, the victories scored by the Jacobites in the campaign of 1745 should not be forgotten: more than once the King of England's troops had been routed and many ascribed these triumphs to the devotion of Charles' troops to the Jacobite cause and, even more importantly, to their fair-haired, handsome, and charismatic leader, who was regarded by many as an almost messianic figure of hope for Scotland.

Months of skirmishes erupted once the Jacobite army reached Scotland. They culminated, of course, in a battle fought on a bleak, high windswept reach of boggy moorland just to the east of Inverness. Culloden was destined to be the last pitched battle ever fought on British soil, and it was also to mark the decisive end to the doomed cause of the Jacobites. The site today, some fifteen minutes by road from Inverness, is one of the most visited in Scotland: a state-of-the-art visitors' center tells the story of the battle through imaginative audio-visual presentations as well as through artifacts (such as some of the hundreds of musket balls that have been found on the battle site) before sending visitors out onto the battlefield site itself. To the north, the site is skirted by a busy B road that crosses featureless farmland, while to the south the land dips to the rich grazing lands of the valley of the River Nairn before rising immediately to the flat summit of Beinn Bhuidhe Mhor (1,798 feet), the highest point of a ridge that marks the first fold of the Grampians. On cold days a biting, drizzle-spitting wind from the Moray Firth often pummels the moor and whistles through the clumps of heather, almost threatening to raise the spirits of the hundreds of Jacobites dead who still lie buried here.

The battle lines drawn up on April 16, 1746, are marked today by rows of flags strung across the gently rolling expanse of moor: blue for the Jacobites and red for the Hanoverians. Those men who lined up where the blue flags now stand carried a rag-bag of hopes in their hearts as they readied themselves for battle. Some were Catholic and wanted a Catholic

Remembering the dead at the site of the Battle of Culloden (Andrew Beattie)

succession, but many Jacobites were actually Protestants who simply believed that a Stuart on the throne would bring back Scotland's lost pride (and its parliament). Others simply carried with them a sense of adventure and the desire to serve their clan and its chieftain. And all of them had pledged unswerving loyalty to the figurehead of their cause—however irrational their belief now seems. In the end as many Jacobite dreams died at Culloden as troops: some twelve hundred of Charles' soldiers were slaughtered in the battle, as opposed to a mere fifty from the Hanoverian side.

Many Jacobite commanders knew that the battle was a doomed enterprise from the start. A number of Charles' key commanders had advised him to withdraw on the evening before the battle, and an attempted surprise attack at dawn had ended in failure when Jacobite soldiers found themselves mired in mud and drenched by rain. Cumberland's troops in contrast were well-fed, well-rested, and well-resourced. In an hour of bloody violence they shattered decisively the hopes of generations of Jacobites: Charles' charging troops were simply impaled on lines of sharpened Hanoverian bayonets and the wounded were slaughtered where they fell.

After the battle, captured Jacobite prisoners were detained in the old High Church in Inverness (though not in the present building, which dates from the 1770s) before being executed in the adjacent cemetery, a grassy spread of tombs that overlooks the River Ness. It is thought that the condemned prisoner sat or knelt on a low gravestone selected for the task while another stone, some nine paces away, which had a v-shaped groove on its upper side, was used by the executioner to steady his musket; both graves can still be seen today. So too can a hole in the cemetery wall that overlooks the river, where a stray executioner's musket ball blasted into a block of pink granite.

The executions were watched enthusiastically from an audience gathered across the river in Balnain House. This whitewashed mansion, capped by two distinctive chimneys, served at the time as a military hospital for the Hanoverians, and perhaps William Augustus himself—who had quickly gained the moniker "Butcher Cumberland" as a result of all the executions—watched alongside his wounded men as the prisoners were led to their deaths across the river. On the battlefield itself those who had fallen were quickly buried in the boggy ground by local people, sometimes in unmarked graves up to four bodies deep; in 1881 the local landowner added some memorial stones and a cairn, which even today are ringed by wreaths of thistles or fresh flowers.

"Like a Bird on the Wing": Bonnie Prince Charlie's Flight across Scotland

Charles, however, escaped from the battlefield unharmed. He fled across northern Scotland and then made for the Inner Hebrides. Everywhere he went he was offered food and shelter. One of the places in which he found sanctuary was a tumbledown house on the west coast that was a hideout of the Jacobite chieftain Cluny MacPherson. The place was known as Cluny's Cage and provides the setting for scenes in Robert Louis Stevenson's novel *Kidnapped.* In the novel Alan Breck and David Balfour find the "strange house which was known in the country as Cluny's Cage" and noted that "a tree, which grew out from the hillside, was the living center-beam of the roof. The walls were of wattle and covered in moss. The whole house had something of an egg shape; and it half hung, half stood in that steep, hillside thicket, like a wasps' nest in a green hawthorn." It was the presence of unfriendly French privateers in Loch nan Uamh, close to the shelter, that caused Charles to abandon this hideout and be on his way; eventually he made his way to South Uist in the Western Isles, where he met a remarkable young woman by the name of Flora MacDonald.

Flora was destined to become one of the great romantic heroines of Scotland. On meeting Charles in South Uist she gave him some of her own clothes to wear as a disguise and then accompanied him "over the seas to Skye." With his bonnet and flowing dress Charles now went by the name of Betty Bourke, an Irish maidservant. On Skye his deception was nearly discovered when he held up his clothes too high when crossing a brook. So, according to James Boswell, when the party came to the next brook, Charles "did not hold up his clothes at all, but let them float upon the water." But Boswell also remarks that some observers of this curious maidservant noticed that the figure walked with unusually large strides, and mused half-jokingly that this was the prince in disguise, never guessing that they had actually stumbled on the truth.

The party's journey across Skye took them to Kingsburgh Castle, where Flora's mother, who was accompanying them, did not wash the bed-sheets in which Charles had slept, instructing her daughter that she should be buried in them when she died—a request that Flora carried out when the time duly came. After Kingsburgh came the port of Portree, where Flora's last duty towards Charles was to bid him farewell from McNab's Inn (a site now occupied by the Royal Hotel) as he set off for the mainland and then exile.

Flora MacDonald led an eventful life after her involvement with Charles. A number of months after the prince left Scotland she was arrested and imprisoned in the Tower of London on suspicion of treason. On her release she married a man from Skye and migrated with him to America. When he was captured during the American War of Independence she returned to Skye where she died in 1790 at the age of sixty-eight. She was buried in a remote hillside cemetery at Kilmuir, right on the island's most northerly tip. The graveyard overlooks the narrow sea passage between Skye and the Western Isles that is known as the Minch, and when there is no veil of mist or curtain of rainclouds to obscure the

Flora MacDonald's grave at Kilmuir, on the north tip of Skye, with the Western Isles clearly visible across the "Minch" (Andrew Beattie)

view, the tantalizing closeness of the islands of Harris and Lewis—across the sea channel that took Charles to Skye—is an exhilarating one. Three thousand mourners turned up for her funeral, joining a procession that wound along the lanes of the blustery Trotternish peninsula for over a mile. Johnson and Boswell had met Flora in 1773 during their tour of the Highlands, when Boswell commented that she was "a little woman, of a genteel appearance, and uncommonly mild and well-bred." Dr. Johnson, who slept in Bonnie Prince Charlie's old bed during their visit, wrote that "her name will be mentioned in history, if courage and fidelity be virtues, mentioned with honour." It is these words of Dr. Johnson that are carved on her memorial headstone, an extravagant affair of white marble topped by a Celtic "ringed" cross that was erected in 1880 and paid for by public subscription. The grave receives a fair few visitors today, partly as this remote site is actually on one of Skye's premier tourist routes; a brief stroll away is the engaging and informative Museum of Island Life, where displays relating to the history of farming, education, and community life in Skye are housed in a series of replica crofters' cottages, while the crumbling ruins of Duntulm castle crown a promontory just a couple of miles up the road.

After his departure from Skye, Charles headed for Borrodale on the mainland. He then set sail for France from the shores of Loch nan Uamh, only half a mile from the place where he had made landfall some fourteen months previously (the spot is marked today by a cairn beside the main A830 road as it skirts the loch between Polnish and Druimindarroch). He lived out his exile in France and Italy, as his father and grandfather had before him, never abandoning the Stuart cause. He married a German princess, in an effort to produce a Stuart heir, and eventually died in Rome, the city in which he had been born. He had been a sworn enemy of British rule of Scotland, of the Hanoverian dynasty, and of English Protestantism, but only a hundred years later his story had been transformed into one of the most shamelessly sentimental myths of "Bonnie Scotland" that so beguiled Victorian England. The *Skye Boat Song* is one of the more enduring legacies of this romantic myth-making. The song, written in the 1870s, recounts Charles' flight with Flora MacDonald from the Western Isles to Skye, the words by Harold Boulton set to a traditional air collected by the musicologist Anne Campbell MacLeod. "Speed Bonnie Boat, like a bird on the wing/Onward the Sailors Cry," commands the first verse. "Carry the lad that's born to be king/Over the sea to Skye."

The final verse tells of the defeat of the Jacobites and the hope that their cause will live again. "Burned are their homes, exile and death/Scatter the loyal men;/Yet 'ere the sword cool in the sheath/Charlie will come again." Another song whose roots lie in the same era, *Take the High Road*, was written in 1746 by Andrew Lang, again to a traditional Highland folk tune. It takes the form of a melancholy refrain written by a Jacobite prisoner in English hands who knows he will never see his true love again. "O ye'll tak' the high road/and Ah'll tak' the low (road) and Ah'll be in Scotlan' afore ye," the prisoner laments. "Fir me and my true love will ne-er meet again/On the bonnie, bonnie banks of Loch Lomond."

"THEIR FEROCITY OF TEMPER IS SOFTENED": THE CRUSHING OF THE CLANS

After Culloden a systematic program of terror was inflicted on those who had supported the Jacobites. One of its orchestrators was General Henry

Hawley, or "Hangman" Hawley, who even in the year after the battle was able to gloat that "there's still so many more houses to burn, and I hope still some to be put to death." In 1747 the British government passed the Act of Proscription, which prohibited any expression of Highland identity, such as the wearing of tartan: in his novel *Butcher's Broom* Neil Gunn condemns this legislation as a "penal enactment against the clansmen designed to destroy all that was distinctive in them, from the allegiance of their spirit to the very pattern of their clothes." Offenders faced the penalty of seven years' deportation if they broke any of the new regulations. In addition, clan chieftains were forbidden from keeping private armies, and those who had supported the Jacobites found their lands and properties confiscated. Chieftains were also stripped of their role as judges: in future Highlanders would be tried in the same courts as other subjects rather than in the courts of their chief.

Major Caulfeild of the British Army meanwhile built yet more roads through the Highlands, extending the network established by his predecessor General Wade, to allow for even faster troop movements across the mountains. The most dramatic and skilfully engineered of these was the steep zigzag path at the entrance to Glencoe that allowed soldiers access to a low pass that led to Kinlochleven; it was christened the "Devil's Staircase" by the soldiers who built it and now forms the most challenging section of the West Highland Way long-distance footpath.

It did not take long for the centuries-old traditions of clan rule to be eradicated. Samuel Johnson, a closet Jacobite sympathizer, realized on his visit to Scotland in 1773, just twenty-seven years after Culloden, that a whole way of life and political culture had already gone. "We came too late to see what we expected," he wrote. Exactly what he expected to experience in the Highlands, he wrote, was "a people of peculiar appearance, and a system of antiquated life. The clans retain little now of their original character, their ferocity of temper is softened, their military ardour is extinguished, their dignity of independence is depressed, their contempt of government subdued, and their reverence for their chiefs abated." People would now have to go much further afield to encounter "savage virtues and barbarous grandeur," Johnson continued, now that the pride of Highlanders had been "crushed by the heavy hand of a vindictive conqueror."

But the restrictions imposed by the Act of Proscription were in place for less than four decades—and judging by the writer Thomas Pennant's comments, that he had seen plenty of men very publicly wearing kilts at a fair in Inverness in 1769, the enforcement of the legislation was not as brutally rigorous as has been suggested. And we know that the men of the island of Seil, in the Firth of Lorn southwest of Oban, ignored the Act of Proscription entirely and wore kilts when on the island, because the pub beside the bridge leading to the mainland is to this day called the *Tigh an Truish,* the House of the Trousers; it was here that men changed out of their kilts and into trousers before heading over the bridge. They would have had no need to do this after 1782, however, for by then the Highlands were calmer and in that year the restrictions imposed by the Act of Proscription were repealed by parliament.

Despite the repeal of the Proscription Act it remained the case that any overt support for the Jacobites was regarded as treason of the highest order. Families who still supported Bonnie Prince Charlie had to be cautious. In the West Highland Museum in Fort William is an "anamorphic painting" of Charles that looks at first sight like a circular smudge of color, but when the smudge is viewed in a circular mirror wrapped around a cylinder it transforms itself into a portrait of the prince. Owners of such paintings were able to keep their support of Charles a secret during any surprise visits from the authorities, so long as the cylindrical mirror and the circular smudge were kept well apart from one another. The museum also holds a lock of Charles's hair, one of his waistcoats, and a set of slightly frayed, buff-colored bagpipes all of which were passed covertly through generations of Jacobite supporters. That these items were so venerated is an indication that by the late eighteenth century Charles had become a cult figure, his memory sacred, any relics connected to him revered beyond measure. Locks of the prince's hair were particularly coveted and can be seen on display in a number of castles and museums. In Dunvegan Castle on Skye is displayed a tiny locket that once belonged to Flora MacDonald: in it is a curly strand of the prince's blond hair that she had clipped herself from his head.

Attitudes took a long time to soften. Yet by 1815 ardor for the Jacobite cause had faded enough for Alexander MacDonald to be allowed to erect a spectacularly tall column at Glenfinnan to mark the place where Charles had raised his battle standard. The monument is framed magnificently by a famous curving viaduct on the Fort William to Mallaig stretch of the West Highland railway line and by the mountains that rise with such drama from the shores of Loch Shiel; it is easily one of the most photographed locations in Scotland—yet surprisingly the figure that crowns the column is not Bonnie Prince Charlie but an anonymous Highland chieftain. Spectacular though the monument is, it is unlikely that it is in the right place: in 1976 a hill fire on the steep, rocky slopes above Loch Shiel exposed some carvings in Latin that appear to commemorate the raising of Charles's standard, so placing the event on the hillside rather than on the valley floor where the monument stands.

The Highlands after Culloden: Landowners and Their Castles

While clan chieftains who had supported the Jacobites were persecuted following the defeat at Culloden, those who had backed the British crown were handed land and titles as a reward. But within a couple of generations these favored chieftains were not really chieftains at all, at least not in the old sense: they had transformed themselves into lairds, landlords who embraced the doctrine of the free market and the lure of profit. Samuel Johnson was of the opinion that these clan chiefs had "denigrated from patriarchal rulers to rapacious landlords." No longer allowed to maintain a standing army, the clan chieftains began to treat their tenants as economic cogs in the great wheel of forging a profit from their lands. And what bounty those lands yielded. With the advent of better roads, and then canals and railways, it was possible for lairds to export the produce of Highland streams and glens, notably salmon and lamb, to the rest of Britain and beyond. Money began pouring in to their coffers. Clan chieftains changed in other ways too: they began speaking the English dialect known as Scots instead of Gaelic; they bought and often lived much of the time in fashionable townhouses in Edinburgh; and they sent their sons to English public schools to be raised as gentlemen.

Many of the roads that transformed the economic fortunes of the Highlands were built by the army. But some were built by the lairds themselves. One of these was financed by Lord Breadalbane and ran from Taymouth to Tyndrum, so providing a link between the central and the west Highlands. The route required thirty-two new stone bridges to be constructed, many of which are still in use today. And along with the new roads came new, planned settlements. These were founded both for economic

Inveraray Castle
(Hchc2009/Wikimedia Commons)

gain and as a blunt but effective method of controlling a population still assumed to be restive after the Jacobite rebellions.

One of these new settlements was Callander, now a popular tourist center on the southern fringes of the Highlands, whose long, straight, main street (lined, inevitably these days, with cafés and knitwear shops) was laid out in the 1770s to plans originally drawn up by James Drummond, third Duke of Perth. Inveraray, whose setting beside Loch Fyne is one of the finest in Scotland, was likewise purposely founded and planned as an administrative center by the Dukes of Argyll. To visitors of Inveraray today the most obvious manifestations of such planning are the town's boulevard-style main street, which is far too grand and wide for a place of this size, and the formidable sandstone building just off the street that once housed the prison and law courts for the region, which have now been renovated as a family-friendly tourist attraction.

The lairds expected to live in a castle, just as their medieval forebears had. But with no military function to fulfill Highland residences began to look much less like castles and more like palatial country homes. The Highland lairds who found themselves most in favor with the British crown were the Campbell family, who were created Dukes of Argyll and were allowed to build a new castle at Inveraray—situated a ten-minute walk away from their new administrative center—to flaunt their power and wealth. Inveraray is unusual among Highland castles in that it has no ancient core: the whole place was constructed in the second half of the eighteenth century as a Loire-style chateau surrounded by formal gardens. Inside, amidst rooms full of portraits and eighteenth-century furniture, the most striking room is the Armoury Hall: stretching right to the ceiling, it is the tallest room in Scotland, and provides a suitable space to show off a vast collection of ancient weaponry—some 1,300 pikes, muskets, and swords—many of which were given to the Campbells by the British government to enforce British rule in the area. The current Duke of Argyll, the thirteenth, lives in a private wing of the castle; his predecessor, the twelfth duke, who died in 2001, once controversially referred to the Glencoe massacre, in which his forebears had participated as slaughterers, as "no big deal."

A number of other castles across the Highlands follow the same architectural fashion as Inveraray, with the difference that, concealed behind an eighteenth-century facade, is the core of a much older castle. The best examples are Blair Castle, near Pitlochry in the central Highlands, the ancestral seat of the Dukes of Atholl; Dunvegan, on the west coast of Skye, the historic seat of the MacLeod clan; and Dunrobin, on the east coast between Golspie and Brora, home to the Dukes of Sutherland. All of these castles offer visitors (and they turn up in their droves) a similar experience: a good deal of paintings and weaponry, some nice eighteenth-century furniture, and laminated cards in several languages in each room to help make sense of it all. At Dunrobin and Blair the medieval cores of the castles have been so altered as to make them invisible. At Blair, for example, there is little to suggest that the elegant eighteenth-century mint-and-stucco dining hall was once the Great Hall of the medieval castle. But at Dunvegan the old medieval fortress is less well concealed: a cramped dungeon dating from 1360, hacked partly from the rock on which the castle sits, is today accessed via a passage that leads off from an eighteenth-century salon whose parquet flooring is laid on top of the original stone floor from the Middle Ages.

Extravagance and opulence was the hallmark of these great Scottish baronial castles. And their owners have always enjoyed showing off their homes to visitors. In 1773 the chief of Clan MacLeod hosted Samuel Johnson and James Boswell at Dunvegan on their journey through the Highlands, leaving them much impressed with his hospitality. During their visit the pair were proudly shown a drinking vessel made from an ox's horn, "hollowed," so Dr. Johnson wrote, "so as to hold perhaps two quarts"; the vessel was fashioned from the horn of a mad bull in the days of the medieval chieftain Rory Mor MacLeod, and to this day the drinking horn is used in initiation ceremonies for a new chieftain. The horn is filled to the brim with claret and, as Dr. Johnson observed, the new chief has to down it "in one draught as a test of manhood." In 1956 the twenty-nineth chief scored a time of 1 minute 57 seconds in his initiation ceremony. (The horn is currently on view in the castle's north room.)

Even grander than Dunvegan is the great castle at Blair, which features a monumental entrance hall (again lined with weapons) and a magnificent wood-panelled ballroom, added in 1876 specifically for the annual ball staged by the duke for his company of Atholl Highlanders. That the duke was allowed to maintain a private army was a unique privilege, afforded to him after a visit of Queen Victoria to the castle; her generosity was a sure sign that by then the memories of Culloden had been subsumed under the nostalgic fantasy version of Scotland created in the Victoria era. Blair, however, loses out in terms of the quality of its gardens, which are nothing to write home about. Those at Dunvegan, with their little wooden bridges and hidden waterfalls, are the most intimate of the three great castles, but the ones at Dunrobin, laid out on terraces below the castle sweeping down to the sea, are the most beautiful and luxurious, with expansive lawns and fancy fountains that create a wonderfully harmonious accompaniment to the castle above them.

Further along the coast of Skye from Dunvegan is Armadale Castle, which faces Mallaig across the Sound of Sleat. Armadale has suffered a different fate on its journey from medieval fortress to palatial chateau. The old medieval fortress that stood here, a stronghold of the MacDonald clan, was destroyed in 1690 in a Hanoverian bombardment, but a century later the MacDonalds constructed a country house on the same site, adding a neo-Gothic-style extension in 1815 that was designed by the fashionable Edinburgh architect James Gillespie Graham. His most striking innovation was a fan-vaulted dining room. In its fussily grandiose architecture the house reflected the family's proud but distant history as Lords of the Isles. Unfortunately the eighteenth-century part of the house was destroyed in a fire and in the 1930s the family hit on hard times. Now the once-palatial home of the MacDonalds is nothing more than a skeleton of stone open to the sky; most poignant of all is Graham's magnificent doorway and the staircase behind it, which are overgrown with grass and trees. Only the lawns, sloping down towards the sea, give a sense of how glorious this house once was—while the pride of the ancient clan is expressed in a nearby visitor center where those claiming MacDonald ancestry can trace their family tree.

Fate has been kinder to a very different castle across the Sound of Sleat from Skye. At the beginning of the twentieth century the MacRae-Gilstrap family attempted to reclaim some of the glory of Clan MacRae by reconstructing one of the clan's former strongholds, Eilean Donan castle near Kyle of Lochalsh, from the broken shell that it had been reduced to during the Jacobite rebellions. Twenty years of almost wholesale reconstruction came to an end in 1932 and the resulting fortress, situated on an island and reached by an elegant arched bridge, is now one of the most familiar sights in Scotland—even if most of it is actually less than a century old. Nowadays the interior is an odd mix of Chippendale furniture, leaded windows, and waxwork dummies slaving away in a mocked-up century-old kitchen.

Different, again, was the experience of the MacDougall clan. When the MacDougall chief turned his back on his Jacobite past and had his estate returned to him, he chose to let his forebears' hereditary seat, Dunollie Castle, fall into romantic, ruinous decay—and such is the state in which it remains, guarding, as it has done for centuries, the approach to Oban harbor from a precipitous spur of rock. But below the ruins the MacDougall chieftain built for himself a very modest country house, which to this day remains the seat of the MacDougall clan and the (private) home of the current chief.

It is worth ending this section with mention of two Scottish castles built since the year 1880: proof positive that the tradition of fortress-building, which goes back to the Picts and the Celts, is a long one in Scotland. Carbisdale Castle was built between 1907 and 1917 on a site overlooking

Carbisdale Castle
(Andrew Beattie)

the Kyle of Sutherland in the far north. The place can only be described as something akin to a wedding cake built out of granite: no castle in the Highlands is built on such a fussily grandiose scale as this one. The place was built for the Duchess of Sutherland by her stepchildren, after a bitter family dispute broke out over the contents of her late husband's will. (The duchess herself was notorious for serving a six week sentence in Holloway Prison for destroying documents pertinent to the settlement of her legal case contesting this will.) Part of the condition of the castle's construction was that it should lie outside the county of Sutherland: the spot chosen was in Ross-shire at the time but the construction of the castle above the main road and railway line into Sutherland meant that it would be highly visible to the family of the duchess's late husband as they journeyed to their estates in the north (travelers on the Duke of Sutherland's private train would pull the blinds down as they passed the castle so it could not be seen). The castle was deliberately designed in three different styles, to give the illusion of the venerability that in reality it lacked. The three-faced clock tower has a blank side facing Sutherland, which is deliberate; the Duchess, it was said, "wouldn't give the time of day to her husband's branch of the family," and reputedly one of the castle's interior rooms was dedicated to opium smoking.

In the 1930s, not long after it was built, the castle fell into the hands of the Salvesen family from Norway, shipping magnates who allowed the exiled Norwegian royal family to use the place for formal gatherings during World War II. The castle was converted into a youth hostel in 1945, albeit a rather unusual one, graced by grand sweeping staircases and crammed with sculptures fashioned from Italian white marble. Unfortunately at the time of writing the castle had been severely damaged by a storm and its future is uncertain owing to the astronomical costs of renovation. The best views of it are from trains on the Inverness to Wick railway line that cross the Kyle of Sutherland on a girder bridge below the castle; there is a good view too from Invershin, on the main road between Bonar Bridge and Lairg on the north banks of the Kyle.

Not all the castles built in the Highlands since Culloden owe their construction to long-standing Scottish families. After Culloden many chieftains, weighed down by debt, were forced to sell their lands, and from the late nineteenth century onwards a new breed of landowner began buying up tracts of the Highlands (and purchasing whole islands too), often sealing their purchase with the construction of a brand new fairy-tale fortress. Most famously, Sir John Bullough, a textile machinery magnate from Lancashire, bought the island of Rùm in 1888 as a sporting estate and twelve years later his son George built Kinloch Castle on the island's rocky coast, with an exterior that boasted colonnades, crenellations, and turrets, all extravagantly fashioned from red sandstone brought from the Isle of Arran. Bullough filled the interior of the new castle with all manner of fashionable accoutrements that included a barrel organ and a ballroom with a sprung floor. The castle was also double glazed and centrally heated, and was the first house in Scotland outside Glasgow to be lit by electricity and the first private home in Scotland with its own internal telephone system. The Edwardian decadence spilled over to the exterior, too, in the form of a nine hole golf course and bowling green (laid with soil brought all the way from Ayrshire) and heated greenhouses that provided homes for hummingbirds, turtles, and alligators. In another part of the island, on the site of a former coastal crofting community named Harris, George ordered the construction of a mausoleum for his father that took the form of a Greek Temple, which now sits in a desolate spot surrounded by ruined crofters' dwellings: an ostentatious luxury that announced the arrival of a new breed of *nouveau riche* landowner in the Highlands and Islands.

POVERTY AND EMIGRATION IN THE HIGHLANDS

In September 1857 Queen Victoria visited some of the "poor" (as she refers to them in her journal) near her new Highland residence at Balmoral. She wrote that a local woman "walked round to some of the cottages to show me where the poor people lived, and to tell them who I was." To one eighty-eight year old woman Victoria gave "a warm petticoat, and the tears rolled down her cheeks, and she shook my hands, and prayed God to bless me: it was very touching."

Her words demonstrate little understanding of the wretched conditions in which most nineteenth-century Highlanders lived. While lairds lived lives of comparative luxury in their baronial castles, the conditions faced by farmers who eked out a living from the thin soils around Balmoral and across the Highlands were often harsh and challenging. As in Ireland, potatoes became the mainstay of the diet of the poor, and as in Ireland, periodic bouts of disease destroyed the crop and caused devastating famines. In 1846, eleven years before Victoria's visit to the "poor" near Balmoral, blight had devastated the potato crop in the Highlands, leaving tens of thousands destitute and starving. As with the Irish potato famine, the response of the authorities had been one of callous disregard. The Highland lairds ensured that exports of oats and barley continued from the region as the famine raged, and although charities (and some philanthropic landlords) certainly gave valuable assistance, government agencies established to distribute food were inefficient and wasteful, and relief was too late in coming. During a later famine, in 1874, Highlanders on the east coast tried to prevent the export of locally grown grain from seaports, and were beaten back with military force.

Most Highlanders lived in gloomy one-story cottages variously known as blackhouses (due to their dark interiors or to distinguish them from newer white-house dwellings with mortared walls) or long houses (due to their shape). The floors of these cottages consisted simply of earth—"no floor but naked ground" as Samuel Johnson observed—with walls of stone and turf and roofs of thatch. Those who lived in these cottages had to cope with daily hardships of disease and poverty in addition to the foul and icy weather the Atlantic threw at them through the winter. Houses were often built on a slope, with cows at the lower end, behind a partition, so that it was easy to get rid of manure. The animals would provide heat, which was also absorbed and re-radiated by the peat and stones of the cottage walls.

In years of shortage cattle would be bled and the blood would be mixed with oatmeal and milk to make unpalatable cakes, which provided families with their only nourishment. Throughout the eighteenth century English travelers recorded the wretched conditions of the people they saw living in such dwellings. In 1769 the writer Thomas Pennant considered the dwellings he saw near Braemar "shocking to humanity... they look, from a distance, like so many black molehills." As late as 1880 Jules Verne describes the "scattered houses" of Iona as "simple dilapidated affairs... almost all without windows, the only light coming from the door, with only a hole in the roof for a chimney, having only pebble and mulch walls, thatch roofs made from reeds and heather bound together with large strands of wrack." In *A Tour to the Western Isles of Scotland* Samuel Johnson writes of the villages in Glen Shiel where dwellings were "as filthy as the cottages of Hottentots" and tended to be constructed from loose stones piled up without cement, with a hole in the thatched roof to allow the smoke from the hearth to escape.

As for the people who lived in such dwellings, Johnson comments on the shoeless children—"gillie-wet-foots" as Walter Scott calls them in his novel *Waverley*—who would gather around his party "without any evil intention but with a very savage wildness of aspect and manner." Johnson wrote too of the "dark months" of winter that inhabitants of these villages had to endure, which were "a time of great distress; because the summer can do little more than feed itself, and winter comes with its cold and its scarcity upon families very slenderly provided." Yet what Johnson and other commentators did not realize was that these dwellings, set low into hillsides as protection against the weather, would often embody the spirit of the communities that built them: each would be constructed by villagers over the course of a single day, the men and women telling tales or singing as they arranged the stones or secured the thatch with ropes against the wind—and at sunset the finished house would be blessed by the local pastor.

Only the New World across the Atlantic seemed to offer any way out of the wretched conditions in which Highland Scots found themselves. The earliest settlement of Highlanders in North America was a community established by emigrants from Argyll in North Carolina in the 1730s. For the next two centuries emigration was endemic to the Highlands: today it is remembered in books and novels, and by a handsome statue of a man and a child looking out to sea at Helmsdale on the northeast coast, commissioned in 2004 and "erected to commemorate [the] resilience [of emigrants] in the face of extreme deprivation and their subsequent achievements worldwide." According to the eighteenth-century travel writer John Knox, some twenty thousand people left the Highlands for America between 1763 and 1775, largely as a result of the high rents demanded by the new, economically driven lairds.

One of these early emigrants was Flora MacDonald, Bonnie Prince Charlie's savior, who in 1774 sailed from Skye along with two thousand other islanders. "Of this family… there will soon be no remembrance in this poor miserable island," she wrote. "The best of its inhabitants are making ready to follow their friends to America." Robert Louis Stevenson acknowledges the rapid rate of emigration in his novel *Kidnapped*, set in 1751. Though the novel is a work of fiction written by a young man of twenty, Stevenson had traveled extensively around the coast of the Highlands by the time he wrote it, and his description in the novel of a ship full of migrants waiting to depart a West Highland harbor is probably based on first-hand experience. Standing on the quayside at Kinlochaline, Stevenson's hero David Balfour hears "a great sound of mourning" emanating from the vessel, and then observes "the people on board and those on shore crying and lamenting one to another so as to pierce the heart… I saw the tears run down the cheeks of the men and women on the boat, even as they bent at the oars, and the circumstances and the music of the song (which is one called *Lochaber No More*) were highly affecting even to myself."

Equally struck by the sight of departing ships were Johnson and Boswell, who saw a vessel named *Nestor* heaving with migrants when they were in Portree on Skye. Later on during their stay on Skye the pair watched locals perform a dance that Boswell supposed "the emigration from Skye has occasioned. They call it 'America.' Each of the couples, after the common involutions and evolutions, successively whirls round in a circle, till all are in motion: and the dance seems intended to show how emigration catches, till a whole neighbourhood is set afloat." Boswell went on to record that when the first ships had left Skye for America, "the people on shore... lay down on the ground, tumbled, and tore the grass with their teeth. This year there was not a tear shed. The people on shore seemed to think that they would soon follow."

A few years later the philosopher and churchman William Gilpin also heard tales of emigration when he visited Killin, in the heart of the Highlands. In his book *A Scottish Tour* he maintains that thirty families—some three hundred people—had been more or less forced to leave Killin after they had expressed dissatisfaction with their landlord, Lord Breadalbane. "The word was given," Gilpin recounts, that on May 1, 1776, the families should convene in the village, "called together by the sound of bagpipes," ready to depart. The migrants then had to walk to Loch Lomond, "all dressed in their best attire, the man armed in Highland fashion," to take boats across the loch; when they disembarked another walk awaited them, to Greenock on the Clyde estuary, where the ships to America were waiting. "They set out not like people flying from the face of poverty but like men who were about to carry their health, their strength, and little property, to a better market," Gilpin recounted.

Not everyone who left was fleeing destitution. Some Catholics were frustrated by the efforts to impose a very harsh, Highland form of Presbyterianism on their communities—such as those who fled from the notorious Colin Macdonald of Boisdale, who forced his tenants into the local Presbyterian kirk with a stick. But the majority were looking for a better life across the Atlantic. Before they got to the Promised Land, however, they had to endure the rigors of the voyage. Ships were often in an atrocious condition and were operated by unscrupulous speculators, such as the notorious George Dunoon of Fort William, and many emigrants succumbed to typhus and dysentery in the ships' unsanitary and cramped living quarters. There were no regulations regarding the conditions on board the ships—unlike on slave ships of the day, where the conditions many Highland emigrants confronted would not have been allowed.

Yet still the tide of migrants swelled. In 1837 émigrés began seeking out another destination, namely Australia, and between 1852 and 1857,

Poster advertising emigration, 1839
(Kelvingrove Art Gallery and Museum, Glasgow/Wikimedia Commons)

in the space of just five years, some five thousand Scottish emigrants landed on its shores, two thousand from Skye alone. In 1851, believing that emigration offered a real solution to the problems of the Highlands, the British government encouraged the foundation of the Highlands and Islands Emigration Society, and awarded the new body funding too. The organization was based in St. Martin's Lane in central London and included among its committee members the Governor of the Bank of England; its patron, who as we shall see in the next chapter took a keen interest in the Highlands, was Prince Albert.

The flood of emigration continued unabated throughout the nineteenth century, rendering villages and islands across northwestern Scotland little more than empty shells. One such was the island of Handa, off the coast of Sutherland in the far northwest of the country. In 1846 the island was devastated by the serious famine that struck much of Scotland that year. When it was over those who had survived simply upped sticks and headed west across the sea, choosing the island of Cape Breton in Canada as the place for their resettled community. This island was by now a long-standing favorite among Highland emigrants, and was divided up along sectarian lines: people from Skye went to Cape North, those from Lochaber to the village of Mabou. By 1900 the Cape had a population of a hundred thousand Gaelic speakers, and even today there are around one thousand speakers of Scots Gaelic living there.

The island of Handa that the migrants left behind has been uninhabited since the last boat set sail over a century and a half ago. It is now a nature reserve, although the ruined cottages of the former islanders remain scattered around the former jetty. Records show that until the devastation of the famine the islanders had lived on a diet of fish, potatoes, and sea birds, and ran their affairs through a makeshift parliament, where men would gather every morning to discuss business and formulate policy under the watchful eyes of the "head of state" who was known as the island's "queen," a position always held by the community's oldest widow.

Follies and Fishing Towns: Tackling Unemployment

During the late eighteenth century the cities of lowland Scotland began to undergo a renaissance in art, science, industry, education, and culture that would transform them into some of the greatest intellectual and economic powerhouses of Europe. Glasgow emerged as a major center of industry and shipping. Writers and intellectuals flocked to Edinburgh. The four great Scottish universities, in Edinburgh, Glasgow, Aberdeen, and St. Andrews secured an international reputation. But little of this seemed to touch the Highlands, which remained desperately poor and backward in comparison.

The divide between Highland and lowland cultures is vividly described by Sir Walter Scott in his 1817 novel *Rob Roy*, which is set around a hundred years before it was written. According to Scott, all Glaswegians knew of the "dusky mountains of the Western Highlands" was that the region "often sent forth wilder tribes" to their city, accompanied by the "hordes of wild, shaggy, dwarfish cattle and ponies" that they had come to sell. The Highlanders themselves were as "wild, as shaggy, and sometimes as dwarfish as the animals they had in charge." Both sides viewed the other with suspicion and distrust. The city folk of Glasgow "gazed with surprise on the antique and fantastic dress, and listened to the unknown and dissonant sounds of their language, while the mountaineers... stared with astonishment on the articles of luxury of which they knew not the use, and with an avidity which seemed somewhat alarming on the articles which they knew and valued."

Nonetheless over time some Highlanders recognized the opportunities that Glasgow provided and gradually came to form a major part of the city's burgeoning labor force. Scott remarks that even though

> it is always with unwillingness that the Highlander quits his deserts... Many of their inhabitants strayed down to Glasgow, there formed settlements, and there sought and found employment, although different indeed from their native hills. This supply of a hardy and useful population was of consequence to the prosperity of the place, furnished the means of carrying on the few manufactures which the town already boasted, and laid the foundation of its future prosperity.

Despite the waves of outgoing migrants, both to Glasgow and across the sea to America and Australia, unemployment remained a serious problem in the Highlands. But in some cases work was deliberately created for the unemployed by philanthropic businessmen and landowners. These included the building of so-called "destitution roads" that were intended to provide work for unemployed laborers: one such was the road that linked the fishing port of Ullapool with the head of Loch Broom. But McCaig's Tower in Oban is the most obvious manifestation of this philanthropy: the structure was the brainchild of a local businessman, John Stewart McCaig, who wanted to relieve seasonal unemployment among local stonemasons, and the structure he commissioned them to build was not a tower at all but a giant classical-style amphitheatre that rises incongruously above the busy harbor town. (Classical purists always point out that despite being inspired by the Coliseum in Rome the building is circular in plan rather than oval.)

McCaig was a prominent figure in nineteenth-century Oban. He was a banker, property magnate, and a magistrate—an odd mixture, it seems, of show-off and philanthropist. His original intention had been to create a museum, an art gallery, and a chapel within the amphitheatre; statues would be positioned around the parapets and the monument would be

"McCaig's Folly" and the harbor front at Oban
(Andrew Beattie)

linked to the center of Oban via a funicular. But none of this was actually realized. Now the whole construction stands as a bizarre monument to the economic destitution of the Highlands during Victorian times and to one man's vain (in both senses of the word) attempt to solve it. (In his book *The Kingdom by the Sea* Paul Theroux describes the amphitheatre as "lovely and skeletal, symmetrical, purposeless" and notes that locals had dubbed the place "McCaig's Folly.") Within the curving walls of the structure there is nothing but grass and benches, and it is the view from the terrace over Oban's harbor and towards the Isle of Mull that beguiles those who slog their way up here from the town center.

Oddly, a similar thing happened on the other side of the Highlands—on the east coast—though the resulting structure is very different. In Ross, Sir Hector Munro, the chief of Clan Munro and former supreme commander of the Indian Army, decided to alleviate local unemployment by commissioning a somewhat eccentric monument that crowns the bald, flat summit of Cnoc Fyrish (1,478 feet), overlooking the Cromarty Firth above the village of Evanton, home to Sir Hector's ancestral seat. Known as the Fyrish Monument, Sir Hector's strange creation consists of a stark row of stone arches capped by rows of battlements. When seen from the main road and railway that run along the north side of the Firth the monument looks like a toothy version of Stonehenge; up close it seems more to be the only remaining part of some long-ruined castle, marooned on the grassy summit of the mountain. The intention was to represent an Indian gateway, in celebration of Sir Hector's capture of the town of Negapatam, near Madras, in 1781, a year before he returned to Scotland and had the monument built. Nowadays, as with McCaig's Folly, an exhilarating view rewards those who walk up to the monument along a forest track that branches off the minor road from Alness to Boath: the panorama stretches from the bulk of Ben Wyvis in the west to the North Sea in the east, and encompasses the whole of the Cromarty Firth. Again, like McCaig's Tower, this scheme was little more than a sticking plaster, and the scourges of population pressure, endemic poverty, and the spread of disease (not to mention the upheavals caused by the Highland clearances, which are covered further on in this section) continued to force many to leave the Highlands.

Not all Highland communities organized themselves around tilling the soil or raising livestock. Coastal villages had supported fishing fleets for centuries and in the eighteenth century some effort was made to introduce commercial fishing to the west of Scotland. In 1788 the British Society for Encouraging Fisheries (an offshoot of the Highland Society of London) founded the settlement of Tobermory on Mull as a commercial fishing center, and the same organization later established the port of Ullapool at the height of the herring boom.

Tourism was another source of income: by 1800 the innkeeper of the famous Kingshouse Hotel, situated in wild and desolate countryside at the entrance to Glencoe and originally built as an overnight refuge for British soldiers pounding the old military road to Fort William, was noticing that his usual clientele of animal drovers and military men was increasingly augmented by well-heeled aristocrats from England who were simply there to enjoy the spectacular scenery. Meanwhile ferrymen on Loch Lomond and Loch Katrine in the Trossachs began to find that their services were in demand by visitors as well as locals. By the end of the century, when settlements such as Oban, Fort William, and Mallaig had been linked to Glasgow by new railway lines, tourists flocked to the Highlands and many settlements found themselves transformed into tourist towns, with a consequent upsurge in employment opportunities for locals.

Often it was local entrepreneurs who capitalized on the boom; when the railway line to Oban was built an enterprising man named Duncan Fraser, previously employed at a hotel on Loch Tay and known as "Boots" Fraser because he cleaned vistors' boots, realized that tourists would soon be coming in large numbers to the West Highlands, and in 1881 he raised enough money to build the baronial-style Loch Awe hotel that overlooks the loch's northeastern tip to this day. In fact the hotel still has its own railway station (Loch Awe) which Fraser persuaded the line's operators to build, immediately below the hotel on the loch shore. The views from the picture windows of the hotel's Victorian-style drawing room are just as magnificent as they were when Fraser chose this site for his establishment. They stretch across the loch to the romantic waterside ruins of Kilchurn Castle, which are beautifully framed by the slopes of Beinn Donachain rising behind them. But tourism only ever provided seasonal employment—few visitors braved the Highlands in winter until the first skiers arrived in the 1930s—and some areas were favored more than others. Only in a few places did the tourist industry provide a solution to the dire economic straits in which many communities still found themselves at the turn of the twentieth century.

Mining and Canals: The Industrial Revolution in the Highlands

Another form of economic activity that provided employment in some Highland communities during the eighteenth and nineteenth centuries was mining. One of the biggest mining concerns was at Bonawe, on the shores of Loch Etive, where in 1753 ironworkers from Cumbria founded an iron smelter after experiencing a shortage of charcoal in the Lake District. The site was carefully chosen: supplies of iron ore and limestone could be brought in by sea (Loch Etive is a sea loch), power from a waterwheel on the River Awe drove the bellows that pumped air into the smelter, and trees from the surrounding forests provided the charcoal. In fact so many trees were cut down that when the writer and naturalist

Thomas Pennant passed along the shores of Loch Awe in 1769 he feared that the works there would "soon devour the beautiful woods of the country." During Bonawe's heyday the iron works supported a whole community, complete with schools and churches; the owners gave workers a plot of land to till, and turned a blind eye to the heavy drinking and the illicit smuggling that was conducted from the darkened wharves at night. Production finally ceased in 1876 when coke-fired ironworks elsewhere in Scotland proved more efficient than Bonawe's charcoal-based furnaces. Today the former smelter is now a slightly over-restored industrial heritage site that sits on the edge of Tainault, a rather ordinary village near Oban; the whitewashed rows of miners' cottages beside the works seem rather more genuine than the rebuilt forges "worked" by plastic mannequins.

Although Bonawe was the most successful iron smelter in Scotland, it was not the first. That honor went to a smelter founded in 1610 by a lowland Scot named Sir George Hay, who founded a smelter on Loch Maree in Ross. Like the Bonawe smelter it made use of ore from Cumbria. The abandoned Inverlochy Castle on Loch Linnhe was also commandeered for use as an iron smelter in the 1730s, its lochside location allowing for the easy delivery of raw materials. Bonar Bridge on the Dornoch Firth in the eastern Highlands was also home to an iron foundry, and when King James IV rode past it in the sixteenth century on his way to the pilgrimage center of Tain he expressed similar fears to Thomas Pennant concerning the loss of trees, and ordered that the depleted oak forests surrounding the foundry should be replanted.

Much of the iron ore that fueled these and other Highland smelters was imported from elsewhere in the country. Some ore was, however, mined in the region, principally on Raasay, a long, spindly island off the east coast of Skye, where relics of the old iron ore mines can be seen all over the island's southern part. Tucked away in the hills just above the village of Inverarish are derelict and roofless mine buildings, while overgrown cuttings and concrete piers of long-dismantled viaducts form the most tangible evidence of a narrow-gauge railway line constructed by German prisoners captured during the World War I to link the mines to a jetty at Suisnish. The jetty here was linked to the higher section of track in the hills by an inclined railway whose steeply-graded trackbed is also still visible. Lime was also needed for the smelting of iron ore, and this was

Derelict mine buildings on the island of Raasay
(Andrew Beattie)

quarried on another island, Lismore, where disused kilns and cottages can still be seen around the settlement of Sailean.

Other commodities mined in the Highlands and Inner Hebrides include marble, quarried on Skye and transported to the pier at Broadford by means of another small railway; gold, which was mined at Baile an Or near Helmsdale further north, where its discovery in 1869 sparked off a mini gold rush; and lead, rich seams of which were discovered in the 1740s by the mining entrepreneur Sir Robert Clifton at Tyndrum in the heart of the West Highlands, where a couple of rows of squat, white-washed, single-story miners' cottages, known as Clifton village, can still be seen today. They form a surreal appendage to a village that otherwise lives off two enormous coach tour hotels and the famous Green Welly Shop that sells outdoor gear and hearty meals to hungry walkers on the West Highland Way. Lead was mined in a number of other locations, and in 1722 the profitable lead mines sunk beneath the village of Strontian on the shore of Loch Sunart yielded commercial quantities of another valuable metal, strontium, which was named after the village and became valuable in the manufacture of alloys.

One Highland town also emerged as a coal-mining center. Pits were first sunk at Brora, on the shores of the Dornoch Firth, in the seventeenth century, under the auspices of the local landowner, the Duke of Sutherland, whose ancestral seat at Dunrobin is just along the coast from here. The mined coal was initially used to heat seawater to produce salt, and in 1630 Sir Robert Gordon complained of the sulphur smell that pervaded the town, writing that "there is not a rat in Sutherland, and if they do come thither in ships from other parts they die immediately, how soon do they smell the air of that country." Later the coal was used in brick manufacture. The mines shut in 1972, but today lumps of coal can still be found on the town's pebbly beach, while opposite the railway station is a row of brick cottages of a very similar style to those constructed in mining settlements in the English Midlands, where the Duke of Sutherland also owned several mines.

It was slate that was the most important commodity mined in northwestern Scotland. Scottish slate was more hardwearing than Welsh slate but was less easy to split and to work with. Southwest of Oban are the so-called Slate Islands, a scattering of islands scarred by gray quarry workings that once yielded an annual toll of nine million slates between them. Seil is the largest of these islands; at its western tip is the village of Ellenabeich, which is connected to a tiny offshore island named Easdale by a ferry journey of barely a minute. Both places are home to low-slung rows of whitewashed one-story dwellings that are characteristic of Highland mining villages.

Easdale itself is currently home to seventy people, but back in the mid-nineteenth century over four hundred people lived on the island and Easdale slates were exported as far away as Australia. Then one night in 1881 disaster struck: a mighty Atlantic storm flooded the quarries, which were right next to the sea and nearly two hundred feet deep in places. Machinery was destroyed and many of the mines could no longer be worked. With shifting fashions in roofing materials the surviving mines in both Easdale and Ellenabeich finally closed in 1911, although some Easdale miners were fulfilling orders for locals into the 1950s. By then the population of the village was barely twenty.

Although the current community on Easdale is thriving, an air of melancholy still hangs around the place, and a stroll around the island on paths strewn with slates reveals vast and very dark pools, now full of rain and seawater, that were once the slate quarries. Ellenabeich, with its direct bus service to Oban, has fared a little better now its mines have gone. Lovingly curated folk museums in both settlements tell the story of these resilient communities.

The island of Kerrera, to the northeast of Seil, also yielded slate from beneath its rocky terrain. Today a short row of whitewashed cottages on the southern tip of the island (one of which is now the unlikely home of a sanctuary for abused parrots) highlight the island's brief history as a mining center: for the venture failed here, and when it did the cottages briefly became home to the main community of lobster fishermen on the Scottish west coast, who packed their catches in ice and sent them by train to Southampton where they were put on the menu for those sailing to America on the great Cunard liners. On the Scottish mainland, slate was mined at Ballachulish near Fort William between 1693 and 1955, and the quarry can still be seen today, right across the road from the Ballachulish visitors' center; a waterfall cascades picturesquely down the sides of the quarry, whose walls glisten shiny black when wet.

The mining of slate, lead, marble, coal, and even gold at least broadened the economic base of the Highlands beyond farming and fishing, but mining was dangerous work and mining communities risked devastation if the price of commodities fell or their local mine became worked out—or a disaster befell them such as it did in Easdale.

Material produced in the mines and quarries of the Highlands had to be moved around. This was not easy on the military roads that had been built across the mountains, which were intended for soldiers' feet rather than wagons laden with coal or ore. But the turn of the nineteenth century saw a transport revolution in the form of canal mania reach the Highlands. In 1801 the engineer John Rennie supervised the cutting of the Crinan Canal, a nine-mile waterway linking Loch Fyne and the Sound of Jura, whose opening meant ships no longer had to navigate around the long peninsula of the Mull of Kintyre to reach the west coast of Scotland from Glasgow. Rennie's original construction was renovated in 1816 by Thomas Telford, who as we shall see was also responsible for many new bridges and roads across the Highlands. Telford's main achievement in water transport, however, was the Caledonian Canal, the waterway that allowed ships to navigate across Scotland along the Great Glen from Fort William to Inverness, so avoiding the treacherous sea passage around the storm-lashed north coast. The route for the canal had been surveyed by James Watt in 1773 but Telford takes the credit for its completion. Although Fort William and Inverness are separated by fifty-five miles of navigable water, only twenty-two of these must be traversed through Telford's cut channel; the rest of the distance involves ships traversing Loch Ness and Loch Lochy, with canals linking those two lochs with each other and with the sea.

The most famous section of the canal is the series of locks known as Neptune's Staircase, where the canal climbs sixty-four feet in just half a mile. The locks are now used solely by pleasure cruisers, but in the early nineteenth century ships would have passed through this flight of locks laden with the produce of factories, mines, fishing boats, and farms. The famous staircase is only three miles from the center of Fort William, and is visible from the trains on the Fort William to Mallaig railway, which cross the canal on a swing bridge immediately below the lowest of the locks.

THE HIGHLAND CLEARANCES: THE CREATION OF A "HOWLING AND SOLITARY WILDERNESS"

No single event in the last thousand years of history has affected Highlanders more than the Clearances. Over the course of just over one hundred years, from the first Clearances in 1762, tenant farmers across Scotland were evicted from their upland farms by the powerful lairds who had taken the place of former clan chieftains. As has been noted, many evicted families left the Highlands completely, and began to forge new lives in the burgeoning cities of lowland Scotland, or further afield, in North America or Australia. Those who stayed were re-housed in purpose-built coastal communities where they were given a minimal farm holding known as a croft.

Many historians have argued that the Clearances were necessary in an era when despite mass, voluntary emigration, the Highland population was mushrooming and the prospect of devastating famine and destitution was very real. One example cited is that of the island of Tiree, whose population grew from 1,500 in 1747 to an unsustainable 4,453 in 1831. In this light, the Clearances seemed a logical, if severe, mechanism for what was unavoidable—namely the dispersal of people to places where they could achieve living standards judged acceptable in the modern world. But for the farming families who were moved, the pace of change was devastatingly rapid for those who had lived a lifestyle that followed centuries of tradition. And some of the evictions were accompanied by brutality and burnings; even if these were not the norm, they are the ones that have stuck in the collective memory of Highlanders, informing opinion about the Clearances that is still held to the present day. Even if the extent of the cruelty of the evictions has been exaggerated in popular imagination, the forced abandonment of the land certainly compromised the very essence of the age-old clan system, namely the concept of *duthchas,* whereby a particular people were bound both to each other and to the land they farmed; and so the very heart of Highland society and culture was ripped out when the uplands were cleared. To this day the desolation of much of the Highlands, and the concentration of population along the region's coastlines rather than in the upland interior, can be related directly to the upheavals of the Clearances.

Before the middle of the eighteenth century tenant farmers were the mainstay of Highland agriculture. Their relationship with their chieftain was ingrained into the way of farming. Some of the produce of the land they tilled they kept for themselves, while the rest was handed over to the head of their clan. Land was often farmed in rigs—elongated, low-crested ridges of soil—in a system of cultivation known as "runrig." By this method soils would be worked into the center of the ridge, providing a depth of soil usually lacking on steep slopes, while water drained away along the boggy hollows between each rig. Each family in a township would be allocated a series of rigs, scattered around the outskirts of the town, so that no one family ended up with the best or worst land.

Before the nineteenth century these rigs dominated the landscape of the Highlands; now they have faded from view, but to this day, a certain angle of sunlight or the way snow melts in spring can reveal the old ridge markings cutting across the countryside. Villagers also reared animals, often a mixture of cattle, sheep, chickens, goats, and hens. The Highland cattle that can still be seen grazing today, distinguished by their shaggy, toffee-colored coats, are descendants of the beasts reared by these tenant farmers. The goats have mostly gone now, although a community of feral goats still makes its home in the woods around Loch Lomond, descendants of those who were let loose as Highland farmsteads were abandoned.

Every summer farmers would move their livestock from low-lying common fields beyond the rigs to the higher pastures, known as "shielings," in an echo of seasonal livestock movement that take place in upland areas all over the world (and most famously in the Alps, where the tradition is known as transhumance). Shepherds would maintain basic bothies, or shieling huts, high in the hills, in which they would live for weeks at a time during the summer, spending their days turning the milk from their animals into butter and cheese. The writer Thomas Pennant visited a shieling hut in 1769 and noted in his *Tour of Scotland* that the building was similar to a *Senne* in the Swiss Alps: bare and stark, it contained little more than "milking utensils and a couch formed of sods to lie on." Today, such buildings are very familiar to walkers in the Highlands, as a sturdy stone hut providing basic shelter from the elements, or as a jumble of stone ruins at the side of a Highland footpath.

The first Highland landowner to evict tenants was John Lockhart-Ross, a career sailor who rose through the ranks of the Royal Navy to the position of vice-admiral and who, in 1762, inherited Balnagown Castle in Ross and the chieftainship of Clan Aindrea. He had the revolutionary idea of draining the peaty bogland on his farm and then introducing sheep in great numbers. These animals were black-faced lintons from the Scottish Borders—nothing like the sheep Highlanders were used to, which were

Shielings on Jura, from Pennant's *Tour of Scotland*
(Wikimedia Commons)

scraggly dog-sized creatures. Lockhart-Ross wanted to see whether the animals would survive the harsh Highland winter. They did, and he decided to convert his whole estate to sheep farming, employing a lowland sheep farmer to look after the flocks. Not surprisingly the people he evicted from upland pastures to make way for these new sheep took umbrage at his actions: animals were shot at night or were driven into lochs. But sheep farming was in the Highlands to stay, and from the 1780s lairds all over the region began following the example of John Lockhart-Ross by introducing what Gaelic speakers knew simply as *na caoraich* mora (big sheep) to their lands. These new sheep were not in fact lintons but another hardy breed of Border sheep known as cheviots.

Landlords soon found the economics of sheep farming to be starkly advantageous. But Highlanders saw none of this financial benefit. In August 1792 the first sustained revolt against land clearances erupted in Sutherland, when four hundred clansmen rounded up six thousand sheep from the new farms around Lairg and began shepherding the animals south in protest at the policies of the lairds. But the great trek petered out at the hamlet of Boath, inland from the Cromarty Firth, and clansmen dispersed when troops were dispatched from Dingwall to confront them. In reality Highlanders were powerless to stop the inexorable rise of sheep farming. In July 1817 an annual sheep and wool market was established in Inverness, with the encouragement of Liverpool merchants and Aberdeen woollen manufacturers, to process the sheep that were colonizing the Highlands. At its height one thousand farmers attended the Inverness sheep market and 150,000 sheep would change hands; and soon after its opening Highland estates were being bought and sold for ten times the amount they had reached in the 1790s.

Tales of the brutality of the evictions are legion. One of the biggest took place in June 1814 on the estates of the powerful Duke of Sutherland and involved the removal of fifteen thousand people. The actual evictions were executed by the estate factor, a bad-tempered Edinburgh advocate named Patrick Sellar, who instituted a reign of terror over Sutherland. Most notoriously, he took to torching the homes of those who refused to move. When 99-year-old Margaret MacKay died of burns inflicted by the flames Sellar was accused of culpable homicide and put on trial. He was acquitted but his role in the killing was enough to ensure his dismissal from the service of the Sutherlands.

Sellar has become the most emblematic figure associated with the cruelty of the Clearances: for years after his death his tomb in Elgin Cathedral was regularly vandalized, and he remains a hated figure in northern Scotland to this day, although the violence associated with the evictions he orchestrated was not typical. Another notorious Sutherland factor involved in the Clearances was James Loch, who justified his so-called "improvements" in a book, *An Account of the Improvements on the Estate of Sutherland,* in which he wrote that the Clearances were "a wise and generous policy and well calculated to increase the happiness of the individuals who were the object of this change, and to benefit those to whom these extensive domains belonged."

More resistance came in the wake of the momentous evictions orchestrated by Sellar, Loch and others. In 1820 Culrain, a small village just inland from the Dornoch Firth, became the scene of a pitched skirmish fought between constables answering to the Sherriff of Ross-shire and local people about to be deprived of their land. Famously most of those involved in the protest were women, who screamed at the sheriff, "we don't care for our lives… we must die anyway" before overturning his carriage, kicking in its panels and shredding the paper bills on which were printed the writs of removal. When the law enforcers sought shelter in the inn at Ardgay, a short distance away, the women simply hurled stones at the windows.

After Culrain the authorities were determined to confront future disruption with brute force. In 1854 police baton-charged a crowd of three hundred women and girls who were protesting against further evictions from Strathcarron, seriously injuring twenty protestors in the process. The violence was witnessed by a Glasgow lawyer named Donald Ross, who in the years that followed was moved to write a series of books about the Clearances. Describing what he had seen at Strathcarron, Ross observed that "the police struck with all their force… not only when knocking down, but after the females were on the ground. They beat and kicked them while lying weltering in their blood." Such was the brutality of the police action that as the violence died down "the limbs [of the victims] were mangled and their clothes clotted with blood."

Ross also condemned the police brutality in a letter to the Lord Advocate in Glasgow, claiming that after the assault "pools of blood were on the ground, that the grass and earth were dyed red with it, that the dogs of the district came and licked up the blood." But Ross's observations were ignored; sentencing one of the women involved in the Strathcarron protests to prison, Lord Justice-Clerk Hope, sitting in Inverness, remarked that "there exists a singular and perverted feeling of insubordination in some districts of the Highlands against the execution of civil process in the removal of tenants. This feeling is most prejudicial to the interests of all, and it is absolutely necessary to suppress it."

To compound the injustices already suffered by evicted Highlanders, in 1834 a hundred-foot-high monument was erected on the summit of Ben Bhraggie, which rises above the village of Golspie on the east coast, to the memory of the first Duke of Sutherland, who had overseen mass evictions from his estates. From the insufferably pompous monument the sandstone duke turns his back on the glens he emptied and looks out towards his great waterside castle at Dunrobin, which he built from the proceeds of his sheep farms (the turrets are just about visible from the monument). The inscription on the monument indicates that it was raised "by a mourning and grateful tenantry to a judicious, kind, and liberal landlord." There is no mention of the suffering that the duke—an Englishman who had come into his estates by marrying the Duchess of Sutherland—had inflicted on the people who lived in this part of Scotland. Not surprisingly a campaign once existed to smash the monument and scatter the remains over the local area; today it is visible from miles around, and can be reached (in about an hour) via a steep path that winds up through the forest from Golspie.

The Clearances took place during an era of growing interest in the Scottish Highlands. Wordsworth venerated the landscape through poetry, J. M. W. Turner through art, and Walter Scott through his historical novels such as *Waverley*. Yet little acknowledgment of the devastation of the Clearances was ever made by the creative geniuses of the Romantic era—despite the fact that they all traveled in the Highlands and would have witnessed plenty of evidence themselves. Furthermore, some travelers in the Highlands viewed the evictions as entirely necessary and justified. John MacCulloch, a Fellow of the Royal Society, for instance, considered the people he came across (other than gentry) as an offence to the landscapes he wished to enjoy. In his 1824 book *The Highlands and the Western Isles of Scotland* MacCulloch wrote of the "former hamlets of the idle and useless population" in Sutherland, and described how a family of dirty, haggard children he saw cooking a meal by Loch Kishorn simply seemed to spoil the view. John Robertson, a journalist for the *Glasgow National*, found the houses of the poor in Strathcarron filled him with "disgust" for their wretchedness, and wrote that "the idea of business has not dawned on [the Highlander's] soul… the iron genius of economical improvements he knows not and heeds not."

Not all observers and writers were as callous. As we have seen, the Glasgow journalist Donald Ross was a sympathetic chronicler of the Clearances, and in 1857 the author Donald MacLeod was moved to write a book entitled *Gloomy Memories*, in which he lamented the devastation wrought by the Clearances. "It is now a lamentable truth that the Highlands of Scotland… are now converted to a howling solitary wilderness, from which joy and rejoicing are fled forever," he wrote. His book was intended as a riposte to a book entitled *Sunny Memories* by the American writer Harriet Beecher Stowe (author of the classic anti-slavery tract *Uncle Tom's Cabin*), which maintained that the suffering caused by the Clearances had been exaggerated and that the tales of poverty and destitution were a slanderous misrepresentation of the truth.

The psychological scars left by the Clearances were profound and long-lasting. They were expressed in poetry and prose by Highland writers, most famously of all by Sorley MacLean, the best-known of all Scotland's Gaelic-speaking poets, who immortalized the Clearances on his native island of Raasay in verse. Raasay had been cleared in 1843, when the debt-ridden chieftain John MacLeod of Dunvegan Castle sold his land to a wealthy merchant trader named George Rainy, who then let out much of the island to a sheep farmer from the Scottish mainland. Rainy had a six-foot stone wall constructed across the island, confining crofters to the rocky northern tip while the rest was given over to sheep to graze and for deer and rabbit to be bred as game.

In his intense and visionary poem "Hallaig" (1952) MacLean describes one of the cleared townships on Raasay, in which the landscape is populated by the ghosts of those evicted: "The dead have been seen alive," he writes in the poem (as translated by Seamus Heaney): "The men at their length on the grass/At the gable of every house/The girls a wood of birch trees/Standing tall with their heads bowed."

The Clearances have also served as a background to a number of novels—not least those of Neil Gunn, the supreme chronicler of the lives of the Highland poor. Early on in Gunn's 1937 *Butcher's Broom* an estate factor, clearly based on Patrick Sellar, is sent to a village in Sutherland and explains that "the whole of the county from one end of the county will have to be gutted out." He goes on to report that he sees the Clearances as a "work of sanitation… the people of the glens live in sloth, poverty and filth… the sooner they are cleared out, the better for themselves, and for those who have the right use of their country at heart." Eviction, Gunn writes, was

> a terrible thing, for it meant the tearing up of life by the roots and the throwing of it on a sea-beach or a foreign strand where everything that made life comely and happy and to be desired would forever be denied; where life itself, through exposure and lack of physical sustenance, would become wretched beyond reason and starve and die.

When the evictions finally begin, "the red wall of fire advanced against the houses [and] the whole scene had something infernal about it… the groups of the homeless were like condemned beings by pits of fire in a smouldering hell."

Children's writers have also set novels against the background of the Clearances. The best-known of these is *The Desperate Journey*, written by Kathleen Fidler, considered the most important twentieth-century Scottish writer of children's fiction. The novel opens with the brutal eviction of a family from their croft near Dornoch on the orders of the Countess of Sutherland, and the burning of their property by Patrick Sellar; the rest of the book follows the fortunes of the family as they travel to Glasgow and then Canada, following the well-trodden route of those who were evicted from their Highland landholdings two hundred years ago.

Villages abandoned during the Clearances can be seen all over the Highlands. Two stand in the lonely but beautiful Strathnaver valley, south of the village of Bettyhill on the north coast, accessed by a road that winds through land still given over to sheep grazing. One of the abandoned villages is Rosal, where Margaret MacKay died in the conflagration ordered by Patrick Sellar; the other, much closer to Bettyhill, is Achanlochy. Both sites now consist of little more than earthy mounds and isolated stones that are slowly sinking into the hillsides. But the scale and impact of the Clearances can be judged from the volunteer-run, endearingly eccentric

The Strathnaver Clearances as depicted on a frieze displayed in the Strathnaver Museum in Bettyhill and created by local schoolchildren (Andrew Beattie)

Strathnaver Museum occupying a former church at the eastern edge of Bettyhill. Amidst the various displays in the museum—rock samples, memorabilia from the Clan MacKay, farming tools, a wind-up gramophone, and an old supply boat for the remote island of St. Kilda—the story of the Clearances is simply but effectively told in photographs and models, with much input from local people, including friezes and other work done by schoolchildren. The church's outsized eighteenth-century pulpit is still intact and it was from here that the Strathnaver eviction notices were read out.

Perhaps the most poignant reminders of the Clearances can be seen in a very different part of the Highlands some fifty miles to the south, at Croick in a remote part of Easter Ross. Here, in 1845, families evicted from nearby Glencalvie were forced to take refuge in the graveyard of the village church. "It was a most wretched spectacle to see these poor people march out of the glen," remarked a report on the eviction in *The Times*. "The whole countryside was on the hills watching them as they silently took possession of their tent [in the churchyard, which was fashioned from] tarpaulin stretched over poles, the sides closed in with horsecloths." Some of the evictees were moved to write inscriptions on the diamond-paned east windows of the church, and these can still be read today—with the help of a viewing platform positioned by the window. "Glencalvie people was in the church here May 24, 1845," runs one inscription, the broken English a clear indication of the writer being a Gaelic speaker. "Glencalvie people, the wicked generation," says another, suggesting that some evictees saw the Clearances as some sort of divine punishment for their sins.

The Plight of the Crofters

Those evictees who did not move out of the Highlands were housed in entirely new coastal communities consisting of groups of crofts. It was assumed that Highlanders in these new communities could eke out a living from growing crops on tiny strips of land, from fishing, and from harvesting the brown seaweed that was then incinerated to make kelp, a vital material used in both industry and agriculture. For a time, kelp manufacture was phenomenally lucrative. In 1803 a number of Highland lairds even lobbied parliament to curtail emigration from the area—by limiting the number of emigrants allowed on boats, ostensibly for humanitarian reasons, but actually so that kelp production could be maintained. Crofters, of course, saw little financial benefit from the miserable business of seaweed collecting. As for the land that surrounded their croft, it was often of desperately poor quality. Planted seeds would often be blown from the cliffs while new crops were blasted by winds laced with salt and sand. In 1815 disaster struck many of these communities when the price of kelp collapsed. In a rapid *volte-face,* landlords then forced entire communities to emigrate; the MacLeans, for instance, paid for the residents of the island of Coll to leave for Canada in 1826.

Given all this it is not surprising that a number of the new crofting settlements were later abandoned. One of these was Badbea, built above precipitous sea cliffs on the northeast coast between Helmsdale and Dunbeath. The stone cottages whose scant remains still cling to the sloping land here were originally built by tenants evicted from nearby Ousdale; conditions were so difficult for crofters that they had to tether their

The abandoned village of Badbea, near Dunbeath, created for those evicted during the Clearances, with its striking monument (Andrew Beattie)

children to posts to stop them from being blown into the sea by the ferocious winds. The settlement lasted a hundred years; the last crofters abandoned the place in 1902, and in 1911 a somber, pyramid-topped stone monument was raised above the former village by the returning son of Badbea residents who had migrated to New Zealand. The severe monument stands to this day, recalling the harshness of life for those forced by the Clearances to exist in such a mercilessly bleak environment.

Those who lived in the settlements that fared better than Badbea nonetheless faced monumental hardship. Neil Gunn set his 1937 novel *Highland River* in one of these communities at the turn of the twentieth century. The village of his novel—clearly based on Dunbeath, where he had grown up, one of a number of settlements specifically created for evictees—comprised little more than a "string of cottages along the bay" and was

> typical of what might be found anywhere round the northern and western shores of Scotland: the river coming down out of the wooded

> glen or strath into the little harbour; the sloping croft lands, with their small cultivated fields; the croft houses here and there, with an odd one on a far ridge against the sky; the school, the post office, and the old church, where the houses herded loosely into a township; and inland the moors lifting to the blue mountains... wealth was unknown amongst [the crofters] and poverty had to be outwitted by all the means in their power.

Winters could be atrociously hard. "For days on end the sea would thunder on the beach with reverberations that could be heard far inland. Sometimes the sound would play on the ear with forebodings of universal doom, and when the light would go dim in the early afternoon and the drizzle thicken into rain, the misery of consciousness would go cold as the mire." The landlord lived elsewhere: "a being apart, who visited his mansion house only at intervals... their rents were collected by a factor who came for the purpose from his lawyer's office in the county town. The people had an instinctive fear of this factor and always assumed their best dress and manners when they went before him to pay their dues."

In the late nineteenth century a disastrous downturn in farm prices brought yet more suffering. But it was now, at last, that some crofters began to protest against the miserable conditions in which they found themselves. They were encouraged in this by a journalist named John Murdoch, editor of the *Highlander* newspaper, who suggested that Highland communities adopt the same organized strategies of defiance against rapacious landlords as had the Irish Land League. That meant rent strikes, and in 1881 members of the crofting community of the Braes, which overlooks the Narrows of Raasay on the east coast of Skye, marched into Portree and bluntly informed their landlord's factor that they would not pay rent on their land until grazing rights on pastures above their village were returned to them. When the rents went unpaid eviction notices were issued. But the crofters burned the notices and tension mounted until a pitched battle erupted between crofters and fifty policemen drafted in from Glasgow. (The site of the battle is commemorated by a cairn at Gedintailor, the most northerly of the three settlements that make up the Braes.) In his "Song About the Skye Crofters" the Skye poet Neil Macleod lamented that the evicted crofters had been "scourged/by lowland poltroons; with sticks at the ready being beaten like cattle... The folk who were friendly, and kindly, warm-hearted, have now been pressed sore by landlords' conceit."

In 1883 another rent strike among crofters on Skye, this time in Glendale, resulted in prison sentences being handed out to crofters, and two years later the Duke of Argyll resorted to sending in a company of marines to clear striking crofters from a settlement on his island of Tiree.

Yet public opinion throughout Britain was siding with the crofters and in the same year as the Tiree evictions a commission began looking into the conditions they faced. Meetings between commissioners and crofters were convened across the Highlands, in schools and churches; those evicted from Strathnaver gave their evidence in the same church at Bettyhill in which the original eviction notices had been announced. The first report of the Crofters' Commission made little impact and the rent strikes continued. But the crofters had found a sympathetic champion of their cause in the form of Prime Minister William Gladstone, and after several members of the Highland Land League won parliamentary seats in the 1885 General Election, Gladstone pushed the Crofters' Act through parliament the following year.

Under the Act crofters gained ownership of the land and dwellings they occupied; now they could not be evicted by landlords and they could pass their holdings onto their heirs. The Act also established a new commission that lowered the rents paid by many crofters. However, the legislation did not encompass the whole of the Highlands, did nothing for the landless farmers known as cottars, and did not restore crofters to the land from which their forebears had been cleared. It was not until the return to the Highlands of soldiers who had fought in World War I that these injustices were addressed—by the Board of Agriculture, which in the 1920s redistributed a fair amount of land to crofters, including land that had originally been cleared by landlords a century or more before.

THE HIGHLANDS DURING WORLD WAR II

Remote from Germany though the region is, the Highlands played a part—and often a vital part—in the military campaigns of World War II. A number of isolated locations along the north and east coasts of Scotland were home to top-secret listening stations, bristling with aerials and humming with surveillance equipment, and the half-collapsed, grassed-over concrete bunkers that can be seen nestling between the weather-beaten cottages of Durness, as well as the forlorn, boarded-up huts beside the beach at Brora, are tangible reminders of the role the region played in intercepting enemy communications. Occasionally enemy bombers were detected from these bases. The bombers' targets included the Fort William aluminium smelter, where one bomb actually smashed through the roof of the power house, without exploding; authorities did their best to camouflage the enormous hillside pipes above the plant, while people living near the smelter in Kinlochleven were given instructions as to what they should do if the Blackwater Dam above the village was successfully breached by a Dambusters-style German raid.

Numerous other roles were afforded the Highlands and Islands during the war. The island of Gruinard, off the coast of Wester Ross, was the scene of some of the most secretive work in the war, namely the testing of biological weapons. In theory the anthrax spores released here could have survived in the soil for a thousand years, but the island was decontaminated in the late 1980s and was finally declared safe in 1990. Further south along the west coast, the sheltered waters of Oban's harbor provided a gathering point for the North Atlantic convoys that kept Britain supplied during the war. A German reconnaissance photo taken from a Junkers 88 in September 1940, and now on display in Oban's War and Peace Museum, clearly shows Sunderland flying boats, the chunky, four-engine aircraft that provided air cover for the convoys, assembled on the water there. Mines were laid around the west coast to prevent German U-boats from getting too close to these convoys—and a memorial to the mine-laying squadron that was based in Kyle of Lochalsh can be seen outside the Lochalsh Hotel, appropriately taking the form of a deep-water mine.

The Norwegian navy trained off Bute, from where British submarines set off to attack German ships in the Norwegian fjords. Meanwhile Russian convoys would navigate the seas off northern Scotland, and Allied servicemen were stationed on lonely Loch Eriboll to watch for German warships hunting them; the foul weather and the dark winter days quickly led soldiers to dub this north coast sea loch "Loch Horrible."

But it was as a training ground for commandoes that the region was provided with its most famous wartime role. The British Army's commando units were created soon after the evacuation from Dunkirk, and the West Highlands were seen as an area that could provide them with a suitably harsh and rugged training environment. In 1940 Inverailort House near Mallaig was commandeered as the commando training base; in February 1942 the training base for the commandoes was moved to Achnacarry Castle, the hereditary seat of Clan Cameron of Lochiel, just northeast of Fort William, and Inverailort became the training center for a different organization, the highly specialized Special Operations Executive (SOE), which also had its own commando units. Recruits at both bases were trained for sabotage operations in Europe and for amphibious landings; they also mastered the arts of self-defence and silent attack. By the end of the war some 25,000 troops had trained at the Lochaber bases. French, Dutch, Norwegian, Polish, and Belgian soldiers were among their number, and in 1942 a team of Czechs who had trained at Inverailort were parachuted into the countryside near Prague to carry out the most high profile assassination of the war, that of Reinhard Heydrich, the Nazi overlord of Bohemia and Moravia.

Notoriously commandos were put through their paces immediately on arrival at the bases. When new arrivals walked from the station to the house at Lochailort they were often met with live ammunition pinging above their heads, while those training at Achnacarry Castle were broken in by an eight-mile march from Spean Bridge railway station and arrived in the castle to confront instructors racing at them down the stairs, weapons already drawn. One of those legendary commandos was Dan Fairburn—the inventor of a knife that still serves as a commando emblem to this day—who told recruits that there were no rules except "kill or be killed." The military engagements in which the commandos fought were suitably tough. The most famous was a raid on the Lofoten islands off Norway, which was aimed at preventing the export of fish oils to Germany, where they were used in the preparation of explosives. Ten ships were sunk, eleven fish oil processing factories were destroyed, and 225 prisoners were captured in this daring raid.

Today the commandos who trained in the Highlands are commemorated by a memorial that stands a mile from Spean Bridge beside the main A82 Fort William to Inverness road. The memorial portrays three commandos (wearing familiar berets and carrying binoculars around their necks) gazing out over the countryside that was their training ground; "united we conquer" are the words emblazoned on the plinth, which was unveiled by the Queen Mother in 1953. A somber circle of personalized memorials close by, installed by families and regiments, remembers former commandos who have served in the British army in the decades since 1945.

To this day, the military retains a strong presence in the Highlands and Islands. Walkers in the mountains are frequently "buzzed" by fighter jets on low-flying training missions, while the deserted tracts of land around Cape Wrath have been used for artillery training since 1933. Today this is the only place in Europe desolate enough for live one thousand-ton bombs to be dropped and detonated, and the road to the Cape Wrath lighthouse passes through a beaten-up landscape of bomb craters and various bits of cast-off military hardware.

Into the Twenty-first Century

Sometime in the 1960s—the exact year remains a matter of some debate—a resident of the tiny hamlet of Arnish, at the northern end of the island of Raasay, decided that his community needed to be linked to the southern, more populated part of the island by means of a proper road. For Calum MacLeod the building of this road, which took him around fifteen years, was a one-man crusade against the erosion of traditional culture in the Hebrides. He completed the road, which winds its way across challenging countryside from Brochel Castle to Arnish, in 1982—by which time constant depopulation meant that only two crofters' cottages remained in Arnish, one of which was his own.

Calum's road has now entered the modern folklore of the Inner Hebrides: the folk band Capercaillie have sung about it, the ceramicist Patricia Shone was inspired to create pottery by pressing clay against the tracks of the famous road and exhibiting the finished works at a gallery in Skye, and in April 2013 Roger Hutchinson's well-received book *Calum's Road* was adapted as a play and staged at the Eden Court Theatre in Inverness. The well-engineered road can still be followed today: those who make it to the remote far north of Raasay, which must be accessed by a short ferry journey from Skye, can admire Calum's dedication and see the plaque honoring his work affixed to the cairn just above Brochel Castle. And they can also ponder the greatest irony of the extraordinary dedication of Calum MacLeod: that at no point in his life did he ever own a driving licence.

Calum MacLeod's crusade was principally aimed at the depopulation, underinvestment, and unemployment that blighted many areas of the Highlands and Inner Hebrides during the twentieth century. Between 1931 and 1951, for example, the mainland between Applecross and Cape Wrath lost a quarter of its population—a devastating loss in an area already thinly populated. But other parts of the Highlands fared better during the twentieth century, as the economy of the region embraced heavy manufacturing and energy production and then broadened its economic base to include education, services, and even high-technology industry.

In 1904 Kinlochleven, a tiny hamlet on the sheltered shores of a narrow sea loch between Oban and Fort William, was chosen as the site for a new industrial revolution in the West Highlands, in the form of an aluminum smelting plant. The smelting required huge amounts of electricity, which was to be provided by turbines built into a dam to be constructed across the Blackwater Valley above the village. Three thousand workers toiled for four years to construct the new dam, which at the time

Hydro-electric power generation at Kinlochleven, with the former aluminium smelter in the background (Andrew Beattie)

was the largest in Europe; the sinuous reservoir behind the structure extends for some eight miles, the eastern tip jabbing like a finger into the bleak expanse of Rannoch Moor. The plant closed in the 1980s, the victim of a fall in the price of the metal and more efficient smelters established elsewhere in the world; an ice climbing wall now occupies the old smelter, part of Kinlochleven's attempt to reinvent itself as a center for adventure tourism now that its industry has gone.

The power station that provided the smelter with electricity still generates power for the national grid, the enormous pipes (often spraying fountains of leaking water high into the air) creating an incongruous scar across the wooded hills that rise immediately above the town. In his 1968 guide to the Highlands W. H. Murray dubbed Kinlochleven "the ugliest village on two thousand miles of Highland coast" and many would concur today. The presence of rows of whitewashed tenement cottages, the high brick building that houses the power station (looking something like an enormous tram shed), and the ugly workers' hostel perched like a medieval castle above the town all ensure that its industrial heritage is ever-present.

Fort William, to the north, was also the setting for an aluminum smelter, with electricity provided by a dam across Loch Laggan; water from the reservoir behind the dam was then fed through fifteen-foot diameter pipes cut through miles of solid rock. That smelter remains in operation today, producing over forty thousand tons of aluminum each year and employing over one hundred and fifty people; the alumina comes by train along the West Highland line and the plant is one of the biggest industrial concerns in the Highlands. Its construction is celebrated by exhibits in Fort William's West Highland Museum, where an enormous slab of shiny aluminum has remained on show since it was presented to the museum in 1965.

With the aluminum smelter at Kinlochleven closed and the old iron smelters on other parts of the west coast also consigned to history, manufacturing industry is now largely a heritage concern in the Highlands rather than an employer. Most of the old mines and quarries that served these industries have also ceased operation, but in 2011 an Australian-owned company named Scotgold began extracting gold from the hills around Tyndrum, an old lead-mining settlement in the heart of the West Highlands, taking advantage of the sudden hike in gold prices around the world; the company later announced that viable reserves of silver were also present in the same mine. At the time of writing Tyndrum, already a busy stop in the West Highlands for walkers and road travelers, could possibly find itself the center of a minor gold rush, with plans afoot for jewelry shops and gold-panning experiences. The town's situation within the Loch Lomond and the Trossachs National Park means, however, that the developers face considerable problems balancing the needs of the mining industry with those of the stunning local environment. Not least among these is what to do with the five hundred thousand tons of waste the mine will produce—and how to minimize the impact of the gold extraction on Tyndrum itself, a place of car parks and garish hotels set in beautiful countryside that still bears the scars of its former lead-mining heritage.

The companies mining at Tyndrum can possibly learn lessons from the operation of the Glensanda quarry on the isolated Morvern peninsula. The quarry here has been sending granite aggregates all over the world since 1986. But extensive efforts have been made to hide the enormous hole in the ground, which cannot be seen except from the air. No roads or footpaths go near the quarry, to which the 160 workers have to travel across Loch Linnhe every day by boat from Oban. It is reckoned that there is enough high-quality granite at Glensanda to keep the quarry going for another century or more.

High rates of unemployment and low incomes have been the economic hallmarks of the Scottish Highlands for generations. The encouragement of smelting, mining, and quarrying has gone some way to alleviate the situation, but population falls were recorded in rural areas such as Argyll and Sutherland, and some Hebridean islands, in the 2011 census. These days, however, out-migration is balanced to a certain extent by incomers (often from England) seeking a new life, particularly on the islands of the Inner Hebrides, and by sometimes substantial growth in Highland towns such as Inverness and Fort William. This growth has been stimulated in part by subsidies from the European Union and the British and Scottish governments, which have been pouring into the region since the creation of the Highlands and Islands Development board in 1965. That body has now been succeeded by a myriad of regional development authorities that encourage economic development through grants and tax breaks.

Today the economy of the Highlands revolves around tourism, whisky distilling, forestry, fish-farming, and power generation from dozens of hydro dams such as the one at Kinlochleven. The oldest whisky distillery is at Glenturret, just north of Crieff, which was established in 1775, and produces the Famous Grouse blend; Pitlochry, the home of Bell's, and Dufftown on Speyside, site of the Glenfiddich distillery, are other important stopping-off points on any whisky-lover's tour of the Highlands.

Commercial salmon farms in the Highlands yield an annual haul of 130,000 tons of fish, while a farm for rainbow trout occupying part of Loch Awe is the largest in Europe, harvesting 1.6 million fish each year. Sea fishing fleets remain busy on the coast, selling on their catch to vast processing plants such as the one on the quayside at remote Kinlochbervie, Scotland's most northwesterly village, from where convoys of articulated trucks ferry the produce all over Europe.

Sometimes the various strands of the Highland economy elide together in a curious blend: whisky distilleries are well-known for pulling in busloads of sightseers, but coaches also pull up outside the Cruachan Power Station on Loch Awe for a journey (by minibus) through over half a mile of tunnels to see the vast turbine hall (big enough to support a seven-story building built on a football pitch) that was hollowed out of the interior of Ben Cruachan in the 1960s. The generating plants at Cruachan and a host of other Highland locations, such as Pitlochry, where the dam across the River Tummel is a popular walk for visitors to that town, were built between 1948 and 1965 as part of a deliberate policy formulated by the wartime Secretary of State for Scotland, Tom Johnson. His grandiose scheme aimed to bring industry and jobs to the region and to ensure that as many communities as possible throughout the Highlands were linked to the national power grid. The workers who built the forty-eight power generating plants were known as the "hydro boys" and included many former German and Italian prisoners of war among their number. When the Cruachan power plant was being constructed it was the patronage of these workers that made the Tight Line Pub in Loch Awe village the most profitable in Britain.

Crofting still remains a vital and viable aspect of the Highland economy. But many crofters are forced to supplement the income from their croft with wages from part-time work, and issues of tenure remain as highly charged as they always have been. In 1998 celebrations erupted across Scotland when the crofting community on the remote Knoydart peninsula staged a community buy-out of the whole estate. Crofting communities remain largely coastal, confined to the islands of the Inner Hebrides and to remoter parts of the west coast. Up in the mountains traditional farms still spread across the hills, with hardy crops such as turnips grown in the valley bottoms and livestock kept on the upland slopes. But farmers struggle perpetually with depressed prices for wool and beef, and in popular areas give over some of their land and buildings to the higher yields from tourists in the form of campsites and bunkhouses. The vital place that livestock farming still occupies in Scotland can be experienced on an annual basis in Lairg at the head of Loch Shin, where the August lamb sale remains the biggest one-day livestock market in Europe.

Four hundred thousand people now make their home in the Highlands and Islands. Inverness, the "capital" of the region, has a population of 63,000—a metropolis in northern Scotland, although the place would be considered just another small town anywhere else in the country. Inverness claims, however, to be one of the fastest-growing cities in Europe, with a flourishing high-tech sector and a thriving role in education too, supporting the principal campus and administrative center of the new University of the Highlands and Islands.

But away from Inverness and centers such as Fort William and Oban, some parts of the Highlands boast population densities lower than anywhere else in Europe outside Scandinavia. The area where people are most thinly scattered is northwest Sutherland, where the single-track A383 from Lairg to Laxford Bridge passes through the most uncompromisingly desolate scenery in the Highlands, and where a single policeman (based at the police station in the hamlet of Rhiconich) covers a beat larger than the area of Greater London. The road that crosses the interior of Mull, from the ferry port at Craignure to the Iona ferry at Fionnphort, also passes through a similar area of spectacularly bleak nothingness.

Regarding rail lines—from a train, the desolation of the landscape is even more palpable—nothing rivals the wilderness of Rannoch Moor, traversed by the West Highland line between the lonely stations serving Bridge of Orchy and Tulloch, or the empty scenery north of Helmsdale on the line to Thurso and Wick. Of areas that bask in their own isolation, the Knoydart peninsula counts itself as one of the most dramatic and unspoilt wilderness areas in Britain. Its sole hamlet, Inverie, is only reachable by boat or on foot; its pub, the Old Forge, is the most remote hostelry in the country. An even larger community, Scoraig on the coast of Wester Ross, which boasts organic vegetable gardens and a primary school, is similarly isolated.

The reason for the sparseness of settlement is largely the Highland Clearances. John Prebble, the most passionate historian of the Clearances, maintained in his classic book on the subject that "there is no satisfaction to be got" from the solitude once the reasons for the desolation are known. Yet it is this very solitude that attracts tourists to the Highlands and islands from all over the world, contributing a huge amount to the Highland economy. And the isolation has gone part of the way to ensuring that the ancient language of Gaelic, the "rude speech of a barbarous people" according to Samuel Johnson, has hung on in so many communities—on Skye nearly half the population is fluent, and there is an important Gaelic-speaking college at Sleat. Where once the authorities tried to extinguish the speaking of Gaelic, it is now taught in schools and is championed by state-sponsored cultural institutions.

There is still one final aspect of the Highlands that has gone unmentioned, and it is familiar to all those who travel in the region in the summer. It is the small winged and biting creature known as the midge, whose favorite haunt is anywhere that visitors to the Highlands gather during the damp, still, summer evenings. It is not just visitors who find midges a painful distraction. Neil Gunn, who grew up in the Highlands, writes in his novel *Highland River* that there would be "Junes and Julys in the Highlands of Scotland that would be pure paradise but for these moor-emanations of some diabolic intelligence." But the author George Hendry takes a different—even positive—view of these creatures that particularly populate fens, bogs, and marshes. Perhaps, he suggests, they provide the true reason for the isolation in which much of the region still basks. In his book *Midges in Scotland* Hendry asserts that "The Scottish Highlands remain one of the most under-populated landscapes in Europe, with a timelessness difficult to find anywhere at the start of the twenty-first century… If, as seems likely, the biting midge is a significant factor in limiting our grossest capacities for unsustainable exploitation, then the diminutive guardian of the Highlands deserves our lasting respect."

Lagangarbh Cottage, Buachaille Etive Mòr
(Bill McKelvie/Shutterstock)

Part Three

IMAGINATION

The Romantic Highlands: Scottish pictures drawn with pen and pencil by Samuel G. Green (London, 1886) (St. Andrews University)

"THE GREATEST OF NATURE'S ROUGH PRODUCTIONS"

It is only comparatively recently that the scenic grandeur of the Scottish Highlands has been venerated and admired. Before the eighteenth century the notion that natural scenery here (or, in fact, anywhere) was worthy of admiration would have been regarded as odd in the extreme, for no-one would have ever considered the landscape of the Highlands to be invested with the qualities we value today—beauty, grandeur, tranquillity. This was made clear by one of the leading philosophers of the late eighteenth century, William Gilpin. "There are few who do not prefer the busy scenes of cultivation to the greatest of nature's rough productions," he wrote in despair, for he was very much a fan of the "rougher" side of nature, and wanted others to likewise embrace his enthusiasm. Resident in Hampshire, Gilpin was a clergyman, a schoolmaster, and an amateur artist; his most unusual claim to fame was that he had invented the word "picturesque." His desire was that his readers should open their eyes to the attractions of wild and untamed areas of country, especially the Highlands.

By 1789, when he published his travelogue *Observations, relative chiefly to picturesque beauty, made in the year 1776, on several parts of Great Britain; particularly the High-lands of Scotland*, in which he fulsomely celebrated the beauty of northern and western Scotland, he was beginning to make headway in his mission. The way in which "rough productions" such as mountains were viewed was undergoing a change, in both the popular and intellectual imagination. The change was gradual, but it was of decisive and absolute proportions—and within a generation it would transform the Highlands into one of the great tourist playgrounds of the world.

The medieval and Renaissance imagination venerated neatness and harmony in the countryside: favored above everything were the "busy scenes of cultivation" that, centuries later, Gilpin was still so keen to dismiss. Well-ordered gardens and ploughed fields bounded by neat hedges were the order of the day. By contrast, mountainous areas such as the Scottish Highlands were seen as being terrifying and untameable: after all, mountains are not mentioned in the account of creation offered by Genesis, and as a result their existence was often thought of as some sort of punishment wrought on humankind by God. This view persisted well into the eighteenth century. In the 1720s Edmund Burt, an early English traveler in Scotland, wrote in his book *Letters to a Gentleman* that the east-west orientation of ridges in the Highlands was due to "water rushing violently from east to west" and "has created arguments for the truth of a universal deluge." The ascribing of the creation of mountains to Noah's flood is an indication that Burt, like many others of his time, was of the view that mountains represented God's curse on humanity rather than any sort of divine blessing.

No wonder that two centuries before Burt was writing, Thomas More had populated part of his island of Utopia with a race of mountain-dwellers, the Zapoletes, whom he described as a "hideous, savage, and fierce race." Mountains contained the lairs of beasts and giants, of witches and unquiet spirits, of demons that brought disease and destruction to those unwise enough to live amidst the peaks and valleys. As a result, few people ever traveled in the mountains—least of all for the pleasure of the scenery. "The Highlands are but little known even to the inhabitants of the low country of Scotland," Burt tells us, "for [potential travelers] have ever dreaded the difficulties and dangers of travelling among the mountains." Any traveler who actually did embark on a Highland journey was wont to make a will before setting out "as though he were entering upon a long and dangerous sea voyage, wherein it was very doubtful if he should ever return."

It was not only Edmund Burt who demonstrated this attitude in his travelogue. Other gentlemen travelers of the eighteenth century happily adopted the same way of thinking. The comments of the playwright and novelist Oliver Goldsmith, who traveled through the Highlands in 1753, are typical: in a letter to his cousin Robert Bryanton he wrote of "this unfruitful country… every part of [it] presents the same dismal landscape, no grove nor brook lend their music to cheer the stranger, or make the inhabitants forget their poverty." The same sentiments persist in the more extensive accounts of the region by eminent men of letters of the age, such as Samuel Johnson and Daniel Defoe. In his three-volume *Tour through the Island of Great Britain*, published between 1724 and 1727, Defoe describes with interest a number of Highland towns but is dismissive of the "frightful" Highland scenery. Beyond the stone bridge of Inverness he found that the landscape

> cannot call for a distinct description, because it is all one undistinguished range of mountains and woods… our geographers seem to be almost as

> much at a loss in the description of this north part of Scotland as the Romans were to conquer it; and they are obliged to fill it up with hills and mountains, as they do the inner parts of Africa, with lions and elephants, for want of knowing what else to place there.

Twenty years later, Samuel Johnson and his companion James Boswell also had very little to say about the scenery of the Highlands in their journeys through the region. Boswell remarks that on their boat trip across Loch Lomond Johnson "was much pleased with the scene," but crossing the Highlands Johnson merely railed at "a uniformity of barrenness [that] can afford very little amusement to the traveller" and complained that the hills "exhibit very little variety." Boswell and Johnson published their accounts in 1774 and were some of the last travelers in the region who were not beguiled by the scenery—something writers just thirty years later could not get enough of.

The Unquiet Spirits of the Highlands

Before the late eighteenth century it was monsters, rather than the scenery, that interested most travelers in the Highlands: and the presence of all manner of spirits and demons was, of course, reflective of mountains being a divine curse. (The existence of similar demons was also a major concern of early travelers in other mountain ranges, most especially the Alps.) The most famous monster of the Scottish Highlands was, of course, the one that was reputed to live in the unfathomably deep waters of Loch Ness. In the seventh century Adamnan, the biographer of St. Columba, even insisted that the famed monster of the loch had attacked one of Columba's companions as he was swimming across the water. Columba, though, on seeing the monster, "raised his holy hand, while all the rest, brethren as well as strangers, were stupefied with terror, and, invoking the name of God, formed the saving sign of the cross in the air, and commanded the furious monster, saying 'thou shalt go no further, nor touch the man; go back with all speed.' Then, at the voice of the saint, the monster was terrified, and fled.... the Brethren were amazed to see that the beast had gone."

To be accurate, Adamnan set his story on the banks of the River Ness rather than the loch itself. But it was the first written record of a watery monster in the region. Tales of many other water-dwelling beasts abound. For instance, people who lived on the shores of the tiny Lochan Lunn Da-Bhra, south of Fort William, had to contend with a water bull that would rise from the loch and feast on livestock that it plucked from the surrounding fields. Elsewhere the rocky slopes provided lairs for witches. Loch Awe, the shores of which are spectacularly skirted by the main railway from Glasgow to Oban, was supposed to have been created by a witch named the Cailleach Bheur, the winter hag of death and darkness. The story goes that every night she would block up a spring on the side of Ben Cruachan, but one night she forgot, allowing the waters from the spring to cascade down the mountainside and fill the valley, creating the loch. The story is told on a mural created by Elizabeth Faulkner that hangs in the turbine hall of the Cruachan power station, which was hollowed out beneath the sides of Ben Cruachan.

Loch Ness was also home to witches, and legend told that somehow a local nobleman, Mòr Mac Aoidh, had forced them to build Urquhart Castle on its shores for him. Meanwhile Rannoch Moor, the bleak West Highland expanse of bog and black pools, was supposed to be the home of the feared water kelpie, or water horse. This "demon of the streams," according to David Balfour in Robert Louis Stevenson's novel *Kidnapped,* was "fabled to keep wailing and roaring at the ford until the coming of the doomed traveller." The naturalist Gavin Maxwell wrote that belief in kelpies was still widespread when he was living in the Highlands in the 1960s. In his book *Raven Seek thy Brother,* the sequel to *Ring of Bright Water,* he maintains that these creatures "were held to inhabit many lochs; they waylaid maidens by night and carried them down into the cold deep, so that they were seen no more. Loch na Beiste (Loch of the Beast) at Kyleakin is said to contain a creature that some describe as having a head covered with a mane, while others who claim to have seen it refuse utterly to give any description whatsoever."

Maxwell is one of a long line of writers who have been regaled with tales of these particular beasts. In his *Journal of a Tour to the Hebrides,* written two centuries before Maxwell, James Boswell tells of a Raasay legend related to him by a local that also concerns a kelpie. The creature, Boswell was told, had made its home in one of the island's pools. One day it captured and devoured the daughter of a local man. In revenge the man set a devious trap to rouse the beast from the pool. When the kelpie lifted its head from the water the man raised up the red-hot poker he had brought with him, and killed it instantly.

Out at sea lurked yet more water-dwelling nasties that were wont to ensnare unwary mariners. Between the islands of Scarba and Jura is a notorious whirlpool that churns the waters of the Gulf of Corryvrechan. In *The Rocks Remain* Gavin Maxwell describes the vortex as "a mad leaping confusion, as if the tides of all the world had met in that one place." He had observed the whirlpool from a boat, just as tourists can today, from launches that set off from Ellenabeich on the island of Seil. The whirlpool was well known to ancient travelers too, who feared it as a visible manifestation of the anger of Hag, the Celtic goddess of storms. Tales were also told on the same storm-lashed coast of western Scotland of an Irish giant named Fingal, who had once built a causeway from Ulster to the Hebrides to do battle with a Scottish giant named Benandonner: the stepped basalt columns on the island of Staffa, and the similar formation on the coast of Antrim known as the Giant's Causeway, are the visible manifestation of this ancient crossing.

The island of Staffa itself, together with a number of tiny islets to its west, were reputedly created by another giant, Torquil MacLeod of Eigg, who had scooped up part of the causeway, stuffed it in a sack and carried it home, dropping parts of it into the sea as he clumped along. Fingal himself was a Farmorian, a breed of giant whose deeds suffuse both Irish and Scottish folklore; his final resting place is supposedly the village of Killin at the head of Loch Tay, now a popular center for walkers in the West Highlands. But in some stories Fingal is not a giant at all but a fierce warrior, while in others he is a pirate who tethers his galley in Fingal's Cave on Staffa, ready to plunder passing ships.

Other beasts of the mountains were foretellers of doom. Before the infamous massacre at Glencoe in 1692 it was said that An Duine Mor, the "Great Man" who always made an appearance in times of crisis, had been seen at Ballachulish at the head of Loch Leven, signifying that a disaster was imminent. Other spirits that foretold the calamity were Bean Nighe, the spectral washerwoman who could be observed cleaning the same shroud again and again, and the Caoineag, a woman who could never be approached but whose appearance was always a harbinger of death. In his classic novel *Waverley* Walter Scott writes of a similar spirit, that of Bodach Glas, the "grey spectre," who appears "when any great disaster was impending, but especially before approaching death"—and who duly makes his presence known to the doomed chieftain Fergus MacIvor.

In the same vein Martin Martin, author of the 1703 book *A Description of the Western Isles of Scotland*, described the mystical powers of animals on Skye: "When the cows belonging to one person do of a sudden become very irregular and run up and down the fields," he wrote, "and make a loud noise, without any visible cause, that is a presage of the master or mistress's death." When James MacDonald was killed at the Battle of Killiecrankie, Martin informs us that back home on Skye his "cows gave blood instead of milk." But not all supernatural beings were associated with death and disaster. According to Martin, "invisible beings" would often help individuals or communities with the answers to their questions, speaking through a man who performed the same function as the Oracle at Delphi. The man serving as the Oracle would be wrapped in cowhide and left for the night until he communicated with the relevant spirits; sometimes a live cat would be roasted on a spit nearby to facilitate the appearance of these magical creatures.

But no aspect of the supernatural was more frightening and more remarked upon than that of second sight. This phenomenon also receives considerable attention in the writings of Martin Martin. On his travels through both the Inner and the Outer Hebrides Martin frequently came across people who could see visions before them. The affliction of second sight, he said, was "a singular faculty of seeing an otherwise invisible object without any previous means used by the person that sees it for that end; the vision makes such a lively impression upon the seer, that they neither see nor think of anything else, except the vision, as long as it continues; and then they appear pensive, or jovial, according to the object which was represented to them." Often the vision is a foretelling of death; one of the eeriest instances involves the young boy Martin encounters on Skye who makes a habit of seeing coffins "close by his shoulder." Another common phenomenon of second sight occurred when ghostly apparitions of floating shrouds appeared above the heads of those who were close to death; the height of the shroud, Martin was told, determined the exact time of the person's imminent demise. He wrote that children and infants were particularly able to view these phenomena, as were horses and cows, and that the affliction was also apparent in other places in which he had traveled, such as Holland, Ireland, and the Isle of Man. But on Skye second sight seemed particularly prevalent, and in documenting it so thoroughly Martin seems entirely willing to believe in its veracity.

In *Ring of Bright Water* Gavin Maxwell maintains that the tradition of second sight was still alive on Skye. "My impression is that a deep, fundamental belief in the existence of second sight is practically universal throughout the Western Highlands and the Hebrides, even among intelligent and well-read people, and that the few scoffers are paying lip-service to the sceptical sophistication they do not share," he wrote. Approaching the subject again in *Raven Seek Thy Brother*, he notes that "among the old people, and not a few of the younger, the world of the supernatural is accepted as unquestioningly as the natural," and relates the tale of a woman of Skye who had had

> a sudden and instant vision of the corpse of a boy whom she had seen ploughing in a nearby field. The boy died by drowning within a week... whatever is foreseen, the image is said always to be of great detail, never a blurred impression. Often it is a funeral, and the face of every mourner is recognizable, together with knowledge of the time and the place; sometimes it is a photoflash, but of equal intensity and shock.

Among the fishermen of Skye superstitious belief in the supernatural extended beyond second sight. In *Harpoon at a Venture,* Maxwell's account of establishing a shark fishery on the island of Soay, he writes that Skye fishermen regarded a woman on board a fishing boat as bringing bad luck, and that "many islanders will not put to sea if they even meet a woman when going down to their boats in the morning." Fishermen also saw eggs as bad luck, and would not have them on board their boats—and nor would they have anyone whom they knew had recently eaten eggs, either.

The Sublime, the Dreadful, and the Vast

The Age of the Enlightenment in Europe, which reached its apogee in the early eighteenth century, had celebrated order, regularity, and a sense of proportion in the natural world. In keeping with these ideals, by the middle part of the century all the great houses of England were surrounded by carefully laid-out gardens, complete with fountains and neat lawns (and even the occasional obelisk) that seemed defiantly to reject the apparent randomness of the real countryside.

But by the later decades of the century, a new fashion was beginning to transform the refined world of English country gardens. Manicured estates were being raked over to create symbolic wildernesses, while pretty fountains were redesigned as gloomy grottoes or dramatic waterfalls. Suddenly the unkempt became fashionable. One case is that of Richard Hill, who succeeded to the Hawkstone estate in Shropshire in 1783. He developed a cave complex in the grounds of his estate, in which a hermit was paid to live, and also constructed a three hundred-foot mound, named Grotto Hill, from which the views were breathtaking. In the decade after his trip to the Highlands Dr. Johnson climbed Grotto Hill and remarked that the "ideas which it forces upon the mind are the sublime, the dreadful, and the vast."

A radical change of sensibility was unfolding. Dr. Johnson's use of that particular word—"sublime"—to describe the view from Grotto Hill was wholly deliberate, for the new and radical doctrine of the sublime delighted in chaos, irregularity, cataclysm, and fear. It was the fashionable embracing of the sublime among writers and intellectuals at the turn of the nineteenth century that transformed the untamed wildness of mountains from something appalling into something that deserved to be savored and celebrated. Empty deserts, impenetrable forests, frozen ice wastes, and, in particular, rugged mountains were newly experienced through fascinated, awe-struck eyes. And there was no better champion of the new way of thinking in the Highlands than William Gilpin, and no better guide to the appeal of the sublime than his *Observations*. Here Gilpin revels in the grandeur of the mountains, in their gloomy colors, in the unparalleled solitude of the moors, in the "vast tracts of land... in a state of nature." For Gilpin, the "poverty [of vegetation]... which no doubt injures the beauty of a Scotch landscape is certainly at the same time the source of sublimity... unadorned grandeur is their characteristic, and the production of sublime ideas, the effect... One genuine Scotch torrent is fairly worth all the serpentine rivers in England." Moreover, he adds, if the landscape lacks the "picturesque" qualities he admired in areas such as the English Lake District, these can be found in Highlanders themselves, in their colorful dress and in the shaggy cattle they accompany to pasture.

Gilpin also makes a point of admonishing Dr. Johnson for expressing such disdain for the "hopeless sterility" of Scottish landscape. Yet in his *Journey to the Western Islands,* Samuel Johnson at least expresses a fascination with the notion of the sublime, even though its intellectual appeal had yet to make him truly enthusiastic about the scenery. As he traveled with Boswell past Loch Ness he mused that the "imaginations excited by the view of an unknown and untravelled wilderness are not such as arise in the artificial solitude of parks and gardens... man is made unwillingly acquainted with his own weakness." Thirty years later, when the idea of the sublime had truly taken hold in the imagination of the Romantics, such feelings were more explicitly evoked in Sir Walter Scott's novel *Rob Roy.* According to Scott, the scenery around Loch Lomond placed man "in a state of inferiority, in a scene where all the ordinary features of nature were raised and exalted... [the loch] affords one of the most surprising, beautiful, and sublime spectacles in nature."

The champion of this new way of thinking was the Dublin-born philosopher and MP Edmund Burke (1729–97), whose 1757 work *A Philosophical Enquiry into the Origin of Our Ideas of the Sublime and the Beautiful* considered the passions evoked in the human mind by apparently terrible scenes. He suggested that things that terrified us also pleased us, through their size, their complexity, their hectic uncontrollability and, in particular, their sense of danger. According to Burke, mountains inspired in the observer feelings of awe, pleasure, and terror—the latter a passion that "always produces delight when it does not press too close." He wrote of the "dark, confused, uncertain images" which influenced the imagination through "grander passions than those which are more clear and determinate."

This fondness for the confused, the uncertain and the wild was why all those neat gardens in English country houses suddenly seemed so unfashionable by the 1780s. Orderliness and regularity were out; untamed wildness was in. If a single year is needed for a date in which the notion of the sublime took hold of European sensibilities then it has to be 1789, when the *siècle des lumières*— the "century of lights" that characterized the Enlightenment—was decisively and irredeemably dimmed on the streets of revolutionary Paris. After the mob had stormed the Bastille and the guillotine had done its work on the Place de la Concorde, reason and order were pronounced dead; the poets, musicians, and artists of the Romantic era lost no time in embracing the sublime, spurning the rationalism and confidence of the Enlightenment as complacent and spiritually moribund.

Above all, the Romantic imagination was to emphasize feelings and sentiment as being the true pathways that writers, artists, and musicians would have to follow in the search for spiritual truth. In his Dictionary of 1755 Samuel Johnson had defined "Romantic" as meaning "full of wild scenery"; this was prescient, because although the word is actually derived from medieval Romances (that is, epic stories), many poets, writers, and artists of the Romantic era (roughly 1780–1840) came to be known for their celebration of the beauty of mountain landscapes, in the Scottish Highlands, the Alps, and elsewhere.

WILLIAM AND DOROTHY WORDSWORTH IN THE HIGHLANDS

One of the most influential eighteenth-century poets who introduced the Highlands to a wider audience (particularly in England) is now largely forgotten. But James Macpherson, while not being a poet of the Romantic school himself, influenced the imagination of Romantic poets such as Wordsworth and Byron by bringing to their attention epic stories that were apparently written and set in the Highlands during the Dark Ages. Macpherson was born in 1736 in Kingussie near Aviemore and was educated at Inverness Grammar School and later at the universities of Edinburgh and Aberdeen. After a career as surveyor-general of Florida he became a Member of Parliament (for Camelford in Cornwall) and a successful merchant. In 1760 he published the lugubriously entitled *Fragments of Ancient Poetry, Collected in the Highlands of Scotland, and Translated from the Gaelic, or Erse language*, and followed this two years later with his two most notorious works, epic poems concerning the mythical giant Fingal and the goddess Temora.

Macpherson claimed the works had originally been written in the third century by Ossian, a legendary Irish warrior who was Fingal's son. The books became a literary phenomenon but Macpherson failed to produce evidence for his sources and many condemned the poems as hoaxes. Samuel Johnson, in particular, was insistent that Macpherson produce the original versions of the poems, but Macpherson never did, claiming that the poems came from an oral tradition and had never been written down. Johnson was unimpressed. Macpherson's poems were "as gross an imposition as ever the world was troubled with," James Boswell quotes the good doctor as fuming.

The controversy surrounding Macpherson's epic poems continues to this day; most scholars assume that the two poems were fanciful fabrications of legends rather than scholarly translations of ancient works that Macpherson had somehow unearthed. Even so, the poems caused a literary sensation (Goethe was a fan) and their depiction of the wild and lawless Celtic lands of old proved inspirational to the Romantic poets who were to flourish in the decades immediately after their publication. Macpherson's memory is still cherished to this day in the southern Highlands: in 1783 a romantic folly set above a waterfall on the River Braan, close to Dunkeld, was renamed "Ossian's Hall" in honor of the legendary Gaelic bard whom Macpherson had championed. The folly, originally named (and still known as) "The Hermitage," resembles a chapel, with its circular frontage fashioned from heavy stone; the terrace offers a spectacular view over the falls and the wild, forested valley through which the water crashes. This seemingly untamed landscape was actually laid out by the Dukes of Atholl in the eighteenth century and the scattering of follies through the woods was an attempt to create a pleasure-ground similar to that of the Hawkstone Estate. Not surprisingly, the Romantic poet William Wordsworth was drawn here, on his 1803 tour of the Highlands, and the poem "Effusion in the Pleasure-Ground on the Banks of the Braan near Dunkeld" was the result. In the poem Wordsworth dubs Ossian's Hall "a quaint medley, that might seem/Devised out of a sick man's dream! Strange scene, fantastic and uneasy/As ever made a maniac dizzy." Nowadays the place is a popular family day out, reached after a shady stroll of barely ten minutes along a woodland path that begins at a car park just off the busy A9; the building is empty, but the elegant cane-back chairs and ornate mirrors that were once installed in it can be seen in the Derby Room in nearby Blair Castle, the ancestral home of the Atholl dukes.

Wordsworth visited the Hermitage in the company of his sister Dorothy and their friend, the poet Samuel Taylor Coleridge. They were, at the time, a few weeks into their tour of Scotland. William did the driving on their trip, sitting at the front of a horse-driven vehicle known as a "jaunting car," while Dorothy and Samuel sat behind him, their backs to the center of the road, their luggage stored beneath them. It was something of a difficult trip: when they had called on the widow of Robbie Burns in Ayrshire they found she was out, and the trio were distressed by the wretched condition of the poor in Glasgow. They found the scenery of the lowlands to be disappointing, and Loch Lomond, the Wordsworths decided, was not as pretty as Ullswater. But walking along its shores during a storm the trio underwent a strange and cathartic experience as they took shelter in a ferryman's hovel. Smoke from the peat fire had rendered the dwelling pitch-black inside. Yet once they were settled, according to Coleridge, the trio nonetheless found themselves "laughing like children at the strange atmosphere... we laughed and laughed again, in spite of the smarting of our eyes."

Like all Romantic poets Wordsworth was intrigued by ancient myth and fable—hence his visit to Ossian's Hall and his interest in the legend of Ossian and Fingal, as told by James Macpherson. But in his description of landscape—of the Alps, of the Highlands, and of course of the Lake District—Wordsworth also embraced the sublime in his poetry. In fact, Wordsworth pays tribute to Edmund Burke, the chronicler of the sublime, in his posthumously published verse autobiography *The Prelude*; and in his collection *Memorials of a Tour in Scotland*, published shortly after that first trip in 1803, Wordsworth's poetry takes on a familiar Romantic hue. In one poem, "The Solitary Reaper," a young woman working alone in the fields was immortalized as "Yon solitary Highland lass,/Reaping and Singing by herself... Alone she cuts and binds the grain/And sings a melancholy strain/O listen! For the vale profound/Is overflowing with her sound." An invitation to supper by the ferryman's daughter at Inversnaid on Loch Lomond also proved inspirational. "Sweet Highland Girl,/a very shower of beauty is thy earthly dower!" Wordsworth proclaims in "To a Highland Girl." "In truth together do ye seem/Like something fashioned in a dream;/Such forms as from their covert peep/when earthly cares are laid asleep."

Wordsworth's sister Dorothy also fell in love with the Highlands. The journal in which she had recorded her visit to Scotland with William was originally intended for private circulation; but it was eventually published in 1874, seventy years after the journey when the Victorian mania for all things Scottish was at its height. In the journal Dorothy described Loch Lomond as "an entire solitude, and all that we beheld was a perfection of

Dorothy Wordsworth
(Wikimedia Commons)

loveliness and beauty," and in her entry for August 27, 1803, she goes on to remark that "nothing was to be seen but water, wood, rocks, and heather, and bare mountains above."

Dorothy did not accompany her brother on his later trip to the Highlands, made in 1831 when he was sixty years old. Instead Wordsworth traveled with his daughter Dora on a journey of several weeks, and walked for twenty miles each day behind their carriage as it trundled along the Highland turnpikes. That year Wordsworth reached the Isle of Mull—much further than he had in the earlier trip of 1803—and wrote poems such as the "Address to Kilchurn Castle," inspired by one of the most dramatic ruined fortresses in Scotland, whose walls crumble into the shores of Loch Awe. "The hour of rest/is come, and thou art silent in thy age," he wrote. "The memorial majesty of time/Impersonated in thy calm decay." The same castle also inspired the artist J. M. W. Turner, who in 1802 painted it as a tiny ruin dwarfed by the surrounding mountains, overlooked by a rainbow curling through a storm-lashed sky.

Kilchurn Castle, Loch Awe: engraving by William Miller after J. M. W. Turner, 1847 (Wikimedia Commons)

MORE ENGLISH POETS: COLERIDGE, BYRON, AND KEATS

Wordsworth and Coleridge developed a somewhat fractious relationship during their trip to the Highlands. Shortly after their visit to Loch Lomond Coleridge decided, in a fit of ill-temper, to split from the Wordsworths and head off on his own. The reasons why he did this are still disputed to this day. According to Wordsworth, Coleridge was rather "too much in love with his own dejection" to be much fun as a traveling companion, but Coleridge, for his part, later admitted that he was dismayed by the wet weather and annoyed by Wordsworth's egotism and hypochondria. Whatever the reason for his desertion it is clear that Coleridge was in a state of advanced depression as he headed off alone through Glencoe to Fort William, wearing out several pairs of shoes as he trudged through the mountains. But Coleridge wrote no poems extolling the scenery through which he passed on his strange jaunt, and the torch of Romanticism in the Highlands was passed from Wordsworth not to him but to George Gordon, Lord Byron.

Byron visited the area around Braemar in the Cairngorms as a boy of eight and then later on as an adolescent of fifteen. Though a very young boy at the time of his first visit, made when he was recovering from scarlet fever, the trip was clearly a formative one. The young George was lodged with a farmer near Ballaterich and made a point of wearing the family tartan of Clan Gordon, which was dark blue with lighter shades of green crossed through by thin yellow lines. His poem "Lachin Y Gair" recalls and celebrates his boyhood in the Highlands in the shadow of the Lochnagar peak:

> Ah! There my young footsteps in infancy wander'd;
> My cap was the bonnet, my cloak was the plaid;
> On chieftains long perish'd my memory ponder'd,
> As daily I strode through the pine-cover'd glade.

Later in the poem he affirms the appeal of the Highlands in a manner that is typical of the Romantics. "England!" he exclaims. "Thy beauties are tame and domestic/To one who has roved o'er the mountains afar… Oh for the crags that are wild and majestic!/The steep frowning glories of dark Loch Na Garr."

In another poem, "When I Roved a Young Highlander," Byron turns his eye towards Morven, near Ballater, in the same part of the Highlands, and again remembers the visits of his youth. "Morven of snow!/To gaze on the torrent that thunder'd beneath,/or the mist of the tempest that gather'd below… I arose with the dawn; with my dog as my guide,/From mountain to mountain I bounded along."

Like Wordsworth, Byron remained a lover of Scotland all his life. In a letter to Sir Walter Scott he once remarked that "My heart warms to tartan or to anything of Scotland," and in his poem *Don Juan* he wistfully recalls "Scotch plaids, Scotch snoods, the blue hills, and clear streams."

John Keats, a near contemporary of both Wordsworth and Byron, was also drawn to the Highlands, although his poetic work inspired by the region was slim in comparison. Instead he expressed his impressions of the mountains in letters and diaries. On a visit to Loch Lomond in 1818 in the company of his friend Charles Armitage Brown, Keats became exasperated by the busy tourist scene around the loch, observing that "steam boats on Loch Lomond and barouches on its sides take a little from the pleasure of such romantic chaps as Brown and I." Traveling from Glasgow to Oban on foot he complained in a letter to his brother Tom about the cost of getting to Staffa: the seven guineas demanded was "like paying sixpence for an apple at a playhouse." He seems to have been more satisfied by a trip up Ben Nevis, however. At the summit—"blind in mist!"—he knocked back a dram of whisky and composed one of his best-known sonnets: "All my eye doth meet/Is mist and crag," he wrote, "not only on this height,/But in the world of thought and mental might!"

THE CREATION OF "SCOTT-LAND"

Wordsworth was not the only writer of the early nineteenth century who extolled the beauty of the Highlands to English-speaking readers. His contemporary Sir Walter Scott (1771–1832) was doing the same—and was a native Scot, to boot. In fact, Scott's work was arguably more influential than that of Wordsworth, as Scott was the first author writing in English to gain an international following and reputation during the course of his lifetime. From literary critic to common reader, from Maine to Moscow, Scott's appeal was wide and irresistible. Much of his life and work is associated with the Borders and with Edinburgh. Yet the Highlands feature memorably in a number of Scott's novels and poems and along with Wordsworth he was responsible for romanticizing the region and for unwittingly encouraging the first tourist onslaught on the glens and mountains.

Just like the poetry of his contemporaries Byron and Wordsworth, Scott's Highland-inspired verse often celebrated the "dark, confused, and uncertain images" of the sublime. One such work is the narrative poem *The Lord of the Isles* (1815) which is set partly around Loch Coruisk on Skye, a dark, needle-like slice of water that languishes in the shadows of the remote Black Cuillin range. "Rarely human eye has known/A scene so stern as that dread lake/with its dark ledge of barren stone," was how Scott evoked the landscape.

> For all is rocks at random thrown,
> Black waves, bare crags, and banks of stone,
> As if were here denied
> The summer sun, the spring's sweet dew,

That clothe with many a varied hue
The bleakest mountain-side.

Another of Scott's narrative poems, *The Lady of the Lake*, was set around the softer, more forgiving landscape of Loch Katrine in the Trossachs and was responsible for a huge upsurge in visitors to that picturesque loch. (Scott's influence on tourism is discussed more fully in a later section of the book.) Scott began writing the poem in 1809 while staying in the area with his family, and it was published the following year, after he had laid it aside for a while to help nurse his young daughter through a bout of serious illness. The poem chronicles the dispute, "in ancient days of Caledon," between King James V of Scotland and the Douglas clan, and true to the epic poem tradition of the Middle Ages it features a narrative that reverberates with the sound of battles and strains with the pain of unrequited love. One strand of the narrative follows a contest between three men for the love of the Highland heroine, Ellen Douglas, "the indignant spirit of the North." One of her suitors is James Fitz-James, the noble Knight of Snowdoun, who encounters Ellen while seeking shelter at a remote chieftain's lair beside the glimmering loch: "The silver light with quivering glance/played on the water's still expanse/Wild were the heart whose passion's sway/Could rage beneath the sober ray." Readers were spellbound. Within eight months of its publication some 25,000 copies of the poem had been sold.

Scott's first novel was *Waverley*, which he published anonymously in 1814 at a time when his poems had already made him famous. (Most readers had already guessed the author's identity when Scott admitted the truth in 1827.) The novel was set during the Jacobite rebellions of seventy years before. A preoccupation with customs and personalities remote from the "civilized" present was a hallmark of the Romantic era, but Scott was the first to explore this theme in fictional form, and with *Waverley* he is credited as having created the historical novel as a distinct genre. The novel and its sequels helped strengthen the revival of the Highlands in the popular imagination—a process already set in motion by Samuel Johnson and William Wordsworth and later furthered by Queen Victoria through her very public adoration of the region.

In the novel a young English aristocrat, Edward Waverley, travels to Dundee to join a cavalry platoon, a decision forced upon him after he tries to forge a marital arrangement with a woman deemed by his family to be unsuitable. In Scotland he becomes militarily entangled in the affairs of a Jacobite chieftain, and romantically entangled with two young women, Flora and Rose. The novel's Romantic credentials are laid bare in one of the early scenes between Edward, "a knight of romance," and Flora, "the fair Highland damsel," who leads the young man along a narrow glen that "seemed to open into the land of romance [where] the rocks assumed a thousand peculiar and varied forms... [below were] eminences and peaks, some bare, some clothed with wood, some round and purple with heather, and other splintered into rocks and crags." Soon they reach a "romantic waterfall" where Flora sings a Highland battle song, accompanying herself on a harp. The scene could easily be found in a kitsch romantic painting, all kilts and rocky crags and dramatic skies. Yet many scholars have argued that Scott is in fact something of a "reluctant romantic," inherently conservative, distrustful of the emotional fervor and the passionate, revolutionary, individualistic creed so venerated by Byron and other Romantic poets.

Rob Roy was published three years after *Waverley,* and is probably Scott's most famous Highland-set novel. The notorious Highland outlaw Rob Roy MacGregor was born around 1670, the son of a chieftain, and became a cattle farmer, but then absconded after borrowing £1000 from the Duke of Montrose and failing to pay it back. That turned MacGregor into a wanted man. He forged an alliance with the Duke of Argyll against Montrose and embarked on a new life as a cattle rustler, a bandit, and a blackmailer; he was captured and imprisoned in Newgate Prison in London but managed to escape deportation to Australia through a royal pardon. After his release he returned to the lonely village of Balquhidder, east of Loch Lomond, where his kinsfolk had made their home. He died in 1734 from wounds sustained in a duel fought with a local rival.

The novel, though, centers not on Rob Roy but on Francis Osbaldistone, the son of an English merchant, who travels to the north of England and then the Highlands to retrieve documents that will rescue his father's business and reputation—and who becomes involved with Rob Roy and the 1715 Jacobite uprising. The legend that was popularized by Scott was that Rob Roy was something of a "Robin Hood of Scotland... the dread of the wealthy but the friend of the poor," as the author himself states in the novel's conclusion. Certainly MacGregor is presented to readers as a

Fight in the Inn at the Clachan of Aberfoil, an illustration from *Rob Roy*

hero, a handsome, athletic swordsman with a shock of red hair from which he gained his nickname (*Ruadh* means "red" in Gaelic and became anglicised to Roy); and he possessed the "wild virtues, the subtle policy, and the unrestrained licence of an American Indian." MacGregor's involvement with the Jacobite rebellion of 1715 is also given a suitably romantic sheen: in the novel, the chieftain insists that although Highlanders are "a rude and ignorant… violent and passionate people" they have been unjustly persecuted, to which his companion Bailie adds "and persecution maketh wise men mad." Thus the historical background to the novel is set out for readers, whom Scott encourages to sympathize with the romance and passion of the Jacobite cause, if not its political intention.

Just as Scott's earlier work had drawn visitors to Loch Katrine, so after 1817 they flocked to places associated with the Rob Roy story, such as the cave on the shores of Loch Lomond that was supposedly one of his hideaways, and the churchyard in Balquhidder where the famed outlaw is buried beside his wife and his two youngest sons. This lonely spot, reached by a dead-end road that beyond Balquhidder peters out into a farm track, is still a popular pilgrimage site of sorts for tourists; the coins left on the grave slabs and the ribbons affixed to the railings around them suggest a genuine affection for Rob Roy and his memory. Yet the stone slabs over Roy's supposed grave are medieval and the inscriptions are quite recent, casting doubt as to whether the famed outlaw is actually buried here.

In the end, the reverence expressed at the grave at Balquhidder perhaps serves as an indication of how Scott's representation of both Rob Roy and of Scotland was deceptive and inauthentic. In his 1983 book *The Highland Clearances* John Prebble suggests that "Scott and his imitators took the Highlander out of his environment, disinfected him, dressed him in romance, and made him respectable enough to be a gun-bearer for an English sportsman, or a bayonet-carrier for imperialism." Scott himself had once written that "what makes Scotland Scotland is fast disappearing," and his words were echoed by his contemporary, the eminent Edinburgh lawyer and intellectual Henry Cockburn, who remarked that "this is the last truly Scotch age." The sentiments of these intellectuals were propagated by a number of Highlanders, such as Alistair Ranaldson Macdonell, the laird of Glengarry, who was the inspiration for the clansman Fergus MacIvor in *Waverley.* In 1815 Macdonell presided over the inaugural meeting of the Society of True Highlanders which, according to the *Inverness Journal,* supported the "dress, language, music, and characteristics" of the "illustrious race" of Highland Scotsmen. Further meetings of the Society saw attendees arriving in Highland dress, serenaded by pipers. Scott thought Macdonell a "treasure," but Robbie Burns despised him for his arrogant indifference to the wretched condition of Highlanders, most of whom lived in abject poverty.

In London fashionable society sided with Scott. People went mad for tartan while aristocrats and newly-rich industrialists flocked to the new hunting estates in the Highlands. All of them were intoxicated by Scott's portrayal of the Highlands. While science, education, industry, and the arts flourished in Glasgow and Edinburgh, Scott had created a parallel country of pastoral romance and proud tradition that was a world away from the cities of the lowlands. His own version of Scotland was untainted by the Clearances (in which Macdonell was a major player) and was one of tranquil lochs, misty glens and gloomy castles. One such fortress was the ruined Dunollie Castle that stands on a rocky promontory overlooking the sea just outside Oban, which Scott visited in 1814, when he was moved to write that he had "seldom seen a more romantic and delightful situation." His influence was pervasive enough for the American travel writer Bayard Taylor to write, in 1844, that "Scotland is Scott-land." Nearly a century and a half later another American travel writer, Paul Theroux, demonstrated a caustic disregard for this "Scott-land" in his 1983 *The Kingdom by the Sea*, dismissing the "flummery of bagpipes and tartans and tribalistic blood-and-thunder that Sir Walter Scott had turned into the Highland cult." Instead Theroux found himself admiring the "courteous, hospitable, hard-working, and funny" Highlanders he came across on his journey around the Highland coastline, who were self-sufficient and independent, epitomizing "what was best in Scotland."

Since the nineteenth century Scott's literary reputation has faded somewhat. Many modern readers will find his novels long-winded, ponderous, and somewhat humourless in style, and these days most people associate Waverley with the main railway station in Edinburgh rather than with Scott—although the station was actually named after the novel and its hero. (Having said that, the writer's former house in Abbotsford in the Borders remains something of a literary shrine.) Scott's motives for the way he presented Scotland were admirable—he wanted to encourage an interest in Scottish history—but his Scotland was remote from the experiences of many: "my heart's in the Highlands, my heart's in the Highlands, a-chasing the deer" was the sentiment he espoused in *Waverley*, ignoring the vicious poverty and harshness of life that pervaded the region at the time, but providing those living in lowland Scotland, in England, and elsewhere in the world with a postcard-pretty portrayal of somewhere most of those readers had never been to.

"Bonnie Lassie, Will You Go to the Birks of Aberfeldy?": Robbie Burns and Duncan MacIntyre

Scott was writing during a golden age for Scottish literature. His most famous near-contemporary was, of course, Robbie Burns, who was mostly associated with Edinburgh, where he was lionized by polite society, and with Ayrshire in southwest Scotland, where he was born and lived for much of his short life. In the autumn of 1787, however, Burns made a tour of the Highlands in the company of William Nicol, a classics master at Edinburgh High School. Burns' choice of traveling companion has intrigued the poet's biographers, who have portrayed Nicol as tetchy, vain, and prickly, jealous of Burns being feted by the likes of the Duke of Athol at Blair Castle while he, Nicol, was forced to seek lodgings in dreary inns nearby and while away his days fishing.

The tour inspired Burns to write a number of poems. One of the best-known, "The Birks of Aberfeldy," was written after a visit to the beautiful forested chasm created by the churning Moness Burn at the edge of the town of Aberfeldy. The poem opens with the exhortation "Come, let us spend the lightsome days/In the Birks of Aberfeldy" and ends with the plaintive refrain, "Bonnie lassie, will ye go/To the birks of Aberfeldy?" (Today a network of carefully maintained paths and sturdy wooden footways takes walkers around the Birks and to the silver cascade of the Falls of Moness that stand at their southern end; a plaque beside a shallow grotto in the cliffside marks the place where Burns was inspired to write the poem.)

On the same tour Burns visited the Falls of Bruar, a similarly wooded gorge also lying in Highland Perthshire (though less chasm-like than the one at Aberfeldy). Burns found the Falls to be "exceedingly picturesque and beautiful" but remarked that "their effect is much impaired by the want of trees and shrubs." He expressed these sentiments poetically too, in "The Humble Petition of Bruar Water to the Noble Duke of Athole"—the Duke of Atholl, whose seat at Blair Castle is a few miles away down the valley, being the local landowner. This poem takes the form of a plea by the waters flowing in the burn to be provided with shade:

> Would then my noble master please
> To grant my highest wishes,
> He'll shade my banks wi' tow'ring trees
> And bonie spreading bushes.

After Burns died the fourth Duke of Atholl, later known as "Planter John," had larch and Scots pine planted around the Falls in the poet's memory so that the waters in the burn could indeed lie in shade. He also built two narrow stone bridges, which span the lower and upper falls to this day, and constructed timber summer houses beside the falls, although these have long since disappeared. Queen Victoria saw the mature trees when she visited the Falls in September 1842 and noted in her journal that "the trees which surround the falls were planted by the late Duke of Athole in compliance with Burns's *Petition*."

A lot has changed, though, since the days of Victoria and Robert Burns: the lower falls at Bruar are a short stroll away from the busy Perth to Inverness road, so the place is busy with trippers (although few make it to the upper falls, fifteen minutes' walk away up through the forest); and over the place where the path meets the road rises a shopping emporium known as the House of Bruar, where coach parties are tempted to buy Scottish-themed clothing, food, souvenirs, and antiques in a commercialized development that has to be seen to be believed. Burns would not have been impressed. What sort of poem he would come up with if he visited Bruar today is unimaginable, but we know that the place that he was least impressed with in the Scotland of the 1787 was Inveraray, which inspired possibly his oddest piece of verse from the Highlands. Unable to lodge in the castle, the palatial residence of the Dukes of Argyll, he was forced to stay in a busy inn in the town, on one of whose windows he allegedly scratched out the following lines with a stylus: "There's nothing here but Highland pride/And Highland scab and hunger;/If providence had sent me here/'Twas surely in anger." The window no longer exists and in fact there is no real proof that Burns was ever guilty of thus defacing the window of the inn.

Back in Ayr Burns fell in love with a woman named Mary Campbell, who nursed him through a serious bout of typhus. Mary was married at the time but became engaged to Burns, who for his part had got a girl named Jean Armour pregnant but had been rejected as a possible son-in-law by Jean's father, who considered the poet's behavior despicable and his prospects low. Burns' response to this tricky situation was a planned elopement with Mary to Jamaica, where he had already accepted a job as a bookkeeper on a sugar plantation. But Mary contracted typhus and died from it, and his plans were never realized.

Burns immortalized his beloved in a number of poems and songs, including "Highland Mary," which opens with the refrain "Oh pale, pale now, those rosy lips, I aft hae kissed sae fondly!" During the nineteenth century Dunoon, a town on the banks of the Clyde estuary flanked by some of the most southerly mountains of the Highlands, claimed Mary as its daughter, although firm proof that she had actually been born here only came to light in 1943. Nearly half a century prior to this, in 1896, the

Burns Society of London had raised a commanding statue of her in the town, which stands there to this day on a high knuckle of rock above the port, welcoming those who disembark from the ferries that cross from Gourock. Mary is portrayed looking towards Ayrshire and holding the Bible that Burns says he gives her in the song (which is now in the Burns Museum in Ayrshire, along with a lock of Mary's hair). The statue, though, is a piece of guesswork, as no-one really knows what Mary Campbell looked like.

Robbie Burns died at the age of only thirty-seven. His contemporary—and one of the greatest Scottish poets of the nineteenth century—Duncan Ban MacIntyre (Donnchadh Bàn Mac an t-Saoir, 1724–1812), lived to the age of eighty-eight. He celebrated the landscape around Glen Orchy in the West Highlands in poems written in his native Gaelic. MacIntyre grew up beside tiny, jewel-like Loch Tulla, north of the hamlet of Bridge of Orchy, and worked for the Campbell family as a forester and gamekeeper. He also served in the militia raised by the Campbells that fought against Jacobite forces in 1745. He never learned to read or write, and a church minister serving on the Isle of Lismore named Donald MacNicol acted as his scribe. MacIntyre's poems included *The Praise of Ben Doran (Moladh Beinn Dobhrain),* a paean to the mountain that rises above Bridge of Orchy: "In her moorbacks wide/Hosts of shy deer bide/While light comes pouring Diamond-wise from her side," he writes of the gray, brooding mountain that now looms over the stretches of the A82 and the West Highland Railway that run north from Tyndrum onto Rannoch Moor.

In the later part of his life MacIntyre moved to Edinburgh and is buried there in Greyfriars Kirkyard; a monument to his memory stands in the forests above Dalmally, overlooking the place where the River Orchy emerges from Glen Orchy and flows into Loch Awe. The monument was funded by public subscription and was raised in 1859 on the place where, in McIntyre's time, the men of the villages had held their parliaments. It takes the form of a columned, circular granite rotunda resting on a sturdy square plinth. There are superb views towards Loch Awe from the monument (which can be reached by road), although the logging activity in the area and an adjacent communications mast make the spot less splendidly evocative than it might be.

The Highlands in Art and Music

At the end of Sir Walter Scott's novel *Waverley,* Baron Bradwardine is presented with a "large and spirited painting" as a gift. The painting depicts Edward Waverley and the chieftain Fergus MacIvor "in their Highland dress; the scene a wild, rocky, and mountainous pass, down which the clan were descending in the background." This painting, by "an anonymous Edinburgh artist," never of course existed, but so many artworks of this kind were being made at the time that Scott's readership would have instantly nodded in recognition at his description. For just as poets of the Romantic era sought inspiration from the wild scenery of Highland Scotland, so did a generation of late eighteenth-century and early nineteenth-century artists, and by the time of *Waverley's* publication in 1814 a steady flow of paintings portraying the dramatic scenery of Scotland was flowing from their easels. Some of these paintings were probably not much good—Scott does not tell us whether the (fictional) painting in *Waverley* was great art or not—but a few of these paintings were later destined to be counted among the greatest achievements of British art.

John Ruskin, the great art critic and social theorist of the nineteenth century and the first Slade Professor of Fine Art at Oxford, wrote extensively on the appeal of wild mountain scenery to Romantic painters in his 1856 book *Of Mountain Beauty*. This was the fourth volume of his seminal five-volume work *Modern Painters*, published between 1843 and 1860. In his book Ruskin argued that the Romantics had changed forever our way of looking at mountain scenery: "Those desolate and threatening ranges of dark mountain, which in nearly all ages of the world men have looked upon with aversion or terror and shrunk back from as if they were haunted by perpetual images of death are, in reality, sources of life and happiness far fuller and more beneficent than all the bright fruitfulness of the plains," he wrote. The new scientific enquiries into the origin and structure of mountains also informed Ruskin's ethereal love for them: he saw their ridges and peaks as the crests of waves blown by some scarcely understandable geological tempest. And like Wordsworth, he also saw mountains as being blessed with spiritual and religious significance. In *Of Mountain Beauty* he observed that when it comes to mountains "the purposes of their Maker have indeed been accomplished… mountains are the great cathedrals of the earth, with their gates of rock, pavements of clouds, choirs of stream and stone, altars of snow... they seem to have been built for the human race."

The Romantic "packaging" of the Highlands in art can be seen in its earliest incarnation in the works of Paul Sandby (1731–1809), a draughtsman and map-maker who became a founding member of the Royal Academy. During the decades following the Battle of Culloden Sandby was commissioned by the army to make drawings of Highland valleys for the surveyors of the new military roads that were designed to facilitate troop movements across the mountains. One of those drawings was of the broad valley of Strathtay. Sandby made two drawings of this valley from identical spots, in 1774 and 1780, and the difference between them is striking. In the second drawing the peaks are loftier and more dramatic, gorse and heather cover the hills rather than pasture, and a kilted Highlander decorates the scene. Clearly the first drawing shows the Highlands of old—forbidding, unappealing, barren—while the second is infused with Romantic sentiment. Sandby later turned to watercolor views of Scotland and several of his works show distinct Jacobite leanings. In *The Taking of Jacobite Prisoners*, for instance, Sandby's sympathies clearly lie with the captured Highlanders rather than their guards.

It was the subsequent work of the English landscape artist J. M. W. Turner (1775–1851) that most popularly brought Romantic sensibilities to bear on the painting of Highland scenes. According to Ruskin, Turner's champion, the artist possessed a prodigious talent for "stirringly and truthfully measuring the moods of nature." Turner's fondness for capturing the drama of mountain scenery took him to Scotland on six separate occasions. These visits inspired ten oil paintings and hundreds of watercolors, prints, sketches, and drawings. Turner drew inspiration from the whole of Scotland, not just the Highlands—during his first visit, in 1797, he got no further than the Borders, where he made a number of sketches of ancient abbeys—but his second, four years later, took him to the West Highlands. Travel was difficult at that time—Telford's efficient road network was yet to be built—and there were very few scheduled coach services beyond Scotland's big cities. Nonetheless Turner's itinerary was ambitious and he managed to visit Loch Awe, Loch Lomond, Inveraray, Blair Atholl, and Killiecrankie, producing a great number of drawings in pencil that evoked the grayness of distant mist-shrouded mountains.

In 1818 he traveled north of the border again to meet with Sir Walter Scott, with the intention of providing illustrations for the latter's book *The Provincial Antiquities of Scotland*. It was not a happy working relationship. Scott later wrote that Turner would "do nothing without cash and anything for it," while Turner for his part could be cold and off-hand in his business and personal dealings; on one occasion he even failed to turn up to a dinner hosted by Scottish artists in his honor. His enthusiasm for Scotland remained undimmed, however, and in 1831 he traveled in the Highlands again, this time to make illustrations for another title by Scott, namely a new edition of his *Poetical Works*. On this tour Turner visited and painted Loch Tarbert and the coastline around Oban, and the islands of Islay, Staffa, and Mull. Two of his most famous Scottish paintings were made on this tour. His impressionistic watercolor of Glencoe is a swirling miasma of grays and reddy-browns, with figures dwarfed by distant mountains, while *Staffa, Fingal's Cave* is a symphony of mist, sea, and storm that was described by one critic as a "sublimity of vastness and solitude." Despite this painting's subsequent fame it remained unsold for thirteen

Everett Millais' portrait of John Ruskin in the Highlands
(Ashmolean Museum/Wikimedia Commons)

years after its execution. Even its eventual buyer, the New York art collector James Lenox, complained the painting was "indistinct," not having got to grips with Turner's handling of color and the expressive dynamism of his work that were later recognized to be the hallmark of his genius. The painting currently hangs in the Yale Center for British Art in New Haven, Connecticut.

Ruskin also nurtured the talents of a number of other English painters who were drawn to the Highlands. Foremost among these was John Everett Millais, one of whose paintings was a portrait of Ruskin himself, set against the backdrop of a waterfall in the Trossachs. Millais was staying with Ruskin and his wife Effie at Brig o'Turk near Glen Finglas when the painting was completed; scandalously, Effie had an affair with Millais and later married him. The other paintings Millais made in the Highlands between 1870 and 1892 were often depictions of bleak lochside or riverside scenes, many of them portraying the scenery of the southern Highlands around Dunkeld. His work, alongside that of Turner and Ruskin himself, inspired many other painters, including those from Scotland itself. These indigenous artists included Horatio McCulloch, whose 1857 painting of the ruins of Inverlochy Castle, part-reflected in water and set against a stormy background, hangs in the National Gallery of Scotland in Edinburgh.

Peter Graham, McCulloch's contemporary, specialized more in painting wild places, overpowering scenery and stormy skyscapes, and *Wandering Shadows,* which can be seen in the same gallery, is no exception: in the painting a dazzling ray of sunlight emerges from curls of clouds to transform a rocky mountainside into a patchwork of reds, grays, and greens, and the solitary sign of life—a man fishing in a splashing burn—only serves to emphasize the loneliness. Painters from abroad also began to show an interest in the Highlands. One was Gustave Doré (1832–83), whose *Paysage d'Ecosse*, now in the Museé des Beaux Arts in the Normandy city of Caen, features a dramatic and desolate landscape washed by milky sunlight that pours from a violent sky and glistens on the waters of a distant loch and on the rocky slopes rising from the water. The scene has a tremendous sense of space and drama about it: an untamed landscape (save for some farm animals coming into view along a track in one corner of the canvas) that is the epitome of Edmund Burke's notion of the sublime.

Doré's *Landscape in Scotland*, c.1878
(Walters Art Museum/Wikimedia Commons)

When Turner painted Fingal's Cave the dramatic feature was already well-known to the public through Felix Mendelssohn's *Hebridean Overture*, which had been composed two years previously. Mendelssohn had visited the Hebrides in August 1829 and had sketched the overture's opening during his travels, even including a snatch of the opening in a letter he sent from Scotland to a friend. Mendelssohn was only twenty years old at the time, and journeyed to Scotland after a few months living in London (he even went out of his way to visit Sir Walter Scott in Abbotsford, later complaining that he had "lost a day for the sake of at best one hour of superficial conversation"). The visit also inspired the *Scottish Symphony*, though this was composed much later in Mendelssohn's life. That said, however, it seems that the Highlands inspired few composers beyond Mendelssohn. Although Malcolm Arnold and Max Bruch wrote pieces inspired by traditional Scottish melodies there was nothing specifically Highland about them, and one has to look to the comparatively obscure likes of Frederic Lamond (1868–1948) and his concert overture *From the Scottish Highlands* for a piece directly inspired by the region.

ROBERT LOUIS STEVENSON AND BEATRIX POTTER

Nothing can compare with the first few decades of the nineteenth century in terms of the sheer productiveness of artists and writers who responded to the scenery of the Scottish Highlands. The later part of the century, by contrast, was much less remarkable in its fecundity. Two figures from the second half of the century do, however, stand out in a survey of literary figures associated with the Highlands, namely Robert Louis Stevenson and Beatrix Potter. Unfortunately the connection of these writers with the region is often forgotten in the public imagination, largely because during their eventful lives both writers sought inspiration for their most famous works elsewhere.

Beatrix Potter (1866–1943) was born into a solidly middle-class family in London who, as was the fashion of the day, holidayed frequently in Scotland. Between the ages of five and fifteen Beatrix joined the family in the rented Dalguise House, a large, rambling Victorian residence overlooking the banks of the River Tay just to the north of the neighboring towns of Birnam and Dunkeld. There she was encouraged in her drawing by Millais, a friend of her father, while the noted Perthshire naturalist Charles McIntosh advised the young girl on the wildlife she encountered around the area. "I remember every stone, every tree, the scent of the heather," Potter later wrote of Dalguise in her journal, "the murmuring of the wind through the trees, the sun sinking behind the mountains... the white mist rising from the river... oh, it was always beautiful. Home sweet home!"

When Potter was a young woman of twenty-seven her family rented Eastwood, another Tayside house near Dunkeld, where Peter Rabbit, Flopsy, Mopsy, Cottontail, and the rest of the happy brood were "born," in a series of illustrated letters Potter wrote to the son of her former governess; the animal characters eventually sprang to life in book form in 1902 (although Potter had published a previous edition of *The Tales of Peter Rabbit* privately after being turned down by six publishers). Potter later wrote that it was her childhood holidays at Dalguise House that had inspired her to create these stories—and that the fairy Mrs. Tiggy-Winkle was apparently based on a washerwoman there named Kitty MacDonald, who according to Potter had "a tiny body, brown as a berry... and much wrinkled." As an adult, Potter lived primarily in the English Lake District, where her work and memory is much cherished. Today Dalguise House serves as an outdoor adventure center for children and is off limits to visitors; a memorial garden in Birnham, across the road from the town's venerable nineteenth-century hotel, celebrates Potter's connections with the area, with sculpted rabbits frolicking among ponds and woody glades. An exhibition in the striking new arts center next door features a number of photographs of Potter and her family in Scotland, and sheds light on the author's early scientific research into fungi, which was ignored by the botanists of her day, largely because Potter was a woman.

Robert Louis Stevenson (1850–94) was born in Edinburgh, the son of Thomas Stevenson and the grandson of Robert Stevenson, Scotland's prolific father-and-son lighthouse builders and engineers. In his short life he traveled the world from the French Cévennes to Australia and from the Highlands to Samoa, where he died at the age of forty-four, having moved to a tropical climate for the good of his health. His wanderlust began in the Highlands, whose wild scenery influenced a number of his works, most particularly his novel *Kidnapped.* That novel was written in 1870 when Stevenson was just twenty years old, and was inspired by a book that his father had bought in a second hand bookshop in Inverness entitled *The Trial of James Stewart*, which he passed on to his son. The book was the official record of the trial of a Jacobite clansman, James Stewart, who had allegedly shot a British government agent named Colin Campbell of Glenure in the Wood of Lettermore near Ballachulish in 1752. Campbell had been sent to the area as a rent collector shortly after the defeat of the Jacobite cause at Culloden; the rented property had been confiscated from the Stewart clan of Ardshiel, who had supported the Jacobites, and the political situation in that part of the West Highlands was very tense at the time. James Stewart was tried and hanged but there was very little evidence linking him to the murder. Robert Louis Stevenson was convinced that a miscarriage of justice had occurred and that the killing had resulted from a feud between the Stewarts and the Campbells; and he used the murder as the background to the action of his celebrated novel.

Much of *Kidnapped* concerns the flight across the Highlands of the novel's hero, seventeen-year-old lowlander David Balfour, who is seen as a suspect in the murder; accompanying him is his guide and friend, the foolhardy and daring Jacobite Alan Breck Stewart. Balfour had wound up in the West Highlands after his uncle Ebenezer tried to have him

From Robert Louis Stevenson's *Kidnapped*: David Balfour and Alan Breck Stewart encounter Robin Oig MacGregor in Balquhidder (Wikimedia Commons)

kidnapped and shipped to the colonies so that the boy would be denied his father's inheritance; the ship, the *Covenant,* is wrecked in a storm on the Inner Hebrides and Balfour manages to escape in the company of Alan, whose boat had struck the *Covenant* in the storm.

Throughout the narrative that follows Stevenson guides his characters across landscapes familiar to him from a childhood that was spent partly in the Highlands and Islands. One section of the novel was written on the island of Erraid, off Mull, during the time that Robert had to stay there while his father was supervising the restoration of the island's Dubh Artach lighthouse. Stevenson made use of the island as the setting for Balfour's shipwreck: the hero describes the place as "nothing but a jumble of granite rocks… the time I spent upon the island is still so horrible a thought to me, that I must pass lightly over it… it was all desolate and rocky; nothing living on it but game birds which I lacked the means to kill, and the gulls which haunted the outlying rocks in a prodigious number."

Later on, having escaped from Erraid, Balfour witnesses the killing of the "Red Fox," Colin Campbell, and escapes into the hills after Breck convinces him that he is a prime suspect: "either take to the heather with me," Breck advises Balfour, "or else hang." Constantly dodging the companies of soldiers who are searching for Campbell's murderer, the pair make for the wilds of Rannoch Moor, and later encounter Robin Oig MacGregor, the son of the legendary outlaw Rob Roy, in Balquhidder, the village where Rob Roy is buried.

Robin, a murderer and a renegade, is portrayed by Stevenson as having all the dash and swagger of his father: "[stepping] around Balquhidder like a gentleman… [walking] into the house of his blood enemies as a rider might into a public inn." At first Robin challenges the pair to a duel, but their host, an accomplished player of the bagpipes, persuades them to settle their differences in a piping contest, which Robin wins comfortably. After this the two men make it across the hills to Edinburgh, where Balfour meets a lawyer who helps him claim his inheritance from the clutches of the dastardly Ebenezer. The novel is shot through with action and danger in the proper tradition of *Boy's Own* adventure yarns (there are virtually no female characters), but although it has received countless screen adaptations the archaic language and complexity of the political setting would make it hard-going for all but the most enthusiastic child readers of today.

The murder of Colin Campbell, and the subsequent execution of James Stewart, is remembered today in a number of memorials in the Appin region around Ballachulish. The actual site of the murder is commemorated by a memorial cairn on the hillside above the road along Loch Linnhe, a mile or so west of the village. At Ballachulish itself, overlooking the southern pier of the road bridge across Loch Leven, a short flight of steps leads to a cairn marking the place where James Stewart was hanged for the murder, on November 8, 1752. Before he died, "James of the glen," as he was known, made a speech in which he asserted his innocence and forgave his accusers; he then mounted the scaffold singing the 35th Psalm, which in the Gaelic-speaking Highlands has been known since as the *Salm Sheumais a' Ghlinne*, or Psalm of James of the Glen. After his execution his body was simply left there to swing, watched over by a constant guard of Hanoverian soldiers. When the body was torn down in a gale in 1755 it was re-hung with wire supports. Eventually, though, the bones fell to the ground, from where they were discreetly collected by a Ballachulish man named John Stewart, and were eventually laid to rest in the coffin of James Stewart's wife in the churchyard at Keil, on Loch Linnhe. As for the murder weapon, today there are four guns in Scotland that are claimed by their owners to be the rifle that was used to kill Colin Campbell; one, an enormously long Spanish-made rifle, which stands the height of a reasonably tall man, can be seen in the West Highland Museum in Fort William.

Ten years after the publication of *Kidnapped* Robert Louis Stevenson was again living in the Highlands, this time in Braemar, and it was here that he wrote his most famous work, *Treasure Island.* Unlike *Kidnapped* that novel takes no part of its setting from the Highlands (although the character of Long John Silver was supposedly inspired by a man from Arisaig on the region's west coast, and his name was possibly taken from a notoriously violent miller named John Silver who lived in Braemar at the time). Braemar is one of the highest villages in Scotland and Stevenson was there for the good of his health; he had moved there from Pitlochry, where the weather was foul, but there was no improvement up in Braemar, where the conditions proved to be "more unkind than man's ingratitude." Stevenson's lodging was "a house lugubriously known as the Late Miss McGregor's Cottage." It stands on Castleton Terrace and today is in private hands, although a plaque above the front door commemorates the writer's association with it.

At one point during his stay in the cottage Stevenson found himself having to entertain his twelve-year-old stepson, Lloyd Osbourne. At first he amused the boy by drawing treasure maps but then the story of *Treasure Island*, which is dedicated to Lloyd, began to take shape. As Stevenson explained in an article in the *Idler* magazine in 1894, "The next thing I knew I had some papers in front of me and was writing out a list of chapters… On a chill September morning, by the cheek of a brisk fire, and the rain drumming on the window, I began *The Sea Cook*, for that was the original title." The novel was eventually finished in Davos, the spa high up in the Swiss Alps where Stevenson had sought refuge during his relentless search for suitable conditions to cure his consumption; when it was accepted for publication as a serial by *Young Folks Magazine* the editor suggested the title be changed to *Treasure Island.*

The Highlands through the Words of Twentieth-Century Writers

As far as the twentieth century is concerned the greatest chronicler of Highland life is the novelist Neil Gunn (1891–1973). Gunn grew up in Dunbeath, a weather-beaten fishing village on the windswept coast between Helmsdale and Wick, which was established to house those displaced by the Clearances; no wonder, then, that in many of his works he describes the struggles of the remote fishing communities of the northeast with an almost mystical awareness. Dunbeath spreads itself out along a deep, narrow valley, spanned these days by a viaduct that carries the main road from Inverness to Wick, and it was in one of the terraced houses under this modern viaduct that Gunn was born, the son of a crofter-fisherman. In Gunn's day the village school, which he attended, overlooked the valley from the south. Today the building houses a cultural center where his work is celebrated; one of his typewriters is even on show.

As a writer Gunn was extraordinarily prolific. Most of his works were novels, but he also wrote books and articles on travel and whisky. His most popular work remains *The Silver Darlings* (1941), a powerful and evocative novel set among the fishermen of Scotland's northeast, who battle against poverty, disease, and treacherous seas to establish a viable herring industry at Helmsdale. The novel is less a story of Highlanders, though, than of Scots seafarers, and the action ranges to and fro across the coast of northern Scotland as far as the Western Isles. Many of Gunn's other works were inspired by a childhood spent beside the sea. They include *Morning Tide*, which centers on the twelve-year-old son of a Dunbeath fisherman, and *Highland River*, which tells how Dunbeath Water (the river that reaches the sea at Dunbeath) becomes a spiritual source of life for a young boy named Kenn. In the novel the young boy catches a salmon in the stream, and "for of all that befell Kenn afterwards, of war and horror and love and scientific triumphs, nothing ever had quite the splendour and glory of that struggle by the well pool… It was a war between an immature human body on one side, and a superbly matured body of incredible swiftness and strength on the other." The struggle between the small boy and the enormous fish is today evoked by a greening bronze sculpture on the quayside in Dunbeath, erected in 1991 by the Neil Gunn Society.

The novelist Neil Munro (1863–1930) was also born in the Highlands, in Inveraray, and edited the *Glasgow Evening News* before turning his hand to fiction. His most famous creation was Para Handy, the skipper of the boat *Vital Spark*, whose exploits first appeared in print in 1905 in the *Glasgow Evening News*. Munro published the stories under the name Hugh Foulis because he thought them too slight to be considered serious works of fiction. His home in Inveraray provided the setting for some of his stories and novels that have endured less well, such as *John Splendid* (1898), which concerns the fate of the manager of a silver mine during the military skirmishes stirred up across Scotland by the English Civil War. The book includes a memorable description of market day in "Inneraora" (Inveraray), when the place "hummed with Gaelic and the round bellowing of cattle… in such a season the bustling town in the heart of the stern Highlands seemed a fever spot… a constant stream of men passed in and out at the changehouse closes and about the fisherland tenements, where seafarers and drovers together sang the maddest love-ditties in the voices of roaring bulls, beating the while with their feet on the floor in our foolish Gaelic fashion."

Munro's work, and that of Neil Gunn, contrasts markedly with that of Alan Warner, the most recent novelist of note to have emerged from the Highlands. Warner burst onto the Scottish literary scene in 1995 with *Morvern Callar*, a dazzlingly stylish novel about a young woman who abandons her dead-end job in a supermarket when she passes off the novel written by her dead boyfriend as her own, and receives a huge advance from a London publisher. The setting is very clearly Oban—although the town is never mentioned by name—and the novel's milieu, of dead-end lives eked out in a town at the end of the line, could not be further from the historical romanticism of Sir Walter Scott or the lyricism of Neil Gunn. The novel was filmed in 2001, by Scotland's leading filmmaker Lynne Ramsay, partly on location in Oban, with the washed-out grays of that town contrasting with the bright colors of southern Spain, where Morvern goes on holiday to escape the drear of a West Highland winter.

In 1998 Warner published his second novel *These Demented Lands*, set on the island of Lismore which lies just offshore from Oban (although Lismore is only ever referred to as "the island," just as Oban is always "the port" in the earlier novel). This second novel reads like a hallucinatory nightmare, an intensely and hysterically imagined story that forms a sequel or companion piece of sorts to *Morvern Callar.*

A number of twentieth-century poets have also chronicled life in the Highlands. The best-known was Sorley MacLean, who was born on the island of Raasay, off Skye, and wrote in Gaelic. After being wounded at the Battle of El Alamein, MacLean served as a schoolmaster in Plockton near Kyle of Lochalsh before living out his retirement on Skye. In "The Island" he likens Skye to a great bird, "your supremely beautiful wings bent/about many-nooked Loch Bracadale,/your beautiful wings prostate on the sea/from the Wild Stallion to the Aird of Sleat/your joyous wings spread/about Loch Snizort and the world."

Roughly contemporaneous with MacLean was Norman MacCaig, who described the area around Loch Assynt in the far northwest of Scotland in poems such as "Midnight," "Lochinver," and "Above Inverkirkaig." He also wrote a poem specifically for television, "A Man in Assynt," in which he evokes "the ruffled foreland… this frieze of mountains" that characterizes the rugged and remote scenery of the northwest Highlands.

Lastly, Christopher Murray Grieve (1892–1972) is a much-respected figure among lovers of twentieth-century Scottish poetry. Grieve wrote under the pen name of Hugh MacDiarmid and with Neil Gunn was a founder member of the Scottish National Party. He lived in a number of parts of Scotland including for a while the Highlands, which inspired his *Sonnets of the Highland Hills*; one sonnet, "The Wind Bags," describes Kildermorie Lodge near Alness on the Cromarty Firth where Grieve lived for a number of years, teaching at a tiny village school. The poem is brilliantly evocative of the bleakness that foul weather can bring to desolate parts of the Highlands. "Rain-beaten stones; great tussocks of dead grass, and stagnant waters throwing leaden lights/To leaden skies: a rough-maned wind that bites with aimless violence at the clouds that pass/Roaring, black-jowled and bull-like in the void." With Neil Gunn, MacDiarmid is considered a leading exponent of the "kailyard" (cabbage yard) school of Scottish literature, which concentrated on the rural environment of Scotland in contrast to the industrial traditions of Glasgow or the literary and intellectual life of Edinburgh.

GAVIN MAXWELL AND THE *RING OF BRIGHT WATER* TRILOGY

Gavin Maxwell's book *Ring of Bright Water* is unquestionably the best-known and most widely-read book ever written on Scottish wildlife. With its abundance of bird and aquatic life, upland Scotland is, of course, a nature writer's paradise, and the shelves of bookshops throughout the Highlands positively groan with titles about everything from golden eagles to red squirrels. But Maxwell's tale of how he raised pet otters in a remote beachside cottage in the West Highlands remains unsurpassed in terms of the affection it has raised among generations of readers; it is nature writing of the highest quality, gripping even to those who have little interest in the subject matter, and the book has not been out of print since its first publication in 1960.

Maxwell was born to an aristocratic family in Dumfries and Galloway and served in the Scottish Highlands with the Special Operations Executive during World War II. After the war he returned to the Highlands and his first book, *Harpoon at a Venture* (1947), told the story of the shark fishery he established on the island of Soay, off Skye. Basking sharks thrive in the waters off Scotland, feeding off plankton, and according to Maxwell they are often "longer than a London bus [with] row upon row of tiny teeth as small and as needle-pointed as a kitten's"; but he goes on to remark that the shark's "movements are gigantic, ponderous, and unfamiliar; it seems a creature from a prehistoric world." Deciding that there was commercial potential in the harvesting of these beasts Maxwell had a harpoon for snaring sharks made to his own design in Mallaig, and when the first shark was caught and hauled ashore both the townsfolk and hotel guests in the town feasted on shark steaks for days afterwards. The shark fishery on Soay, however, proved difficult to establish and rapidly became beset with problems, not the least of which came when the sixteen tons of shark flesh held in the factory store turned rotten, creating a stench of extraordinary putrescence. "For a wave of air so noisome, so active, and so evil, it is hard to find a comparison," Maxwell wrote. By then Maxwell's harpoon ship was developing woodworm and he was told that "half the garden fences in Mallaig" were held up by his discarded harpoon sticks. Eventually a lack of capital caused the venture to fail, and Maxwell shut up shop, wrote his book and then set off on a very different venture—traveling around the marshes of southern Iraq with his friend, the explorer Wilfred Thesiger.

Thesiger's travels in this isolated part of the world resulted in his famous book *The Marsh Arabs,* a classic of post-war travel writing. While Thesiger spent his time in Iraq fascinated by the people living among the marshes, Maxwell was drawn to the wildlife, especially the otters that lived among the reeds of the watery region where the two great rivers of Iraq, the Tigris and the Euphrates, merge. Asking around for an otter to take home as a pet, Maxwell eventually arranged for one to be delivered to him at the British consulate in Basra—a "very small medievally conceived dragon"—that he named Mijbil. "I became, during a year of his constant and violently affectionate companionship, fonder of him than of almost any human being," Maxwell later admitted. Mijbil was a species of otter that was unknown to zoologists and eventually it was scientifically christened *Lutrogale perspicillata maxwelli,* or "Maxwell's Otter," much to the author's delight.

Not without some difficulty Maxwell brought Mijbil back to London and, after living with the creature in his flat, which proved a disastrous experience, he moved with it to a remote cottage on the west coast of Scotland and the "bright, watery landscape" of the place that he named Camusfearnà. Into this new environment "Mij moved... with a delight that communicated itself as clearly as any articulate speech could have done." Needing money to keep the dilapidated cottage going, Maxwell decided that his next book should recount his experiences of raising Mij; the title, *Ring of Bright Water,* refers to the stream that curled around his beachside cottage, forming a "glittering horseshoe... a ring of bright water whose ripples travel from the heart of the sea." The book was an immediate success and sold by the hundreds of thousands throughout the world, even though Maxwell saw it as "no more than a personal diary" of his life with Mij and another otter, Edal, in his remote Scottish paradise.

Ring of Bright Water was followed by two sequels, *The Rocks Remain* (1963) and the *Raven Seek Thy Brother* (1968). These books recount the growing community of otters at Camusfearnà, and the attachment of the creatures to their keepers, who included a teenage boy named Terry Nutkins who had his finger bitten off by Edal but nonetheless grew up to become a prominent wildlife writer and broadcaster. Maxwell's motivation for adopting the lifestyle of a modern-day hermit was, he admitted, a search for "freedom from the prison of adult life and [an] escape into the forgotten world of childhood... man has suffered in his separation from the soil and the other living creatures of the world." The appeal of Maxwell's book may be due to the basic emotion it evokes, of living in a natural and isolated paradise that conforms to the very earliest forms of human existence. Certainly Maxwell's Highland hermitage has precursors in western Scotland, where in the early Middle Ages Celtic monks lived in similarly isolated locations on the coast, often treating the wild animals that lived nearby as their soul mates and companions.

Yet the modern world was quick to encroach on Maxwell's remote cottage. For a time, thanks to the popularity of *Ring of Bright Water,* the otter Edal was the most famous living creature in the world, and public fascination with Maxwell and his otters meant that Camusfearnà became deluged with uninvited visitors. This was despite the place-name being an invented one, concocted to keep the location of the cottage secret. But Maxwell had given enough topographical information in *Ring of Bright Water* for readers to work out that his cottage was situated at Sandaig, just below the minor road that skirts the Glenelg peninsula south of Kyle of Lochalsh (and not to be confused with a different Sandaig on the Knoydart Peninsula further south). He admitted in *The Rocks Remain* that readers had seen "the disguise of place names as a challenge" and with the popularity of the first book "the privacy of Camusfearnà came abruptly to an end... a steady stream of rubbernecks arrived daily, often with loose and undisciplined dogs, to bang on the single door of the house and demand, as if it were their right, to see the otters and all that had figured in the story."

Raven Seek Thy Brother was published a year before Maxwell died. By that time Camusfearnà was no more; the cottage had been gutted by fire and Maxwell was living on the island of Eilean Bàn, situated in the narrow gulf between Kyle of Lochalsh and the port of Kyleakin on Skye. With the lighthouse recently automated, Maxwell was able to live in the former keepers' cottage, which is now a small museum (unfortunately only visitable by appointment) dedicated to his life in Scotland: among many photographs, letters, and books are a pistol he used while serving with the SOE and a facsimile of the first handwritten page of *Ring of Bright Water* (the original is in the Scottish National Library in Edinburgh). Appropriately otters can still be seen from the purpose-built hide overlooking the

Gavin Maxwell's former home on the island of Eilean Bàn, in the shadow of the Skye Bridge, is now a museum dedicated to his memory (Andrew Beattie)

rocks here, but the concrete piers of the Skye Bridge that rise from the island, and the consequent rush of traffic above visitors' heads, rather compromise the appeal of the place as a wildlife observatory. And the whole place offers a somewhat reverential view of Maxwell's life: visitors might best remember that not everyone who knew Maxwell viewed him with such high regard. His friend Richard Frere, whose memoir *Maxwell's Ghost* was published in 1977, wrote of his first meeting with Maxwell as being "abrupt and uneasy" and that "it was said that he drank like a fish, spent money like water, tipped massively with condescension, drove his powerful car with fury and to the public danger, and, it was added with a snigger, was always surrounded by young boys. Few of the local rustics had much good to say of him, except to his face." Yet Frere became close to this fascinating and enigmatic man, and the rest of the book provides a highly personal though always honest portrait of Maxwell during the time that his beloved home at Sandaig burned down and then, in the final months of his life, the years of chain-smoking and whisky-drinking began dealing serious blows to his health.

Sandaig is much more isolated than Eilean Bàn and receives far fewer visitors. The road journey from Kyle of Lochalsh through Shiel Bridge and then along Glen More to the village of Glenelg is spectacular, but a good map is needed to follow the forest tracks and muddy paths leading down to Sandaig from the isolated house at Upper Sandaig where Maxwell used to have his post and supplies delivered (there is no vehicle access to the beach itself). Since Maxwell's time the dunes have become overgrown with bracken and gorse, and little is discernible of the "ring of bright water" once formed by the burn as it bubbled over the sand and into the Sound of Sleat. A cairn (placed in position by Richard Frere) marks the place where Maxwell's cottage stood and where his ashes are buried. Not far away, close to the burn and shaded by trees, another cairn carries the inscription: "Edal, the otter of *Ring of Bright Water,* 1958–1968. Whatever joy she gave to you, give back to nature." Both cairns are smothered with pebbles and shells left by respectful well-wishers. Maxwell's old boat cradle can also be seen, rusting away close by, although the growth of vegetation in summer often obscures it. Here the boat *Polar Star* had once lain "high and dry on her massive wheeled cradle, her bronze propellers glinting wetly on the grass below her stern."

In 1969, the year that Maxwell died, *Ring of Bright Water* was made into a film, in which the author was played by the actor Bill Travers. The film deviates from the book in a number of ways, most conspicuously introducing a romantic interest for Maxwell's character, in the form of a local doctor played by Virginia McKenna; and in the film Mij comes from a pet shop in London rather than from the marshes of southern Iraq. Although the singing of the title song over the end credits by Val Doonican is not exactly the film's high point, there is some outstanding wildlife photography, and the playful otters are fun and appealing, if somewhat destructive of the human environments in which they are placed (such as, at one point, the London to Inverness sleeper train).

The film was one of a number of wildlife-oriented family films that were briefly fashionable in the late 1960s: McKenna and Travers, who were married when the film was made, had three years earlier starred in *Born Free,* a film about the raising of a lioness cub named Elsa, who for a time was as well-known as Edal the otter. Location filming for *Ring of Bright Water* took place in the village of Ellenabeich on the island of Seil in the Inner Hebrides, whose distinctive rows of whitewashed former miners' cottages look just the same today as they did when the film was made. The busy fishing harbor at Mallaig also gets a brief look-in in a couple of scenes.

The Highlands in Film and Television

Ring of Bright Water is certainly not the only film to have made good use of Scotland's scenic coastline. *Local Hero,* made in 1983, features an equally picturesque setting amidst the soft coastal landscape of the West Highlands. The film is a quirky tale about a multinational oil company based in Texas that attempts to buy up a remote Scottish fishing village and turn the site into an oil refinery. "This will be the petro-chemical capital of the free world… it will even survive the next ice age," gushes an oil executive, clambering around a huge model of the beautiful landscape they plan to destroy. But the young junior executive who comes over from Houston is seduced by the slow pace of life in the village and comes up against some locals who are prepared to indulge in some unexpectedly hard bargaining

The village of Pennan, location for *Local Hero* (Tom Jervis/Wikimedia Commons)

when it comes to selling their land. Gently pro-environment and anti-big-business, this comedy provided an early outing for the actors John Gordon Sinclair and Peter Capaldi, and for the director Bill Forsyth and producer David Puttnam; the head honcho of the Texas oil giant is played by the American veteran Burt Lancaster, who flies noisily into the village on a helicopter in the final scene.

The broad, sandy beach on which a number of scenes were filmed is the one at Morar, near Mallaig, one of the best-known bucket-and-spade holiday beaches in Scotland; the film's fictional village of Ferness is actually Pennan, a seaside village situated away from the Highlands on the blustery east coast of Scotland between Banff and Fraserburgh. A hundred miles separate the beach and the village, which in the film are supposed to be adjacent. Bill Forsyth maintains that the only person who ever noticed this was a geology student at the University of St. Andrews who commented that the stone from which the houses in the village are built was geologically incompatible with the rocks backing the beach. With its deadpan humor *Local Hero* has garnered something of a cult reputation over the years, and today at least one off-beat travel agency offers a trip around the various locations where the film was shot.

Local Hero and *Ring of Bright Water* offer viewers a glimpse of Scotland's coastal scenery under the soft light and gentle weather of summer. But winter on the coast of Scotland is a very different affair. *Breaking the Waves*, a 1996 film made by the Danish director Lars von Trier, is set in a remote fishing village outwardly similar to that in which the action of *Local Hero* takes place. But in *Breaking the Waves* the attitudes of the villagers during the hard Scottish winter are as harsh and as cold as the squally weather and iron-gray skies. The film was made by a Danish crew but with a cast of largely British actors, and tells the story of a naïve, emotionally fragile young woman named Bess MacNeil (an extraordinary performance by Emily Watson) who marries an oil worker (played by the Swedish actor Stellan Skarsgård) only for him to be seriously injured in an accident on an oil rig. She then attempts to cure her husband's paralysis by engaging in casual sexual encounters with strangers from the town and from the boats that moor occasionally out at sea. Not surprisingly Bess is spurned as an outcast by the town's strict religious community, whose church has no bells and whose elders conduct funeral services that readily condemn to hell those who they consider to have sinned.

Some of the most striking scenes of this long, austere, and challenging film were shot at the stark, whitewashed church that stands on an isolated spot at Lochailort in the West Highlands; the harbor at Mallaig, the beach at Morar (clearly a popular location venue for filmmakers), and remote roads across the Isle of Skye also help to create a setting as harsh and raw as the drama of the film itself, which won the Grand Jury Prize at the Cannes film festival.

A more recent film that also sets an emotionally raw story amidst the bleakness of a seaside winter in the Highlands is *Shell* (2013), the action of which takes place entirely in a filling station situated beside a remote and often deserted stretch of coastal road. Shell is a seventeen-year-old girl who serves customers in the filling station's shop and looks after her epileptic father in the cramped, tatty residential apartment that adjoins it. The film magnificently captures the rhythm of life in the off-season in northwestern Scotland: the rain batters down remorselessly, the wind flaps at the awnings of the filling station, and Shell admits to a passing motorist that in winter they often do not see a car for a week. The sea, the mountains and the backdrop of the An Teallach range in Wester Ross provide a compelling setting for this bleak tale (the tumbledown filling station that the filmmakers built looked so authentic that passing motorists often stopped there, thinking it would supply them with fuel). The film was shot at Dundonnell near Ullapool, where the fifty-strong crew provided a welcome boost to the local hotel and catering trade when they made the film in October 2011. On the film's release the Highland Council announced that it was pleased with the result and expected it to boost tourism in the region—an odd response given the film's uncompromisingly bleak setting.

Away from the blustery coast of Scotland the typical lochs-and-glens scenery of the Highlands has provided settings for dozens of films over the decades. Most employ the scenery as an appealing and dramatic backdrop to the film's action—but in one film at least the scenery of the Highlands is presented as a complete turn-off. Danny Boyle's raw, unsettling and often very funny 1996 adaptation of Irvine Welsh's novel *Trainspotting* is one of the most striking films ever made in Scotland. Much of the action takes place in a dreary suburb of Edinburgh, where the main characters live a deadbeat life of drinking and drug-taking in a squalid flat. But at one point they abandon their sordid lives in the city and come to the

Highlands intending to do a spot of healthy hiking. As the train trundles away from Corrour station, having deposited our heroes in the middle of Rannoch Moor, one of the characters, Renton, played by Ewan MacGregor, grimly demands "Now what?" only to be met with the curt response from the rather more enthusiastic Tommy, "We go for a walk." "What?" "A walk." "Where?" Tommy points in the direction of a distant peak dusted with snow. "There!" "Are you serious?" At this, Tommy gushes over the scenery and asks, "Doesn't it make you proud to be Scottish?" This question elicits a response from Renton that has since entered the annals of cult movie history. "No!" Renton sounds off. "It's shite being Scottish! We're the lowest of the low… the most miserable, servile, pathetic trash that was ever shat into civilization." Not surprisingly the quartet ends up back in Edinburgh pretty quickly. To this day, nearly twenty years after the film was made, fans of the movie come to the wooden bridge over the burn near the station to recreate this famous scene for themselves.

The characters in Robert Louis Stevenson's adventure yarn *Kidnapped* spend rather more time on Rannoch Moor—hiding amidst the deserted bogland as fugitives—and inevitably the moor has had something of a starring role in the numerous film adaptations made of the novel over the years. One adaptation, made in 1971, starred a mustachioed and tousle-haired Michael Caine as the Jacobite hero Alan Breck Stewart, who supports a broad Scots accent with definite hints of London cockney. The film gives the character of the young hero, David Balfour, a putative love interest in the form of a buxom young farm girl, but does away with Balfour being a suspect in the murder of Colin Campbell of Glenure, which was the narrative focus of Stevenson's novel (elements of *Catriona,* the sequel to *Kidnapped,* were incorporated into the screenplay). The pace of the film is somewhat sluggish but the scenery is undeniably pretty. *Kidnapped* has been adapted for television and film at least twelve other times since the advent of moving pictures, including a silent film from 1917, a Disney version from 1960 in which Peter O'Toole made his first ever screen appearance, and versions made in both East and West Germany, in 1968 and 1978 respectively.

In 1995, with the release of the epic films *Rob Roy* and *Braveheart,* Hollywood seemed suddenly to embrace Walter-Scott-style, blood-and-thunder, tartan-and-bagpipes sagas set in the Highlands of old. Both films tell the story of Scottish rebels. In *Braveheart* Mel Gibson (who also directed the film) plays William Wallace, who raised a Scottish army against the English invasion of Edward I in the early fourteenth century. Gibson's account is bombastic and somewhat fanciful, unfolding over a three-hour running time (with some extraordinarily shot and very drawn-out battle sequences). The opening sequence, all misty mountains and faux-Celtic music playing over the main titles, gives a good flavor of what is to come. Only a small part of the film was shot in the Highlands—principally the opening scenes detailing Wallace's childhood in a rain-lashed Glen Nevis—and much of the rest was made in Ireland (and is set in England and the Scottish lowlands).

The scenery of the Highlands is much better seen in *Rob Roy*, which was shot entirely on location in Scotland, with a number of scenes, once again, filmed in Glen Nevis. Owing nothing to Walter Scott's novel, the film stars Liam Neeson as the eponymous Highland hero who risks his life to secure his honor after he is falsely accused of stealing. Another tartan-soaked Hollywood vision of the Highlands is *Highlander* (1986), though unlike *Braveheart* and *Rob Roy* this is nonsense, telling the story of a supposedly immortal warrior who was born in the Highlands and has somehow ended up in contemporary New York. "I am Connor MacLeod of the Clan MacLeod. I was born in 1518 in the village of Glenfinnan on the shores of Loch Shiel," announces the "Highlander" (Christopher Lambert) shortly before his showdown in the Big Apple with the evil Kurgan. "And," he goes on, almost as an afterthought, "I am immortal." Sean Connery plays the Highlander's mentor as a curious Spanish-Scottish version of Obi Wan Kenobi (from *Star Wars*) in a film rich in terrible acting, hopelessly portentous dialogue, and woefully strung-out action sequences.

A number of scenes in *Highlander* were filmed at Eilean Donan Castle, the island fortress near Kyle of Lochalsh picturesquely linked to the mainland by an arched bridge. The architectural ensemble of bridge and castle seems to perfectly fit the shape of a rectangular cinema screen, and not surprisingly this castle has a regular featured role in many other Highland-set films. These include *The Master of Ballantrae,* a 1953 swashbuckler starring Errol Flynn, loosely based on a Robert Louis Stevenson novel, and set during Bonnie Prince Charlie's 1745 uprising; and more recently the James Bond film *The World is Not Enough* (1999) in which the castle appears as the northern base of the British secret service. In 2012

Bond made a return to the Highlands—where he was born and brought up, according to Ian Fleming's original novels—in the magnificent *Skyfall.* But the production crew only spent two days in Scotland, filming Bond driving through gloomy Glen Etive with spymaster M at his side. The sequences that followed, an explosive finale set in Bond's allegedly ancestral Highland home, were actually filmed on a set constructed in very different surroundings near Elstead in Surrey.

Giving Eilean Donan Castle a run for its money as a location for filming in the Highlands is Ardverikie House, the epitome of a gray-granite Scottish baronial pile. The place boasts a profusion of pointed conical turrets and a picturesque backdrop of forest and mountain for the cameras to lovingly frame and drift over. No wonder filmmakers love the trek to the shores of Loch Laggan, situated on the Spean Bridge to Kingussie road, to film here. The house stood in for Balmoral in *Mrs. Brown*, the screen account of the relationship between Queen Victoria and her Highland servant, John Brown, and often featured in the BBC's popular Sunday evening comedy-drama *Monarch of the Glen*. The estate is in private hands and the house opens its doors only rarely to visitors—much to the disappointment of *Monarch of the Glen* fans who come to stare at its closed front gates.

Other soft-focus tartan-and-shortbread television dramas from the Highlands have included the detective series *Hamish Macbeth,* filmed in the colorful seaside village of Plockton near Kyle of Lochalsh, and the long-forgotten afternoon soap opera *Take the High Road*, which crews from Grampian Television filmed in Luss beside Loch Lomond. And then there is the animated children's TV series *Balamory* which takes the colorful houses picturesquely gathered around the harbor of Tobermory on Mull as the inspiration for both its title and its chocolate-box setting.

Children have also been well served by feature films set in the Highlands. In 2012 the Pixar division of Disney released *Brave,* a tale of a tomboyish Scottish princess, characterized by spectacular computer generated animation and Highland clichés (kilts, castles, lochs, and mists a-plenty). In 2007 a film adaptation was made of Dick King-Smith's children's novel *Waterhorse*, in which a young boy finds a mysterious egg on the shores of Loch Ness that hatches into a monster; exhilarating scenery, an impressive computer-generated monster, and a winning performance from the child actor Alex Etel as the boy Angus distinguish this engaging family movie, in which both Urquhart and Eilean Donan castles make brief appearances.

Waterhorse is one of a number of feature films inspired by Loch Ness and its famous monster, which are among the most iconic features of Scotland for foreigners who know little about the country. One of the earliest was *The Secret of the Loch,* made in 1934, in which a scientist and journalist join forces to attempt to prove the monster's existence, and which was edited by a young David Lean at the start of his career. The most notable West of Scotland-set film from this golden era of British filmmaking, however, is the 1945 *I Know Where I'm Going*, which was filmed and set on the Isle of Mull, and tells the story of a headstrong young woman from Manchester, Joan Webster, who comes to the island hoping to marry a wealthy landowner but finds herself bewitched by both the scenery and the local laird, Torquil MacNeil.

Picturesque castles, rollicking ceilidhs, and noisy bagpipers decorate the scene while the supporting characters include an eccentric aristocrat who trains hawks and a haughtily obnoxious schoolgirl played by twelve-year-old Petula Clark. Fierce gales underscore the blossoming romance between Joan (played by Wendy Hiller) and MacNeil (played by Roger Livesey), who nearly drown in the Corryvrechan whirlpool while in a boat, though Livesey calmly continues to smoke his pipe even when it looks like the end is nigh. Other films made at this time include an adaptation of Neil Gunn's novel *The Silver Darlings,* which looks rather dated now despite fine location filming on the Highland coast, and *The Brothers*, set amidst long-standing rivalries between two families on a Scottish island, into the midst of which comes a young housemaid who drives the island's men to lust and murder.

A number of films purportedly set in the Highlands have in reality been filmed elsewhere, in England or Ireland. But there is at least one film with a defiantly English setting that was actually filmed in the Highlands. In his diaries from 1973 Michael Palin indicates that the National Trust for Scotland vetoed most of the proposed filming locations for *Monty Python and the Holy Grail* after reading the script, announcing that the film's tone was "not consistent with the dignity of the fabric of the buildings." In the end Palin, John Cleese *et al* shot the film at Doune Castle, a privately-owned fortress near Callander, before the production moved to Ballachulish and Glencoe, and then on to Killin on Loch Tay. Everywhere they went the cast and crew were beset with problems of incessant rain and difficult-to-access mountainside locations, and at the end of each day's filming the mud-spattered cast fell over themselves in their haste to race back to hotels where the hot water was only switched on for a few hours each day.

While filming at Killin Palin grumbled that "we couldn't even find a shop to buy a postcard with 'Greetings from Dull' written on it" (there would be no difficulty today, particularly since the village of Dull twinned itself with the town of Boring in Oregon in June 2012 for the specific purpose of promoting tourism to both places). Such was the film's low budget that Palin often found himself driving the production unit's rented van up and down the main road through Glencoe dressed in his knight's costume of chain mail, while villagers from Ballachulish were recruited as extras for some of the battle scenes for the princely fee of £2 ($3.50) per day.

Part Four

VISITORS

Salmon fishing near Taymouth Castle, *The Illustrated Dramatic and Sporting News*, April 1884

The first "visitors" to the Highlands were of course the first settlers, who came here when the ice from the last ice age finally melted away. The first chapter of this book has provided an account of the visitors who came afterwards: the Romans and then the Vikings; the Irish monks who, guided by the example of St. Columba, became the first travelers in the Highlands as we would understand the term today; and the English, who in the Middle Ages came as invaders, but who by the end of the eighteenth century were visiting as tourists, beguiled by the scenery that was so venerated by the thinkers of the new Romantic age.

In fact tourists were fairly thick on the ground even before the influential writing of Wordsworth and Keats: as early as 1759 Lord Breadalbane had been driven to comment that "it has been the fashion this year to travel into the Highlands," and by 1773 the venerable aristocrat wrote that he was beginning to find the number of English visitors seeking lodgings at his home to be something of a burden.

That year, 1773, turned out to be the most auspicious year in the history of Highland tourism, as it was then that Samuel Johnson and his companion James Boswell made their tour of the region. Both published widely-read accounts of their journeys and, as we have seen in the previous chapter, the Romantic poets soon trailed in their wake; all unwittingly served as the first tourism promotion agency for the Highlands, popularizing the area for "ordinary" visitors, who began to visit in large numbers in the early years of the nineteenth century when the Napoleonic Wars rendered travel to the burgeoning tourist spots of Europe off-limits. By the 1820s hostelries that had previously only seen the likes of livestock drovers, traders, and smugglers pass their way were beginning to open their doors (and improve their accommodation) for tourists. At the same time, spa towns and coastal resorts on the fringes of the Highlands also became fashionable as destinations for the new generations of travelers, just as they had in neighboring England.

In the twentieth century long-distance hiking, "adventure" tourism, and skiing have been added to the tourism mix that the Highlands has to offer. Nowadays visitors come from all over the world, and in summer the mountains resound to a mix of foreign languages; everything from German to Korean can be heard in the most popular spots. But none of these tourists could ever have made inroads into the Highlands without there being a means of bringing them to the mountains in the first place.

THE ROADS TO THE ISLES: FROM DROVERS' TRACKS TO DUAL CARRIAGEWAYS

Farms and settlements in the Highlands had been linked together by a network of paths well before the advent of the Middle Ages, thanks to the footfalls of generations of farmers, traders, monks, and cattle thieves, known as "reivers" to Highlanders. In the seventeenth and eighteenth centuries a number of these paths became the favored routes taken by drovers and their animals, linking farms in the Highlands and Inner Hebrides with the great livestock markets in Falkirk and Crieff in the south, where animals were sold to English livestock dealers, and where drovers would spend their earnings on the drink and prostitutes available in the towns. One Highland drover from this era whose name slipped into legend was John Cameron of Corriechoille, near Spean Bridge. He was raised in drove traditions as a boy, minding the stock for the passing drovers who were taking a dram at his father's toll house; in his adult life he drove stock across the mountains to Falkirk for fifty-five years, and he died in 1856 a rich man.

Drove roads such as the ones trodden by John Cameron became intensively used, and tiny settlements such as Bridge of Orchy on the main route from Skye to the lowlands would see a hundred thousand head of cattle and ten thousand sheep pass through each year. Drovers usually walked back home unaccompanied after selling their animals at market: traveling through the Drumochter Pass in 1861, Queen Victoria recorded in her journal seeing "many drovers, without their herds and flocks, returning… from Falkirk." Not surprisingly the life of drovers has proved an inspiration for poets and novelists, not least Kathleen Fidler, the most accomplished twentieth-century Scottish writer of children's fiction. Her 1955 novel *The Droving Lad* concerns an eleven-year-old farm boy whose father keeps cattle on the slopes of Loch Leven, and who leads his father's animals across the Highlands to the great cattle fair at Falkirk—only to meet with disaster when the family's prime bull is stolen.

A number of drovers' routes required the animals to take to the water and swim across narrow sea inlets or wide rivers. As they swam, their masters would herd them as best they could from boats bobbing alongside. The writer Edmund Burt, traveling through the Highlands in the 1720s, saw such a crossing, and observed that the cows took "to the water like

The Kingshouse Hotel, Glencoe, formerly a drovers' hostel and military rest-stop, now one of the most famous hotels in the Highlands (Andrew Beattie)

spaniels... their drivers made a hideous cry to urge them forwards... I thought it a very odd sight to see so many noses and mouths just above the water." One such route was from the north tip of the island of Kerrera to Dunollie, across the narrow sound at the entrance to the bay in which Oban sits. The stone enclosures at Slatrich Bay on Kerrera, where the animals were gathered before making the crossing, are still visible today.

Many of these ancient drovers' paths were turned into more substantial roads in the eighteenth century, following the crushing by English forces of the Jacobite rebellions in 1715 and 1746. The fear of further rebellion meant that thousands of troops had to be stationed in the Highlands (particularly around Fort William and Inverness), and these men needed to be moved around the region swiftly in the event of further rebellion. So the army instigated a frenzy of road building, under the auspices of General Wade and then Major Caulfeild. (The routes taken by some of these roads have already been discussed in Part Two.) To help with the movement of troops a number of refuges were built in remote spots where companies of soldiers could be billeted for the night. The most famous of these is the Kingshouse Hotel on the borders of Rannoch Moor and Glencoe, which became popular both with soldiers and drovers crossing the mountains, and is today the haunt of tired and thirsty walkers on the West Highland Way. Kathleen Fidler describes the place as the venue for "a great cooking of broth… and setting of meals before strangers" in *The Droving Lad*. Her novel is set in the early nineteenth century, when the inn was a place where drovers could gather to discuss the state of the roads on their journey ahead—and whether it was better to pay the tolls to use the new roads or to save their money and use the older paths trodden by their forebears.

The roads built by Caulfeild and Wade served their purpose for only a few decades, and in 1803 the great engineer Thomas Telford was commissioned to construct a new generation of roads to supersede them. He built them with gentle gradients, sturdy bridges across rivers (rather than fords) and a good depth of gravel to protect the hoofs of animals as well as the springs of carriages. By 1822 some 920 miles of roads had been constructed under Telford's auspices. Some of these lie under the tarmac of today's main roads through the Highlands, which were simply built over the top of them; others are now just paths and tracks. The trail that walkers on the West Highland Way follow across Rannoch Moor, between Bridge of Orchy and the entrance to Glencoe, follows one of Telford's old roads, which itself became redundant in 1933 when the modern A82 Glasgow to Fort William road was built along a slightly different course to the east of it.

Telford's other engineering projects in the Highlands included a number of new bridges, such as the handsome seven-arched bridge across the River Tay linking the small towns of Dunkeld and Birnam, commissioned by the fourth Duke of Atholl and completed in 1809; the bridge still carries traffic and a plaque on the parapet, unveiled by the eleventh duke in 2009, celebrates the bicentenary of its opening. Telford's most characteristic bridge, however, is one of his earliest—an elegant but very steep humped-backed bridge known as the "Bridge over the Atlantic" at Clachan that still carries the B844 from Oban across a narrow sliver of sea to the island of Seil.

More recently, a number of road projects across the Highlands have been carried out with funds from local and national government, and from the European Union. The most visually striking—and expensive—of these are the new bridges that carry roads across the wide sea lochs and estuaries that punctuate the west coast of the Highlands, which is one of the most indented and irregular in the world. In the late 1970s the Ballachulish ferry, which took motorists on the A82 across a narrow inlet of the sea that stretched over ten miles inland, was replaced by a new and very substantial cantilever bridge, whose bottle-green girders still guide traffic way above Loch Linnhe; and in 1994 the same improvement was made at Kylescu in the far northwest, when a graceful, award-winning bridge was built over the mouths of Lochs Glencoul and Glendhu, so replacing a ferry journey or a hundred-mile detour inland.

The most controversial piece of new road infrastructure by far has been the bridge linking Kyle of Lochalsh with the Isle of Skye, opened in 1995 to replace the brief ferry journey from Kyle across to Kyleakin. This brought an end to the waiting "queue of stationary vehicles," which according to the naturalist Gavin Maxwell in his book *Raven Seek Thy Brother* would "occasionally stretch for a quarter of a mile or more inland." The bridge was privately financed by an Anglo-German consortium and cost £30 million ($50.6 million) to construct. On its opening the tolls were some of the highest anywhere in Europe, but a concerted campaign by locals forced the authorities to remove the toll booths in 2004 and there is now no charge to use the bridge.

The First Travel Writers

The eighteenth and nineteenth centuries were the era of the gentleman travel writer. Dozens of men, often middle-aged and frequently clergymen, would travel in the British Isles, Europe, America, or even further afield, and then publish their observations in volumes to fill the libraries of well-to-do armchair readers who preferred to stay at home in the city rather than embark on adventurous journeys of their own. By the end of the nineteenth century the genre was so popular that Mark Twain was able to satirize it in his classic book *An Innocent Abroad,* which described his travels through Europe in a way that often mimicked and mocked the style of those who had gone before him. Mark Twain did not include Scotland in his travels but plenty of others did. Among the first was a resident of Skye named Martin Martin, whose 1703 book *A Description of the Western Isles of Scotland* recounted his travels through the Inner and Outer Hebrides.

In the book's preface Martin admits that these islands were, at that time, "but little known, or considered, not only by strangers, but even by those under the same government and climate." Martin was a Gaelic speaker and clearly knew the region well, but little is known about his life and background beyond the fact that he was born around 1669 and spent the later part of his life in Paris, Leiden, and London. His research in the Inner and Outer Hebrides was sponsored by Royal Society, and it is clear that one of Martin's purposes was to describe the area with a view to suggesting improvements that could be made to the economy and living conditions of the people living there. (One of his suggestions was that the government in London should do more to encourage commercial mining, fishing, and sheep farming in the islands.)

The book is something of an unstructured and muddled affair, however, a hodgepodge of observations into the history and geography of the Hebrides which focuses on some islands and ignores others, and is stuffed so thoroughly with descriptions and facts that no room is left for the author's personality to seep through. Martin was writing well before Romantic sensibilities had informed intellectual views on landscape, and he says virtually nothing about the scenery through which he traveled—dramatic, dull, bleak, or otherwise. Instead he indicates in his preface that he has "everywhere taken notice of the nature and climate of the soil, of the produce of the places by sea and land, and of the remarkable cures performed by the natives." The latter is a particular source of fascination: throughout Martin describes a veritable cauldron of cures and remedies used by locals to treat their aches and illnesses. He also looks at "instances of heathenism and pagan superstition, [although] only a few of the oldest and most ignorant of the vulgar are guilty of them." As we have seen in Chapter Three, the most notorious of ancient beliefs that he describes is the phenomenon of second sight, though other instances of paganism are also dealt with, particularly in Catholic areas of the Hebrides (Martin's devout Presbyterianism lends the work a fairly obvious and unashamed bias).

The Isle of Skye receives particular attention in the book. Martin says little about the Cuillins, the dramatic spine of mountains for which Skye is famous, beyond their role in influencing the island's climate, maintaining that they are "the cause of much rain, by breaking the clouds that hover about [the mountain range], which quickly pour down in rain upon the quarter on which the wind then blows." He is more interested in the island's economy and society, his research revealing that there is little arable farming, with the island's inhabitants living mainly off the bounty of the sea. "The natives preserve and dry their herrings without salt, for the space of eight months, provided they be taken [from the sea] after the tenth of September," he writes. "They use no other art in it, but take out their guts, and then tying a rush around their necks, hang them by pairs upon a rope made of heath." The fish thus dried are reported as being tasty and "free from putrefaction."

At Bernisdale Martin is told that the shellfish are "plumper" during the time of the waxing of the moon and when there is a southwest wind. Away from fishing, marble is quarried—"I have seen cups made of the white [marble] which is very fine"—but there is clearly an opportunity to diversify the local economy. "In many places the soil is proper for wheat, and that the grass is good, is evident from the great product of their cattle," he observes. "So if the natives were taught and encouraged to take pains to improve their corn and hay, to plant, enclose, and manure their ground, drain lakes, sow wheat and peas, and plant orchards and kitchen gardens, they might have as great plenty of all things for the furtherance of mankind, as any other people in Europe."

Martin's book is a long way from being a travelogue that can sit comfortably beside those of Paul Theroux or even Samuel Johnson. There are no reflections on people the author meets, and the section on Staffa has nothing about Fingal's Cave. The next major book about the Highlands, though, takes the genre a stage further. It was written by an engineer named Edmund Burt who had been contracted to work on the new military roads, and its author is, like Martin, rather more interested in the economy and society of the Highlands rather than the scenery. Burt's book, *Letters from a Gentleman in the North of Scotland,* takes the form of a series of letters that he wrote in the 1720s to a London friend. Unlike other travelers in the Highlands Burt actually lived in the region, taking trips from his home in Inverness into the surrounding countryside. He describes at first hand the "melancholy consequences of the want of manufactories" in Inverness, and the limited diet of the poor of that town, including "their wretched food [that] makes them look pot-bellied." And he is appalled both by the "most horrid look" of the seals he sees from the bridge over the River Ness and by the washerwomen with "feet red as blood with cold" who spend their days stamping on their washing in tubs beside its banks. But Burt admits that describing the landscape through which he travels beyond Inverness is his "most difficult task."

True to the pre-Romantic sensibilities of the early eighteenth century, he finds no dramatic scenery or sublime grandeur. Instead he is made miserable by the all-pervading "horrid gloom" of the mountains and by the "dirty yellowish" color of the gushing mountain streams. Out in the hills he comes across "huge naked rocks [that] produced the disagreeable appearance of a scabbed head" and wonders "of what use can be such monstrous excrescences." In short, he much prefers Richmond Hill just outside London to anything the Highlands can offer. On one trip he "hugged himself" when he "got clear of the mountains" and their "barren and tedious" scenery. Yet Burt is impressed by the honesty and kindness of Highlanders, and says that he feels safer traveling in the mountains than he would walking "from London to Highgate."

Forty years after Burt's peregrinations an Anglo-Irish cleric named Richard Pococke was busy following in some of his footsteps. Born in 1704, Pococke's father was headmaster of King Edward VI School in Southampton and his uncle was a clergyman in Ireland, which gave the young Pococke a route into the Church that eventually culminated in his appointments as Archdeacon of Dublin and Bishop of Meath and Ossory. But throughout his life Pococke combined serving the Church with the life of a travel writer. In the 1730s he traveled extensively in continental Europe and the Middle East, and during these extensive journeys he proved himself something of an eccentric, climbing up to the Mer de Glace in the French Alps in a turban, sandals, and a kaftan. Widely-read travelogues describing his journeys followed.

His first visit to Scotland came in 1747, the year after Culloden, and he visited for a second time in 1760 when he embarked on an extensive tour that took him from Dumfries and the Borders all the way to Orkney. His accounts of these journeys were published as *A Tour in Scotland,* and take the form of letters to his mother or sister, both of whom are addressed rather stiffly as "Dear Madam." The text that follows the opening appellation is similarly formal. Pococke is very thorough on the architecture, geology, ecclesiastical history, and monuments of Scotland but like Martin Martin he rarely says anything about the people he meets, nor does he describe the scenery through which he travels (although the landscape around

Loch Awe and Loch Leven is described as "beautiful"—an adjective that Martin never comes close to using).

On his trip Pococke traveled along the new military roads, which he noted had the distance from Edinburgh marked off on milestones, and he sought lodgings with clergymen, although the Duke of Atholl also put him up in Blair Castle. In a letter to his sister Pococke gives an exhaustive description of the Battle of Culloden in typically dry and ponderous detail, even including a map showing the battle plan. But his description is devoid of any sentiment—and so are his meticulously recorded dimensions and plans of castles and churches. Even a trip to wild and remote Cape Wrath provokes a painstakingly detailed description of the flora and fauna he encounters there, with no real comments about what the place was actually like. Perhaps not surprisingly Pococke's papers languished unpublished for a hundred years after his death, finally seeing the light of day in 1887 as a result of the efforts of the Scottish Historical Society.

The next book to be shelved alongside those of Burt and Martin was written by John Knox (1720–90): not the Scottish firebrand preacher of the same name but a bookseller on London's fashionable Strand who took up writing in his retirement. Knox had two sponsors for his sixteen trips to Scotland. One was the Highland Society of London, a "convivial club" according to Knox, "who met to enjoy themselves according to the customs of their country" (which largely seemed to involve listening to bagpipe music and drinking whisky). The second was the British Fisheries Society and its funding of Knox's tours lends his book the same flavor as Martin's: like his forebear Knox suggested a number of ways in which the economy of the Highlands could be improved (such as developing new fishing ports along the lines of those recently established in Nova Scotia).

Opening his book *A Tour Through the Highlands of Scotland and the Hebride Isles* with a rather dry survey of Highland history and economy (including a description of some of the first Clearances), Knox then praises the "entertaining [and] instructive" work of Thomas Pennant but pours scorn on that of Dr. Johnson, whose book, he suggests, would be "invaluable" were it "stripped of some illiberal epithets"—a reference to Johnson's Jacobite sympathies. This lengthy introduction is then followed by a description of his tour. He likes Strathearn and finds a number of other valleys "pleasant" but, true to form with his fellow eighteenth-century writers, he says little about the scenery and his writing mostly consists of a dry survey of historical sites, agricultural production, quarrying, and commercial fishing. Yet a wry journalistic comment does sometimes get through: approaching a pub in Inch Kenneth, "we had the mortification to find the doors shut and the people in bed," while an evening spent with the corporal at the military barracks in Glenelg ends in a good deal of snuff being taken and whisky imbibed.

One of the authors Knox admired was Thomas Pennant, whose work he praises fulsomely, finding it to be both "entertaining" and "instructive." Knox was a better critic than he was a writer and Pennant's work has indeed endured much better than his own. Pennant, one of the most eminent naturalists of the day and a fellow of the Royal Society, undertook his first Scottish tour in 1769, traveling twelve hundred miles in nine weeks (which later led James Boswell to complain that his travels were rather superficial). He was a Hanoverian—but he was unfailingly compassionate towards the recently defeated Highlanders: "Their forbearance proves them to be superior to the meanness of retaliation... [they are] hospitable to the highest degree," he wrote. In his book Pennant considers the history, geology, customs, tradition, wildlife, and architecture of the places through which he travels, writing about them all with undisguised

Illustration from Pennant's *A Tour in Scotland and Voyage to the Hebrides,* 1774

enthusiasm (in Fortingall near Aberfeldy he measured the circumference of the famously ancient yew tree that stands beside the church and found it to be just over fifty-six feet).

Yet what is most striking about both his *Tour in Scotland,* published in 1771, and his later *Tour in Scotland and Voyage to the Hebrides* of 1774, is how infused his comments are with the new sentiments of the Romantic and the sublime. Entering the Highlands at Dunkeld, Pennant writes: "the pass... is awfully magnificent; high, craggy, and often naked mountains present themselves to view... overhanging and darkening the Tay, that rolls with great rapidity beneath." From the estate of the Duke of Atholl further along the valley he admires "the most beautiful and picturesque views of wild and gloomy nature that can be conceived." To the west, around Loch Tay, the mountains have "an alpine look, but particularly resemble the great slope opposite the Grande Chartreuse in Dauphiné... a most romantic situation, prettily wooded [where there are] beautiful walks amid the trees." The Fall of Fyers near Loch Ness takes the form of a "vast cataract, in a darksome glen of a stupendous depth," while the "scenery begins to grow very romantic" as Kinlochleven is approached from Fort William, with "vast mountains" rising above bodies of "solemn water." The gulf between Pennant's style and that of Martin Martin could not be wider, and Pennant's is unquestionably the first piece of modern travel writing on the region. "He's the best traveller I ever read," Samuel Johnson later wrote. "He observes more things than anyone else does... Pennant seems to have seen a great deal which we did not see. When we travel again let us look better about us."

Boswell and Johnson

It was Pennant's writing that, in part, inspired Johnson to visit the Highlands and the Hebrides. He did so in the autumn of 1773 in the company of his friend and future biographer, James Boswell. Both men subsequently published journals recounting their journeys: Johnson's was published as *A Journey to the Western Isles of Scotland* while Boswell entitled his work *A Journal of a Tour to the Hebrides.* Johnson's was the work that most clearly follows the lexicon of the modern travel book, its author relentlessly curious (and often highly compassionate) about the places he traveled through and the people he encountered, from lairds and gentry to impoverished folk eking out a living in the Highlands or on the islands of Skye and Coll.

Boswell's work, which is twice as long as Johnson's, is less an account of Scotland and the journey Boswell undertook with his friend, and more an observation of Johnson himself: "my principal object was to delineate Dr. Johnson's manner and character... I shall be the one who will most faithfully do honour to his memory," he noted. In many ways Boswell's work foreshadows the biography of Johnson that he would famously write after the great man's death, with instances of Dr. Johnson's famed conversation and wit preserved word for word in the journal, sometimes in the format of a script for a play.

Boswell (1740–95) was much the younger of the two men who set out north from London in August 1773. He was a Scot, born in Edinburgh and a graduate of that city's university, and had traveled widely in Europe (writing a book on Corsica) before meeting Johnson in 1763 when he was just twenty-two. Johnson (1709–84) was by then a giant of English letters: an essayist, a poet, a critic, and a lexicographer, and the dominant cultural figure of his age. In the year of their great journey Johnson was a comparatively old man of sixty-three, while Boswell was just half his age. But Johnson noted that he had found "in Mr Boswell a companion whose acuteness would help my enquiry, and whose gaiety of conversation and civility of manners are sufficient to counteract the inconveniences of travel." Both had Catholic and Jacobite sympathies, though kept them hidden—their tour took place, after all, less than thirty years after the defeat of the Jacobite cause at Culloden. Although both emphasize the Highlands in the titles of their publications, their journeys and journals actually covered much of mainland Scotland, including the areas away from the mountains: they traveled in the Borders and in Ayrshire, and along the northeast coast around Nairn and Elgin, as well as in the Inner Hebrides and the West Highlands. They did not visit any part of the country north of Inverness, however; the two men's curiosity and ability to put up with poor roads and chilly accommodation apparently did not stretch to a visit to Caithness, Sutherland, and Ross, let alone Orkney or Shetland.

They set out from London in the middle of August, arriving in the Highlands in the autumn—a late season for traveling, but necessitated by Boswell having to attend the Court of Session in London where he practised as an advocate. In the Hebrides they caught the brunt of October

BOSWELL'S

JOURNAL OF

A TOUR TO THE HEBRIDES

WITH SAMUEL JOHNSON, LL.D.

ILLUSTRATED.

JOHNSON ON A HIGHLAND SHELTIE.—*Page* 225.

(FORMING VOL. V. OF BOSWELL'S LIFE OF JOHNSON.)

LONDON:
OFFICE OF THE NATIONAL ILLUSTRATED LIBRARY,
227, STRAND.

gales, which left them marooned on islands several times, waiting for the wind to drop. This caused Dr. Johnson to suffer terribly from seasickness (Boswell, it appears, had better sea legs). A particularly nasty gale blew up as they sailed from the Isle of Skye to Mull, where in the words of Dr. Johnson they "were doomed to experience… the danger of trusting to the wind, which blew against us, in a short time, with such violence, that we, being no seasoned sailors, were willing to call it a tempest." The storm blew them off course and resulted in an unscheduled landing on the island of Coll.

While journeys between the islands of the Inner Hebrides were undertaken on fishing boats, on land the two men traveled on horseback, trotting along the military roads constructed earlier in the century; and at Boleskine they stayed in the lodging that General Wade had built while surveying his new military road, just as Richard Pococke had done some thirteen years previously. The lodging was, according to Johnson, "a house of entertainment for passengers and we found it not ill stocked with provisions." The quality of the road Wade had built was the subject of much comment as they traveled along it: at one point beyond the north banks of Loch Ness Dr. Johnson noted that the military road coped with a severe gradient by zig-zagging up a hillside, the road "cut in traverses, so that as we went upon a higher stage, we saw the baggage following us below in a contrary direction." Further on in the "dreariness of solitude" the pair passed a group of soldiers mending the road, and gave them a present, as a token of how well they had been treated when they had stayed in Fort Augustus near the shores of Loch Ness. Away from the military forts that sprinkled the Highlands, they also stayed at inns and in the grand houses of Scottish lairds, the quality of whose libraries always drew comments from the two literary travelers; and on one occasion they slept in a barn, amongst the hay, with pillows borrowed from curious villagers.

Throughout the journey Dr. Johnson expressed curiosity about practically everything: how it took an hour to make a pair of brogues from bark or animal hides; how the oatmeal cakes on Skye were "coarse and hard, to which unaccustomed palates are not easily reconciled," and how barley cakes were thicker and softer; and how most men began their day with a glass of whisky, a morning dram referred to as a *skalk*. The influence of the weather on people, agriculture, and wildlife was also a point of considerable observation and discussion. On Skye Dr. Johnson admired the quality of gooseberries he picked, and pondered the preponderance of weasels on the island (and the lack of mice or rats); he maintained that there were no beautiful women on Skye because of their exposure "to the rudeness of the climate." The quality of meals was also much discussed: in a number of places on Skye Dr. Johnson's dinner was "much exhilarated by the bagpipes." When the bagpipes were silent, conversation at dinner often resembled that of a London coffeehouse, revolving around literary scandals and reputations and Whig and Tory politics. (Surviving mementoes of the two men's wining and dining include the china tea cups and punch bowl preserved in Eilean Donan castle, from which they drunk during their time on Raasay.)

In short, Johnson's work was the first popular and widely read Highland travel book as we would recognize it today, and although the actual scenery through which he passed was rarely mentioned (and almost never praised) it was responsible in some measure for transforming the trickle of tourists who at that time ventured into the Highlands into something of a stream.

Sir Walter Scott and Queen Victoria: the Creation of "Romantic Scotland"

Johnson and Boswell might have inspired intellectuals and poets to travel in the Highlands. But it was Queen Victoria and the writer Sir Walter Scott who were largely responsible for the huge increase in tourists who descended on Scotland during the nineteenth century. Scott's popularity led to his readers wanting to visit the places in which his Romantic poems and novels were set, while Queen Victoria's very public love affair with the Highlands made a trip to the mountains a hugely fashionable undertaking for many of her wealthier subjects south of the border. Together the writer and the monarch transformed the stream of visitors into a fully-fledged, raging torrent.

As we have already seen, Scott's early poem "The Lady of the Lake" proved to be a huge and immediate hit on its publication in 1810. The romance of the poem, and the drama of its setting around the beautiful Loch Katrine, inspired hordes of Scott's faithful readers to head for the Trossachs. Soon after the poem's publication a ferryman on Loch Lomond, whose shores lie only four miles distant from the western tip of Loch

Katrine, was recorded as bemoaning the enormous popular success of poem and the resultant lack of tourists on Loch Lomond. "I wish I had Scott to ferry over Loch Lomond," he grumbled. "I should be sinking the boat, if I drowned myself into the bargain; for ever since he wrote his 'Lady of the Lake,' as they call it, everyone goes to that filthy hole Loch Katrine... and I have had only two gentlemen to guide all this blessed season."

The ferryman's wishes were granted a few years later when Scott set some of his novel *Rob Roy* on Loch Lomond, "this noble lake," and indicated that readers would "hardly comprehend [its beauty] without going to see it." But the rowing boat operators were only kept busy for a little while: in 1843 the first pleasure steamer arrived on Loch Katrine, putting them out of business. When it mysteriously sank, local rowing boat operators were naturally blamed. But in 1845 the passenger steamer *Rob Roy* was launched, succeeded in 1899 by the *Sir Walter Scott.* This noble vessel, the only steam-driven pleasure steamer in Scotland, continues to ply the waters of the lake to this day, powered by its original engine (though these days using environmentally-friendly smokeless fuel rather than coal).

One of Scott's many enthusiastic readers was a Polish journalist and academic named Krystyn Lach Szyrma, who spent two years at Edinburgh University in the 1820s and heard Scott speaking in the city about his work. After reading "Lady of the Lake," Szyrma was inspired to visit Loch Katrine, where he quickly discovered that others had got there before him. "The genius of Sir Walter Scott has taken these places out of oblivion," he later wrote. "Deserted and unknown beforehand, they are now swarming with people who come from many distant parts, anxious to see their beauty." Another enthusiast was the writer and politician Sir John Sinclair, who wrote to Scott to inform him that the publication of "Lady of the Lake" had "increased the number of tourists [in the Trossachs] beyond measure," and tried to get Scott to compose a sequel to the poem, to be called "Lady of the Sea," which would be set in Sinclair's native Caithness and would be written with the express purpose of boosting tourism there.

The publication of the *Waverley* novels from 1814 onwards brought yet more visitors to Scotland—this time to Loch Lomond and the West Highlands rather than the Trossachs. Scott himself was ambivalent about all the visitors: "Every London citizen makes Loch Lomond his washpot and throws his shoe over Ben Nevis," he once wrote dryly. Nonetheless in

1822 Scott was responsible for organizing the welcoming party that greeted King George IV on his first visit to Scotland, a shindig that the author turned into a riot of bagpipes and tartan, propagating his own fantasy vision of Scotland so adored by early tourists. In its obituary of Scott the *Edinburgh Evening Courant* gave full recognition to the writer's promotion of tourism in the country, commenting wryly that in St. Andrews there were complaints that no-one came to the town as it had never been mentioned in any of Scott's works. The most blatant espousal of Scott as an unofficial tourist promoter for Scotland came later on in the century, when the ferry company Caledonian MacBrayne sponsored the publication of lavishly illustrated "West Highland Editions" of Scott's *Lord of the Isles* and *A Voyage to the Hebrides*. The books included advertisements aimed at tourists and it is not difficult to guess at Scott's reactions to these editions of his work had he still been alive.

George IV had been the first monarch to visit Scotland since 1650. In 1842, some twenty years after his triumphant visit, his niece Queen Victoria followed for the first time. It was less than a hundred years since her Hanoverian forebears had defeated Bonnie Prince Charlie and his Highland followers at Culloden. That battle had not only seen the defeat of the Jacobite claim to the throne; it had also resulted in the humiliation of Scottish self-determination. Yet when Victoria and her consort Prince Albert crossed the border into Scotland for the first time Scots greeted their monarch with unbridled enthusiasm, flattered by her interest in this far-flung part of her Empire.

For her part Victoria repaid their welcome by falling in love with Scotland, and with the Highlands in particular, even if she was presented with the same "fantasy" Scotland as her uncle had been, a mix of mists and bagpipes and tartan and castles, where the history was as romantic as the scenery was rugged. We know what Victoria felt about the Highlands because she kept a journal recounting her trips that was eventually published for public readership. According to the journal, on that first visit in 1842 she was overwhelmed by "Lord Breadalbane's Highlanders, all in the Campbell Tartan" lined up outside his house in Taymouth, and was delighted to see that nearby were

> a number of pipers playing, and a company of the 92nd Highlanders, also in kilts. The firing of the guns, the cheering of the great crowd, the

> picturesqueness of the dresses, the beauty of the surrounding country, with its rich background of wooded hills, altogether formed one of the finest scenes imaginable. It seemed as if a great chieftain in olden times was receiving his sovereign. It was princely and romantic.

A later visit in 1847 to the west coast of the Highlands, including a trip by boat into Fingal's Cave, brought the comment that the area was "so beautiful, and so full of poetry and romance, traditions and historical associations."

These sentiments were straight out of a novel or poem by Scott. Although the writer died ten years before Victoria's first visit he would no doubt have been overjoyed by the Scotland she experienced. And Victoria loved Scott and his historical sagas: the first novel she had ever read was his *Bride of Lammermoor* and in 1861, when her beloved Albert lay dying, she read him another novel by Scott, *Peveril of the Peak*, which is the writer's longest novel and, even his fans would acknowledge, not his best. Nonetheless a black border was drawn around the page that Victoria was reading when Albert died, and the volume, thus embellished, still sits on the shelves of the library at Windsor Castle to this day.

Albert had been as entranced by Scotland as his wife on their first visit in 1842. He was, Victoria noted, "in perfect ecstasies" as they rode through the Pass of Killiecrankie, for the mountains and forests had reminded him of his native Germany. On another occasion, as they passed along the valley of the Dee with its "beautiful wooded hills," Albert was "reminded... of the Thüringer Wald," a region of hills and thick forests in central Germany long associated with romance and legend. And Albert thought the locals were of a similar mind-set to the stoic inhabitants of the Harz Mountains and the Bavarian Alps: "The people are more natural, and are marked by their honesty and sympathy, which always distinguishes the inhabitants of mountainous countries who live far away from towns," he once wrote. He shared the same Romantic ideal of brave, chivalrous Highlanders as Victoria—one that was a world away from the reality of the poverty that afflicted the area.

Moreover, the beginnings of Victoria's love affair with the Highlands also happened to coincide with some of the most brutal of the Clearances. This did not escape the attention of at least one commentator, Thomas Mulock, who edited the *Inverness Advertiser* and was the author of *The*

Western Highlands and Islands Socially Considered (1850), a book that laid bare the wanton cruelty of the Clearances. "We recommend Her Majesty," he seethed, "to try her hand at transferring to her [sketch book] Kildonan and Strathnaver landscapes, interspersed with the blackened ruins of burnt-down cottages, where dwelt in former days the 'loyal and peaceable and high-spirited race of peasantry'" whom the monarch seemed to so thoughtlessly revere.

Balmoral

So seduced were both Albert and his wife by the Highlands that after their third visit they resolved to seek out a permanent residence for themselves amidst the forests and glens. Balmoral Castle, a stately home owned by the powerful Gordon family of Aberdeen, seemed ideal. In 1848 the couple took out a lease on the property and a crowd of eighty thousand Highlanders turned out to watch them make their first official visit to the residence, which sits beside the River Dee near Braemar. "It was so calm and solitary," Victoria wrote of that first visit. "All seemed to bring freedom and peace, and to make one forget the world and its sad turmoils." On seeing the crowds one local journalist foresaw the surge in popularity that the area would experience and remarked that Deeside was about to be "desolated by cockneys and other horrible reptiles."

This did not matter to the Royal Family. In September 1853 the foundation stone for the new palace was laid during a small ceremony. "A mallet will be delivered to her majesty by Mr. Stuart, the clerk of works," announces the printed program for the ceremony, and at that point "her majesty will strike the stone and declare it to be laid." Along with the foundation stone some coins of the realm were also buried, together with a time capsule of sorts that contained a parchment commemorating the laying of foundation stone, signed by the queen. By that time Albert was already organizing a wholesale reconstruction and enlargement of the original sixteenth-century residence. It was he who decided on the round towers and conical turrets that characterize the exterior of Balmoral, which are straight from an illustration to a folk tale collected by the Brothers Grimm. But where the exterior of the new residence was German, the interior was Scottish, very Scottish. There was tartan everywhere, porridge every morning for breakfast, and every spare inch of wall was soon covered in hunting trophies such as stags' heads. Many sniffed at the excess: one of Victoria's ladies-in-waiting, Augusta Bruce, once commented that there was "a certain absence of harmony of the whole."

Victoria and Albert, for their part, were thrilled with their new tartan paradise, and Albert even created a new, special Balmoral tartan for himself and his wife to wear when they were in residence in the palace. Balmoral "has become my dearest Albert's own creation. Own work, own building, own laying out," Victoria later confided in her journal. Her husband, who had a great interest in science and engineering, also commissioned Isambard Kingdom Brunel to build a new bridge across the Dee, linking the main road along the north side of the Dee Valley with the palace gatehouse on the south side. Brunel built a bridge of functional elegance, using steel forged by a firm in the Wiltshire town of Chippenham that had been involved in the building of the Great Western Railway, and his unadorned, straightforward bottle-green construction still forms the approach to the palace to this day.

Reconstruction of Balmoral took four years. From the 1850s onwards Victoria and Albert made frequent visits, staying there in both winter and summer. A number of major political events were celebrated at the castle, such as the fall of Sebastopol in September 1855, when Albert led a party of staff and villagers to a nearby cairn and lit a bonfire, to the accompaniment of ceremonial gunfire and the playing of Victoria's favorite piper. This and other more mundane pleasures were recorded in Victoria's journal, which had originally been published privately and circulated to only a few of the queen's intimates; but in 1868 it was published for a general readership as *Leaves from the Journal of Our Life in the Highlands.* In her preface to the published edition Victoria claimed that she wanted to "provide mere homely accounts of excursions near home… [and for readers] to be allowed to know how her rare moments of leisure were passed in her Highland home, when every joy was heightened, and every care and sorrow diminished, by the loving companionship of the Prince Consort."

The journal turned out to be a publishing sensation and tens of thousands of copies were purchased in England by a public who, like Victoria and Albert, had fallen in love with the Highlands—but who were also eager for a peek behind the public façade of the royals. (Victoria grew to resent the popularity of her published book: even in "the complete

Balmoral, c. 1900
(Library of Congress, Washington DC)

solitude" of Glencoe, according to her journal, she was "spied on by imprudently inquisitive reporters, who followed us everywhere." One reporter, who had a telescope, had to be told to leave the scene by her loyal servant John Brown.) Readers of the diary soon became acquainted with a typical day for Victoria at Balmoral. She loved walks, picnics, and pony rides, which were taken in all weathers, while Albert loved hunting, shooting, and fishing. But the Prince Consort was a notoriously bad hunter: once, so frustrated was he by his lack of success at deer-stalking, that when a tame stag came to the kitchen window for food he raised his rifle and shot it. Not everyone liked Balmoral. When Tsar Nicholas II of Russia came to stay he complained that "the weather is awful, wind and rain every day, and on top of it no luck at all—I haven't killed a stag yet."

As the tsar observed, the weather at Balmoral, then and now, is notorious. Braemar, the nearest settlement, is not only the place in Britain with the coldest average temperature (a mere 6°C (43°F) annually), it also claims the lowest temperatures ever recorded in the country: on both February 11, 1895, and January 10, 1982, the mercury fell to a bone-chilling

Monarch of the Glen by Sir Edwin Landseer
(Museum of Scotland/Wikimedia Commons)

-27.2°C (-19.9°F). The fourth Earl of Clarendon, English diplomat and statesman, complained that he was affected by frostbite while staying at Balmoral even though he never ventured out of the front door, and even the tsar, who knew a thing or two about living in cold countries, claimed the place was colder than the wastes of Siberia. But Victoria embraced the cold: on chilly days she would fling open the windows and insist that members of her family and other visiting guests accompany her on her expeditions that would invariably culminate in a blustery and austere picnic. Once their guests had returned from one of these expeditions they would find that the interior of the palace did not offer much comfort: rooms were small and cluttered, and visiting government ministers often complained that they had to write their dispatches sitting on the bed in their room as there was no room for a desk.

A new term was created out of Victoria's love for Balmoral. "Balmorality" signified patronage, a certain sense of respectability, and a rugged engagement with the great outdoors. The term could perhaps be summed up in the painting of a stag known as *Monarch of the Glen* that was painted by Sir Edwin Landseer in 1851. Landseer was a favorite of Victoria and at Balmoral gave her lessons in painting. The stag he portrayed in the painting was noble, dignified, and honorable, and by implication its hunter shared the same characteristics and sense of purpose: in short, both were vested with a sense of Balmorality.

On Albert's death Victoria entered a period of mourning that was famously to last until the end of her life. During this time she increasingly sought solace and refuge at Balmoral, often deliberately seeking out the companionship of her Highland servant, John Brown. One of nine children of a local farmer, Brown "advanced step by step by his good conduct and intelligence" (according to Victoria's journal) until he became her constant companion and confidant. "His attention, care, and faithfulness cannot be exceeded," Victoria wrote. "He has all the independence and elevated feelings peculiar to the Highland race, and is singularly straightforward, simple-minded, kind-hearted, and disinterested; always ready to oblige; and of a discretion rarely to be met with." In 1871 she presented Brown with a full set of Highland regalia, including various inlaid ceremonial swords, pouches, and sporrans, which were inscribed "VR to JB, 21st March 1871" (these items can be seen today in the West Highland Museum in Fort William). The precise nature of the relationship between servant and monarch was much discussed at the time and still is a matter of debate, although rumors that Victoria secretly married Brown and had a child by him seem wildly speculative. (She allowed him to sleep in the bedroom directly next to hers, something that would be unheard of for any other commoner.) After Brown's death in 1883 Victoria wrote in a letter to Viscount Cranbrook that "perhaps never in history was there so strong and true an attachment, so warm and loving a friendship between sovereign and servant… [he was] one of the most remarkable men." Victoria had a statue to Brown erected in the grounds of Balmoral after his death, when she retreated even further into a state of mourning.

No wonder that the relationship between Victoria and her Highland servant has been pored over by writers on page and screen for well over a century. Perhaps the best-known examination was in the 1997 film *Mrs.*

Golden Jubilee postcard of Queen Victoria (1887) featuring Balmoral
(About.com)

Brown (released in the USA as *Her Majesty, Mrs. Brown*) in which the two principal roles were played by the Glasgow-born comedian Billy Connolly and the distinguished film and stage actress Judi Dench. In a narrative that roams from Osborne House in the Isle of Wight to Windsor Castle and Balmoral, Brown is shown in the film to be the one person who can draw the queen "out of a state of unfettered morbidity" and reconnect with her people. For her part, Victoria tells Brown that "without you I cannot find the strength to be who I must be." Yet in his absolute devotion to the queen, in a relationship that could be tetchy as well as tender, Brown also invokes the jealousy of Victoria's advisers, servants, and her family, notably her gauche son Bertie, the Prince of Wales, who reacts to Brown's death from pneumonia by throwing a bust of him from the Balmoral gatehouse, smashing it to smithereens.

In the later years of Victoria's reign, with both Albert and John Brown dead and Victoria herself an old woman, Balmoral began to take on an entirely new character. Many visitors now found it to be charmless, gloomy, and dour. Henry Campbell-Bannerman, Liberal Party leader during Victoria's last years and prime minister shortly after her death, likened Balmoral to a convent and remarked that once dinner had been served each guest simply retreated "to his cell," while in *Mrs. Brown* the prime minister Benjamin Disraeli grumbles about having to come "six hundred miles from civilization" to visit his queen.

Once Victoria was gone the monarchs who followed her maintained a varied relationship with her Highland refuge: the two Edwards hated the place but the two Georges loved it. Edward VII, a king who lived for food and pleasure, dubbed the library at Balmoral "a mausoleum of the great unread" and scuppered the notion of Balmorality by inviting his mistress to stay, while Edward VIII preferred the weather of the French Riviera and the sophistication of cocktail parties in London and rarely stayed in the remote and chilly Highlands. When Edward brought his American mistress Wallis Simpson to Balmoral she also hated it, and when she saw Albert's interior decoration she simply remarked tartly, "all this tartan has to go." George V, however, ventured that "I am never so happy as when I am fishing in the pools of the Dee, with a long day before me," while George VI and his wife, Elizabeth Bowes-Lyon, whose father was the Earl of Strathmore, also loved Balmoral: Elizabeth (the mother of the current queen) was an expert fly-fisher and when a fish bone became caught in her throat she famously dubbed it "the salmon's revenge." In stark contrast to Edward VII this royal couple were upholders of Victoria's famed Balmorality—and not surprisingly the future Queen Mother clashed with Wallis Simpson on one of the few occasions that the two women found themselves at Balmoral together.

Nowadays some aspects of life at Balmoral would be familiar to Victoria. The current Royal Family spends its summers here and although there are Land Rovers and electric lights, the shooting and fishing scene remains the same. Something that has changed, though, is the manner by which the Royal Family reaches Balmoral. From 1866 Victoria traveled to the palace by train from London, alighting at Ballater station, the terminus of a branch line from Aberdeen, before traveling the last few miles by coach; famously, although she was a fan of rail travel, she did not want a rail line built any closer to Balmoral than Ballater. Her guests, including (in 1889) the Shah of Persia, came the same way. When the Russian tsar visited some seven years later the little station at Ballater was fitted out with electric lights and was decorated in the Russian imperial colors of yellow and black, while according to Victoria's journal, "blazing torches, held by Highland troops, made a path through the night" for the esteemed guest's carriage as it made its way to Balmoral. The branch line from Aberdeen to Ballater closed in 1966, and the last royal train departed from the station the year before; now the old station buildings at Ballater, painted a smart red and white, stand as a reminder of royal patronage, and house a café, an exhibition space (with a mock-up of part of the royal train), and the town's tourist office. The royals and their guests now travel by car to Balmoral, as they have done, on and off, since the 1930s.

Some things have remained the same. The queen always makes a point of attending the Highland Games at Braemar, which Victoria herself championed. Prime ministers are also still invited for a weekend as a matter of course. It was at Balmoral that Harold Wilson, reputedly the queen's favorite prime minister, announced his intention to her to resign—in a manner that appears extraordinarily casual. According to Wilson's own account, the queen had driven him and his wife Mary to a lodge on the estate, where she made tea while Mary laid the table. Afterwards the queen put on an apron and washed the dishes while her prime minister leant casually on the worktop and told her his intention—the reasons for which remain one of the most compelling mysteries of recent British politics.

Although Wilson apparently enjoyed his stays in Balmoral, Mrs. Thatcher hated the place. She found it difficult to wear wellingtons and once gave the queen some washing-up gloves for Christmas as she had seen her washing dishes in Balmoral without them. In his memoirs Tony Blair describes weekends spent at the palace as "a vivid combination of the intriguing, the surreal, and the utterly freaky," and mentions an unlikely barbecue where the food was cooked by Prince Philip. Meanwhile his wife committed a faux-pas by wearing a trouser suit on one visit and by yawning during a visit to the Braemar games. As for royal visitors of recent years, Princess Diana spent part of her honeymoon at Balmoral and even shot a stag, pretending to love the experience while actually resenting the cold and the rain. And of course Prince Charles and their children were staying at Balmoral when Diana died. It was then that the famous church across the road from the palace driveway, in the hamlet of Crathie, became the center of world attention, when the queen viewed the flowers that had been laid outside it (Crathie Parish Church itself had been built by Victoria in 1895 and the Royal Family always attend services there when they are in residence).

These days Balmoral is actually open to the public, although access is granted to only a few of the rooms, such as the grand Ballroom, and in August, the busiest month for Highland tourism, it is closed as the Royal Family is always in residence. Visitors who come here then have to content themselves with visiting Crathie Kirk, buying a souvenir Balmoral mug at the gift shop by the gatehouse (from which there is no view of the palace), and admiring the memorial to men from the Balmoral Estates who gave their lives in World War I. (The memorial's white marble face is adorned by two rows of swastikas—a symbol which, in 1922, had none of the sinister associations it would later acquire.) As might be expected, the small towns near the palace, such as Braemar and Ballater, bristle with top-class hotels and the classier type of souvenir shop, the latter propagating the well-worn vision of Scotland that had drawn Victoria here in the first place, and that her fondness for the Highlands merely enhanced.

By Train through the Highlands to Fort William and Mallaig

Early visitors to the Highlands such as Samuel Johnson, James Boswell, Lord Byron, and William Wordsworth traveled around the region by road. In 1773 Johnson and Boswell hired ponies to carry them along drovers' paths but, where they could, they also made use of the military roads built by Generals Wade and Caulfeild. These new roads could only get them so far. Leaving Inverness for the Highlands Johnson was aware that we "were now to bid farewell to the luxury of travelling, and to enter a country upon which perhaps no wheel has ever rolled." In Skye the situation was even worse: on that island Johnson found "no roads, nor any marks by which a stranger may find his way"—although in neighboring Coll he noted that the laird was slowly building a road suitable for carriages that would link his house with the harbor. Only three decades later Wordsworth was able to use a horse and carriage in the Highlands, such were the improvements to the roads.

Two hundred years later, those who follow the same routes today often do so in coaches, hundreds of which pound the major roads of the Highlands during the summer. One of the busiest of these is the A82, the "Road to the Isles" linking Glasgow with Fort William and Mallaig. In the tiny former mining village of Tyndrum, holidaymakers traveling by coach along that road can stay in one of two colossal coach tour hotels that rise like cathedrals to modern tourism above the old miners' cottages and pebble-dash council houses.

Tyndrum is not only a stop for road travelers: it is also a stop on the most famous railway through the Highlands, the West Highland line, which was built in stages between 1881 and 1901 and like the A82 links Glasgow with the West Coast towns of Oban, Fort William, and Mallaig. (The first sod was cut at Inverlochy by Lord Abinger, chair of the West Highland Railway Company, on October 23, 1889, with an ornamental shovel that can be seen in the West Highland Museum in Fort William.) Many consider a trip on the line to be one of the great railway journeys of the world—and this journey, along with a trip along the "Far North" line from Inverness to Thurso, has been vividly described by the railway writer Michael Williams in his engaging travel books *On the Slow Train* and *On the Slow Train Again*. The train ride from Glasgow to Fort William certainly beats a trip along the A82, especially in summer when the road thunders all day long to the sound of passing coaches and juggernauts.

Heading northwest from Glasgow the line spectacularly skirts Loch Tarbert and Loch Lomond before dividing at Crianlarich, with one spur heading west to Oban and another much longer one heading north to Fort William. Tyndrum, the first stop beyond Crianlarich, actually has two stations—a lower one on the line to Oban and an upper station, high on the hillside above the town, on the Fort William spur. Beyond Tyndrum Upper the trains for Fort William head north and pass through tiny Bridge of Orchy before traversing Rannoch Moor, one of Scotland's great expanses of nothingness. Back in the late nineteenth century the construction of the line across this bleak area of moorland involved laying the track bed on a mattress of tree roots, brushwood and thousands of tons of earth, to prevent the rails from sinking into the peat. (Earlier in the century Thomas Telford had given up the idea of driving a proper road across this landscape as he thought it would just sink.)

Nowadays the trip across Rannoch Moor is the undisputed highlight of the journey from Glasgow to Fort William, a spectacular ride across one of Europe's most desolate stretches of countryside. No road follows the trackside and access to the lonely stations at Rannoch and Corrour (the latter the highest on the line and built for a private hunting estate) involves tortuous journeys from a different direction along miles of single track roads. It is at these stations that the Caledonian Sleeper (nicknamed by loyalists the "Deerstalker Express"), which leaves London's Euston station every evening (except Saturday) at around 9:15PM, disgorges clutches of bleary-eyed walkers early each morning in summer; those lucky hikers walk straight off the platforms and into some of the most fantastic walking countryside in the world. But even in summer those walkers need to be properly equipped. A notice at Rannoch station reads: "At 1000 feet, Rannoch Moor provides one of the wildest and most forbidding landscapes in Britain—treacherous mires, boulder-strewn moorland, complete lack of shelter, and exposure to wind and rain make this an inhospitable environment. Walkers are warned this is not an area to trifle with."

In fact the treacherous Moor has threatened railway users since before the line was even built. When the line was being surveyed in 1889 a group of middle-aged directors and contractors came to this bleak spot to survey the route, and famously ended up floundering through one of the most ferocious blizzards the Moor could throw at them. They would have perished had they not been rescued by some local shepherds, who discovered that the men had gone out on the Moor in tweeds and plus-fours.

The Caledonian Sleeper itself is one of the few trains in Britain that still ooze the glamour and romance of a past era of rail travel. At Euston the attendants ("hosts") greet their passengers by name and ask them how they would like their morning coffee. After dinner, as the train surges north, passengers can relax in the lounge car with its leather sofas, and order drinks from the neighboring bar, which only closes when the last passenger has drained their nightcap and padded off down the corridor to bed. Unlike virtually every other passenger train in Britain the train consists of rakes of carriages hauled by a locomotive. These carriages that cross Rannoch Moor are only a third of the original train: at Edinburgh, in the early hours of the morning, other sections peel away and head for Aberdeen and Inverness. Hugely expensive to travel on (and even then subsidized by the tax-payer) the Caledonian Sleeper is unquestionably the most evocative way to travel from England to the West Highlands. Oddly, as a result of a quirk of Britain's railway privatization policy, the train is actually owned and operated by the German rail consortium Deutsche Bahn.

Just after 11:00AM, some fourteen hours after its departure from Euston, the train rolls into the same modest terminus at Fort William that the first ever official train on the line steamed into on Saturday, August 11, 1894. The opening of the new route understandably caused a surge of public interest. The correspondent of the *Railway Gazette* wrote that the line "throws open to the public wide and interesting tracts of country which have been almost as much unknown to the ordinary tourist as central Africa was ten years ago." The railway author John Thomas commented in his book *The West Highland Railway* that "never before in Britain had such a spectacular length of line been opened in one day… and never before had opening day guests been taken on so spectacular and exciting a trip. Here was a railway fascinating beyond words, every foot of it with a place in the past, a story in every mile."

The principal impetus behind the construction of the line had actually been the movement of livestock. Kathleen Fidler's children's novel *The Droving Lad* opens with an old drover, seeing that railways are coming to the Highlands, commenting that "soon we shall be putting the cattle on the train and sending them straight from here to the London market, instead of driving them down over the hills to Falkirk in a big herd"—but on the line's opening tourists quickly became a vital source of traffic and revenue. In those early days travelers could buy luncheon baskets when they passed through Crianlarich, and the lineside for the next twenty miles was littered with discarded plovers' eggs and champagne corks thrown from the windows. Today's train is somewhat less luxurious—champagne is certainly not available from the refreshment trolley—but one thing has not changed about the line since its opening, and that is the number of trains that operate along it every day: only three each way. Despite the low amount of passenger traffic, each station along the length of the line was originally built with a proper waiting room and staffed ticket facilities. In most cases today the stations are unmanned and the old buildings deserted. At some of the more remote stations, such as the one at Bridge of Orchy, however, the smartly-kept former booking offices and waiting rooms have been converted into bunkhouses for walkers; the arrival every morning of the sleeper train from Euston must serve as an unusual wake-up call.

Train plying the West Highland Line between between Fort William and Mallaig passing over the Glenfinnan Viaduct, built across the valley where Bonnie Prince Charlie raised his standard in 1745 (Nicolas17/Wikimedia Commons)

In contrast to trains on the Glasgow to Fort William section of the line, the run from Fort William to Mallaig hugs valley bottoms and the shores of sea lochs rather than traversing upland moors. But the journey is no less spectacular for that. Both Mallaig and Fort William stations are more or less at sea level but the journey between them involves a succession of climbs and descents, the trains groaning and squealing on the tight curves and steep gradients. Miles Kington, in his book *Steaming Through Britain*, summed up the journey as "going across the back of a glove… you go a long way up and a long way down but every now and then you glimpse a long snake of water snaking down to the sea. It is this coexistence of wild mountain scenery and the invisible nearness of the sea which gives the Mallaig line its special flavour." Even the travel writer Paul Theroux, generally disdainful of mountain scenery, was won over when he traveled along this route in 1983. He noted in his book *The Kingdom by the Sea* that the landscape through which the train passed was "splendid… but the train itself was dull and the passengers watchful and reverent, intimidated by all the scenery."

The scenery is, indeed, overwhelming. After leaving Fort William the line skirts the shores of Loch Eil before crossing the spectacular Glenfinnan viaduct, whose twenty-one curving arches take the line around the head of Loch Shiel. From here there are stunning views of the monument erected to commemorate the landing at this location of Bonnie Prince Charlie and his gathering of the clansmen who were to form his vanguard in the 1745 Jacobite Rebellion. The viaduct, one hundred feet high, is one of Scotland's most stunning engineering achievements; although it was constructed from concrete it still blends in beautifully with the surrounding countryside. Its builder was Sir Robert MacAlpine, who was known in engineering circles as "concrete Bob" because of his fondness for that building material. It was work on this and other viaducts that meant that over four thousand navigational engineers were required to work on the line during the four years of its construction. (A rumor once persisted that a horse and cart had fallen into one of the hollow piers of the Glenfinnan viaduct during construction, and were still blocked up in it; these rumors were investigated by sensing equipment in 2001—but the horse and cart were actually found to be entombed within the piers of another viaduct further up the line, not Glenfinnan.) At Glenfinnan Station, abandoned long ago by train staff, a small museum has been set up in the old booking hall, crammed full of old ticketing machines and station signage from days gone by. An old sleeping car that once plied the London to Scotland route stands outside, alongside a robust-looking, modern snow plough.

Beyond Arisaig ("Britain's most westerly station," as it proudly proclaims on the station signboards) the scenery changes: the train leaves the steep valleys and instead rumbles alongside magnificent beaches of white sand, affording enticing views across the Sound of Sleat to Skye. Then comes the final set of buffers, and the fishing and passenger port of Mallaig. It was the fish landed at Mallaig that provided the reason for this line's construction: mindful of the dire poverty of the West Highlands in the nineteenth century, parliament voted to fund the construction of a line that would allow fish to be landed and then sent to Glasgow within the space of a day. In 1901, when the line opened, Mallaig was a scattered settlement of twenty-eight weather-beaten cottages, but with the coming of the railway the place rapidly developed into the country's busiest herring port. In the port's heyday itinerant laborers, mostly women, worked away in the sheds on the quayside turning the landed herrings into kippers that were loaded onto trains at the adjacent station. Incoming trains brought wagons laden with coal, which was in turn loaded straight into the waiting steam-driven shipping vessels for boiler fuel. In his book *Harpoon at a Venture* Gavin Maxwell describes the "slum" of wooden shacks in which these migrant workers made their home; to him, Mallaig was a "frontier town" of "energy and squalor and opportunity." But then, as now, Mallaig drew in plenty of tourists. Maxwell wrote that the "cargo of holiday-makers" the train "disgorged" at Mallaig in the summer of 1945 consisted of "would-be mountaineers in huge climbing boots and swathes of rope, brightly-tartanned Highlanders from Glasgow and the industrial cities, earnest hikers with gigantic rucksacks and skinny legs, and the sad-looking elderly couples who seem to visit the Hebrides annually to lament the climate." Nearly seventy years on not much has changed.

For decades Mallaig lived off its enormous herring catch. Miles Kington wrote that herrings "fell out of every boat, every nook and cranny," and added that "if you wanted to cook a fish on your shovel on your way home, you just picked one up off the quay. There's the legendary story of the man at the station who asked the driver if there were any spare fish on board. 'Aye, third car down', he said. The man opened the door to the third car down and ten ton of fish fell on top of him." Now, though, the herring trade has died, but prawns and haddock are still landed by the Mallaig fishing fleet, giving the town some of the freshest and flakiest haddock and chips in Britain. Unfortunately the fishing catch is now moved out by road. But the Mallaig line lives on, its three daily passenger trains crammed with tourists from all over the world anxious to experience a "Harry Potter moment" as they cross the Glenfinnan viaduct, which is a familiar scene in the films made from the novels. The luckiest get a seat on the steam train that has been running on the line in summer since 1995, the brainchild of a farmer and railway enthusiast from the North of England named David Smith, who ensures that the trains are hauled by K1 class steam locomotives that were originally designed for the line by Sir Nigel Gresley. If it were not for the revenue earned from these trains this section of the line might be under serious threat of closure; the line from Glasgow to Fort William, meanwhile, earns part of its keep from the heavy freight trains that serve the aluminum smelter in Fort William, which has proved to be the line's savior.

OTHER HIGHLAND RAILWAYS: BY TRAIN FROM INVERNESS TO THURSO AND KYLE OF LOCHALSH

In many ways it is surprising that the "Far North" line that runs along the remote east coast of Scotland north from Inverness was ever built; it is doubly surprising that trains still run on it today. The line was constructed along a tortuously winding course between 1862 and 1874 and when it opened was served by only two trains per day (now there are four each way). One hundred and eighty miles in length, the line runs beside beaches, firths, lochs, and moorland, linking tiny stone-built fishing villages with Inverness and with the two principal settlements in the distant northeast, Thurso and Wick. The former, the largest town on Scotland's blustery north coast, is a passenger port: from its harbor at Scrabster ferries cross the choppy Pentland Firth to Orkney. Wick, on the other hand, is centred on a dour fishing harbor and is regularly blasted by icy winds from Scandinavia. Neither Wick or Thurso are Highland towns; they are separated from the mountains by the bleak and boggy fastness of the Flow Country, a flat expanse of forest and peat over which the train rumbles on the last part of its journey. But between Inverness and Forsinard, where the trains run into the Flow Country, much of the scenery seen from carriage windows is one of mountains and moors, less spectacular though more desolate than the lines in the West Highlands. And north of Brora the line actually runs right by the waves, along a rough and wild stretch of coast where communities of seals make their homes amidst black rocks continuously drenched by the frothing gray waters of the North Sea.

Much of the scenery through which the line passes is unremittingly bleak—and the stations along the line are spectacularly remote. (Altnabreac station in the Flow Country claims pride of place as the most isolated in Britain.) Paul Theroux remarked that "Lairg station was two miles from Lairg, but even Lairg was nowhere" and described the thrill of alighting from the train there—"the clang of a carriage door, and then the train pulled out and left me in a sort of pine-scented silence." Twelve years later another British-based American travel writer, Bill Bryson, also came this way and was also enthralled by the overwhelming emptiness of the scenery. "We rattled on through an increasingly remote and barren landscape," he wrote in *Notes from a Small Island,* "treeless and cold, with heather clinging to the hillsides like lichen on rock...now and then we passed through winding valleys speckled with farms that looked romantic and pretty from a distance, but bleak and comfortless up close. We were entering one of those weird zones, always a sign of remoteness from the known world, where nothing is ever thrown away. Every farmyard was cluttered with piles of cast-offs, as if the owner thought that one day he might need 132 half-rotted fence posts, a ton of broken bricks, and the shell of a 1964 Ford Zodiac." Beyond Golspie, with its council estates of pebbledash bungalows, Bryson noted that the train passed "for a seeming eternity through a great Scottish void, full of miles of nothingness, until, in the middle of this great emptiness, we came to a place called Forsinard, with two houses, a railway station, and an inexplicably large hotel. What a strange lost world this was."

Part of the impetus for this line's original construction in the nineteenth century came from a local aristocrat and railway enthusiast named George Granville, the third Duke of Sutherland. He had previously worked in the engine sheds of the London and Northwestern Railway at Wolverton and when he returned to the Highlands he built a station adjacent to his residence at Dunrobin Castle, with a short length of track to serve it. Eventually the line on which the duke played trains was incorporated into the finished line from Inverness. Dunrobin Castle has always been a station on the line and on one occasion the duke was able to drive Queen Victoria's train right up to the front gates of his estate. To this day the station remains the only one in Britain to serve a private residence; recently restored and smartened up, the interior is host to a cramped museum of railway memorabilia.

The purpose of the rest of the line, however, is hazy. There have always been fewer tourists in northeastern Scotland than in the West Highlands and the line has never moved large quantities of fish or freight—although in northwest Sutherland hints remain here and there in the landscape of a line that would have run northwest from Lairg to a proposed whaling station on the coast at Kinlochbervie, which in the end never got off the ground. That the Thurso line survived the mass railway closures of the 1960s is something of a miracle. In 1983 Paul Theroux thought the line was "on its last legs... slow and dirty, but I liked it for being derelict and still stubbornly running across the moors." He saw lots of train-spotters on the line and considered their presence a bad omen. "They were always a sure sign that a branch line was doomed," he observed. "The railway buffs were attracted to the clapped-out trains, like flies to the carcass of an old nag." An upgrade to the signalling system, which means that the line can be operated by only a handful of personnel, has helped save it, and recently things have been looking much brighter. In 2002 a station at Beauly was re-opened after being close for forty years in an attempt to persuade Inverness commuters to use the southern part of the line, and in 2013 another commuter station was opened at Conon Bridge, between Beauly and Dingwall.

The other Highland line from Inverness, which links the capital of the Highlands with the west coast port of Kyle of Lochalsh, highlights the role of railways in Scotland in bringing goods and people to the islands of the Hebrides. When the line was built the village where it terminated—then simply known as Kyle—consisted of little more than a couple of crofters' cottages looking across the narrow Sound of Sleat to Skye. It was the railway company that added "of Lochalsh" to the name of the village, believing "Kyle" on its own to lack sufficient grandeur for the terminus of their railway—and in so doing they created one of the most evocatively named railway destinations in the world. The station was built on a jetty, so sheep rounded up on Skye could be offloaded from boats and loaded right onto trains, but it was not long before passengers were also a vital part

Caledonian MacBrayne ferry crossing to Skye from Mallaig (Andrew Beattie)

of the through-traffic at Kyle of Lochalsh, thanks to the ferry service across to Kyleakin.

Steam boat services such as the one linking Kyle of Lochalsh and Kyleakin had actually begun at the turn of the nineteenth century, and in 1831 the *Steam Boat Companion to the Highlands and Western Isles* was able to indicate that "the stranger can now explore [Scotland's] mountains, islands, lakes, and valleys, with the greatest facility and expedition; and a journey which one hundred years ago would have been considered the business of a week, and the boast of a life, may now be performed in the course of a day." But these services were organized on a rather piecemeal basis until 1851, when the steamship firm David Hutcheson and Co. was created to run services from Glasgow to Inverness, making use of the recently-built Crinan and Caledonian canals. This, however, was a very slow route: passage along the Crinan Canal involved navigating eleven locks, resulting in a journey that even Queen Victoria found "tedious" in 1847. As railways were constructed across the Highlands Hutcheson's routes linking towns on the mainland became redundant, and instead the company concentrated on operating passenger ferries from mainland railheads such as Oban, Mallaig, and Kyle of Lochalsh out to the islands of the Inner Hebrides.

Changes of ownership led to the company adopting the name Caledonian MacBrayne, and today "CalMac" ferries busily ply a myriad of routes across the churning seas off western Scotland, from brief journeys of no more than ten minutes (such as the route linking Islay and Jura) to rocky three-hour rides from Ullapool out to Stornoway and the Western Isles. Oban has always been the company's busiest passenger port; as at Kyle of Lochalsh the jetty is right next to the station, allowing Victorian (and present-day) travelers the delight of walking off the train and then straight onto the boat. Then as now, passengers who leave Oban by boat glide past by the island of Kerrera, a rocky sliver that effectively serves as a natural breakwater for the Port of Oban, sheltering it from the Atlantic storms; and as they pass the island's northern tip they see a spiky monument that rises in honor of David Hutcheson, who is buried in a cemetery in the town. It serves as an appropriate reminder to today's ferry passengers of the entrepreneur who had opened up passenger routes to the Isles to the first nineteenth-century tourists. As for Kyle of Lochalsh, the brief ferry service across the Sound of Sleat to Kyleakin came to an end when the road bridge to Skye opened in the 1990s, and today trains draw up on a deserted quayside from which no ferries depart; the bridge might well have improved the economy of Skye but now rail passengers who arrive in Kyle of Lochalsh have to continue their journey over to the island by bus—which quite possibly began its journey in Inverness at about the same time as they did.

That it is still possible to travel to Kyle of Lochalsh, Thurso, Fort William, and Mallaig by train is also something of a miracle. Many Highland lines were closed in the 1960s during the infamous cuts to rail services made by the transport minister Dr. Richard Beeching. Abandoned bridges, overgrown cuttings, and collapsing embankments can now be seen in many parts of the region. One lamented line is the one linking Stirling with Crianlarich, which provided a through route from Edinburgh to the West Highlands. The old station in the popular center of Callander has now been commandeered as a giant car and coach park, where a handsome old road bridge that once crossed the tracks has been preserved (with a grassy embankment where they used to be). Another Beeching cut was the line from Oban to the slate-mining village of Ballachulish. Opened in 1903, it was the last to be built in the Highlands, and it might have survived had it been originally built a further fifteen miles to Fort William. This line crossed Loch Etive on an elegant cantilever bridge at Connell now used by traffic on the busy main road from Oban to Fort William; the single-lane status of the bridge, and the typical stone viaduct sections at either end, are give-aways as to its origin as part of a railway line.

To the north of here much of the old line hugs the shores of Loch Linnhe and has been converted into a picturesque cycle path, while just before Ballachulish a lone semaphore signal standing by a grassy bank marks the line of the former track bed and surprises motorists driving along the adjacent A82 towards Glencoe. Originally, Beeching had wanted to close all lines north of the Caledonian Canal—thus putting an end to rail services to Thurso, Wick, and Kyle of Lochalsh—yet somehow these lines survived, and even in economically straightened times their future is reckoned to be more secure today than it has been at any time since World War II.

In the 1990s another type of railway arrived in the Highlands—namely the funicular railway, in which cars are hauled up steep slopes on rails by means of cables; such railways scatter the Alps but none existed in Scotland until the construction of the funicular up Cairn Gorm. The line, opened in 2001, was built to replace a suspended cableway that often had to be closed because of high winds; much of the £20 million ($33.7 million) bill for its construction was paid for by local and European development agencies, anxious to bring money and jobs into the area. A Swiss firm was involved in the construction of both the passenger cars and the track, which is raised on concrete stilts along its length to make snow-clearing easier (and runs through a tunnel in the upper stage for the same reason). But this means that the line forms something of a scar as it ascends the mountain. At the top, the views from the Ptarmigan restaurant reach as far as Ben Nevis, on a good day—but are more likely to be of mist, with anything from spitting drizzle to heavy snowfall assaulting those who cluster on the outdoor terrace. It is nearly always blowing a gale up here, too.

In a nod to environmental preservation, walkers are not allowed to access the mountains from the top station, though of course skiers can do so in winter. In North Wales a tourist railway had been constructed up Mount Snowdon in the late nineteenth century using Swiss technology and locomotives, but nothing similar has ever dragged visitors to the summits of high peaks in Scotland; and the closest the Highlands have ever got to the "great little trains of Wales" was a narrow gauge line built in 1983 along a mile of Mull coastline to get visitors from the ferry terminal at Criagnure to Torosay Castle, which ceased operations and was torn up for scrap in 2011.

THOMAS COOK AND MASS TOURISM

The opening of the new railways meant that yet more visitors could descend on the Highlands each summer. With an extensive and reasonably fast network of coaches, trains, and ferries to take them from place to place, even averagely wealthy Victorians could now enjoy the history and scenery that they had read about in the novels of Sir Walter Scott and the journals of Queen Victoria. The scenery and culture they saw had by then been carefully packaged for consumption by the public (although it is worth remembering that this popularization of the Highlands went hand-in-hand with a genuine, parallel revival in Scottish poetry and literature). One of the best examples of this was the nineteenth-century revival of the Highland Games, which are nowadays easily dismissed as tartan-draped shindigs aimed at tourists, but which have their origins in the competitions held by clan chieftains (beginning with Malcolm Canmore in the Middle Ages) to select the best fighting men. Canmore famously offered his men a specific challenge, namely a race to the summit of Creag Chionnich from Braemar; his challenge is the origin of the hill race that still forms part of the Braemar games to this day.

Nowadays the Highland Games here, traditionally held on the first Saturday in September, can attract an audience of fifteen thousand or more. The queen usually attends, just as her great-great-grandmother Victoria used to in the nineteenth century. Informal gatherings known as *ceilidhs* were also revived during Victoria's time. A *ceilidh* usually involves the performance of music, songs, dances (such as the "Gay Gordons"), and poetry; the most "genuine" *ceilidhs* are those that often break out spontaneously on long winter evenings in remoter communities in the Hebrides.

One key individual who was instrumental in popularizing trips to the Highlands was a remarkable entrepreneur whose name is still indelibly linked with organized travel. Thomas Cook left school at the age of ten to

Thomas Cook, inventor of the package holiday
(Wikimedia Commons)

become a gardener's boy near his home in Leicester. In his adult life, his Baptist faith and missionary zeal led him to organize trips and holidays that would induce those who had wandered from the path of righteousness back towards temperance and moral restraint. A trip "provides food for the mind," Cook wrote; "it helps pull men out of the mire and pollution of old corrupt customs... it accelerates the march of peace and virtue and love."

In 1845 the first group of what Cook called his "excursionists" left Leicester for a holiday in the English Lake District; in the following year another group headed for Scotland. That group had Ayrshire and "the land of Robbie Burns" in its sights rather than the Highlands. Cook did fit in the time to take his tourists to Loch Lomond, however, and the following year he led a specifically Highland-themed trip from Glasgow that took holidaymakers through the Crinan Canal and then to the islands of Bute, Iona, and Mull, before dry land and excursions to Glencoe, Fort William, and Inverness beckoned. (A highlight must have been a boat trip to Staffa—although enterprising locals on Mull had been taking visitors over to Staffa since 1821, and the ruins of a stone shelter built for those early tourists can still be seen on the island's grassy core.)

Those first tourists were moved around by coach on the old military roads, and by David Hutcheson's growing fleet of ferries, but as railways were built across Scotland train became the principal mode of transport. Throughout the 1850s and 1860s Cook was shepherding five thousand tourists around Scotland annually and usually spent two months of each year there. "Sir Walter Scott gave a sentiment to Scotland as a tourist country, and we have spent nearly twenty-three seasons in attempts to foster and develop that sentiment," he wrote in July 1868, although by that time the managers of the various Scottish railway companies were offering him less favorable terms for group travel and Cook was developing Switzerland as a new destination for his excursionists. Nonetheless in 1885 he presented a sturdy winged bookcase, complete with 250 volumes, to the inhabitants of Iona, after bringing several tour parties over to the island. The bookcase still stands in the Iona Heritage Centre, complete with volumes that bear titles such as *Ragged Homes and How to Mend Them* by Mrs. Bayly and *The Christian Mother at Home: her duties and delights* by J. F. Winks—alongside many Dickens novels and a set of Chambers Encyclopaedias.

All these visitors needed to stay in hotels. In places like Oban, hotels appeared along the seafront, much as they did along the fronts of many British seaside towns. In the mountains many hunting lodges were commandeered as hotels and to this day they remain sought-after places to spend the night. Among these are the Tongue Hotel overlooking the Kyle of Tongue on the north coast, which was once a hunting lodge of the Duke of Sutherland, and the stately Inversnaid Hotel, on the east shore of Loch Lomond, a former hunting lodge of the Duke of Montrose. Grand hotels were also built at major railway stations to cater for tourists. The most luxurious was the Station Hotel in Inverness, which now carries the name the Royal Highland Hotel; its grand staircase, still intact, was used as the model for the one on RMS *Titanic*. A publicity brochure from the 1880s indicates that breakfast here consisted of salmon, steak, ham, chicken, and tongue, while a piano was at "the free disposal of occupants in every private sitting room."

It was Cook's new breed of travelers who helped to transform some Highland towns into tourist-swamped honey-pots. Inverness, with its smart new hotels and its rail link and its proximity to Loch Ness, was a case in point. In the Middle Ages the city had grown up as an important center of trade and ship building, though its prosperity attracted raiding parties that swept down from the Highlands at regular intervals. Then came the hotels and the tours along Loch Ness by bus and cruise ship, and Inverness transformed itself into a major stopover point for tourists. Yet the city is actually rather undistinguished, and many visitors, both in Victorian times and now, are just passing through, taking advantage of the best transport links in the Highlands: coaches fan out from the bus station to virtually all parts of Scotland, there are direct mainline rail links to London (including a sleeper service), and from the international airport east of the city (by far the busiest in the Highlands) there are daily flights to Gatwick, Belfast, Bristol, and Amsterdam as well as the far-flung islands to the north and west of Scotland. In the town itself the nineteenth-century castle perched picturesquely above the river is closed to the public (it houses the local sheriff's court) and once visitors have dutifully looked round the excellent history museum and art gallery they are left with a meager itinerary that takes in such delights as an ordinary nineteenth-century cathedral and the Kiltmaker Visitor Centre, the latter offering a chance to see displays of costumes used in the films *Rob Roy* and *Braveheart* and an opportunity to purchase all manner of tweed and tartan.

Inverness has very few literary links—the writer Neil Gunn lived here for a while, working as an excise officer for a local distillery, but he moved away when his novel *Highland River* was published—and perhaps not surprisingly the town has received some disparaging coverage from travel writers over the years. The Orkney poet Edwin Muir called Inverness "inconveniently crowded with vehicles of all kinds, most of them stationary" in his *Scottish Journey* of 1935. While traveling around the coast of Britain for *The Kingdom by the Sea* Paul Theroux stayed in one of the town's many bed and breakfasts and found it "operated by a quarrelsome couple…it was a cold house. The bathmat was damp." The only words the taciturn proprietors said to him were "six pounds," and Theroux found himself "too bored to do anything but set off immediately for Aberdeen." Bill Bryson looks on the place more favorably in *Notes from a Small Island*, though admits Inverness "was never going to win any beauty contests." Although the River Ness was "green and sedate and charmingly overhung with trees" and was lined with "big houses and trim little parks… two sensationally ugly modern office buildings that stood by the central bridge blot the town centre beyond any help of redemption… everything about them—scale, materials, design—was madly inappropriate to the surrounding scene… [they were] awful, awful beyond words." In those days the blocks contained the offices of local business enterprise boards; nowadays, one of them is the tourist office, busy with people seeking constructive ways of getting out of the city and into the mountains.

OBAN: "EVERY VARIETY OF PLEASURE-SEEKER IS TO BE FOUND THERE"

On the other side of Scotland, Skye and the islands of the Inner Hebrides proved immensely popular with visitors in the late nineteenth century, and in summer Oban, the principal gateway to these islands, gave the impression of being about to sink into the Firth of Lorn, so weighed down was the town by tourists. Like Inverness, Oban has garnered a reputation for itself as somewhere to pass through rather than stay: the airport is tiny and the rail links are limited, but unlike Inverness Oban is a key ferry port, and its setting is much more dramatic, with the mountains close-up and the town spreading itself picturesquely around a fishing harbor and up the neighboring slopes. Here is where Oban's tourists while away their time waiting for the next train or ferry. The Glasgow-based poet Alexander Smith, who married a woman from Skye named Flora MacDonald (who was a descendant of her famous namesake), described a visit to Oban in his book *A Summer on Skye*, published in 1865. According to Smith, during winter Oban was "a town of deserted hotels" but in summer the place was

> not a bad representation of Vanity Fair. Every variety of pleasure-seeker is to be found there and every variety of costume… a more hurried, nervous, frenzied place than Oban, during the summer and autumn months, is difficult to conceive. People seldom stay there more than a night… the tourist thinks no more of spending a week in Oban than he thinks of spending a week in a railway station. When he arrives his first question is after a bedroom; his second, as to the hour at which the steamer from the south is expected.

Jules Verne, whose travels in Scotland inspired his novel *The Green Ray*, remarked that Victorian Oban was full of "families whose only occupation is to watch the sea going in and coming out" who rubbed shoulders with "highly respectable ladies and gentlemen, stiff and motionless on green benches with red cushions" and a few "passing tourists with... deer stalkers on their heads, long gaiters on their legs, and umbrellas under their arms, who arrived yesterday and will leave again tomorrow."

After World War I the growth in car travel brought yet more people to the Highlands—and introduced a new type of recreation, the touring holiday. It was at this time that many landladies began converting their homes into bed and breakfast accommodation. In June 1938 the novelist Virginia Woolf passed through Oban on one of these newly-fashionable motoring holidays and wrote in a letter to her sister, the artist Vanessa Bell, that Oban seemed to her to be "the Ramsgate of the Highlands" and that its heavy granite buildings made it "grim" and "without frivolity." Woolf traveled on from Oban to Skye and her letter goes on to reveal the typical experience of a certain breed of cultured tourist who chose to abandon a home in London for a holiday in Scotland. "We've driven around the island today, seen Dungevan [she means Dunvegan], encountered the children of the twenty-seventh chieftain, nice red headed brats: the castle being open I walked in; they very politely told me the castle was shut to visitors, but I could see the gardens... it's no use trying to buy anything, as the price... is at least six times higher than in our honest land... the old women live in round huts exactly the shape of Skye terriers."

On a postcard to the artist Duncan Grant Woolf complained that on the island there were "no railways, no London papers, hardly any inhabitants... [it was] remote as Samoa; deserted; prehistoric." It was the first time Woolf had been to the island, despite it providing the setting for her classic 1927 novel *To the Lighthouse,* which had been written eleven years previously. Although the novel is ostensibly set in the Hebrides, the setting was inspired by Godrevy in Cornwall, where Woolf spent many childhood holidays. One of her correspondents who had read *To the Lighthouse* shortly after its publication complained to the author in a letter that she had got the description of the flora and fauna of the Hebrides completely wrong—surely something of a pedantic criticism for a novel that was soon to earn its place as a classic of modern literature.

The art deco façade of the Regent Hotel, on the seafront in Oban (Andrew Beattie)

Oban today remains solid and Victorian, its austere buildings, enlivened occasionally by a conical turret or two, making it the town in the Highlands that most closely resembles Edinburgh. Paul Theroux called it a "dull clean town on a coast of wild water and islands." Only the cream-colored curves of the art deco façade of the Regent Hotel on the sea front add a much-needed touch of lightness—though when the sun comes out the place is enlivened by the brightly colored hulls of ships in the harbor: russet reds, deep purples, and egg-yolk yellows are all vivid and alert in the glare of northern sunlight. And Oban remains a place through which people merely pass rather than stay. This was emphasized further in the 1950s when the first Atlantic undersea cable made landfall here. The cable linked Washington and the Kremlin by way of Newfoundland and Oban, and the spot where it rose from the water is now marked by some derelict low-rise buildings fringing a nondescript beach. The undersea cable is no more, rendered redundant by satellite technology, and still tourists do not stay in Oban for long: the town's attempt to brand itself the seafood capital of Scotland has been the latest in a long line of attempts to rectify this state of affairs.

Jules Verne (1828–1905) wrote a number of novels inspired by the theme of travel—the mere titles of his most famous books, such as *Journey to the Center of the Earth* and *Around the World in Eighty Days* are suggestive of journeying as a principal theme—and in 1859 his visit to Scotland inspired one of his strangest books, *The Underground City*, a dark tome set beneath Loch Katrine. In 1879 he returned to Scotland; this time he came to bustling Oban, from where he visited Mull and Iona. His diaries from the trip show that he followed a route from Glasgow to Oban that was more or less identical to that taken by the characters in his novel *The Green Ray*, which is the most resonant expression in fiction of the popularity of West Highland travel in the Victorian era. The novel's heroine is a headstrong, romantic young woman of eighteen named Helena Campbell, whom the author later admitted was inspired by Diana Vernon, the heroine of Scott's *Rob Roy*. Helena reads in a newspaper of the "green ray"—an optical effect caused by the sun setting over the sea—and is determined to see it for herself; so she sets off from Glasgow to Oban with her two grumpy uncles, who serve as her guardians.

They travel first on the steamer *Columba*, which according to the *Baedeker* of the day was "probably the finest river steamer in Europe," offering passengers the use of drawing rooms, baths, and a post office on the nine-hour journey, and Verne clearly writes from experience when he remarks that the ship boasts "every possible comfort in her lounges and dining rooms." Passing through the Crinan Canal they are serenaded by a bagpiper; then they head across the fabled Gulf of Corryvrechan and its whirlpool, where they encounter a rowing boat "caught up in the swirling waters and heading for certain destruction"—and Helena's insistence that the stricken fisherman, Oliver Sinclair, is rescued sets off the novel's central love story. Much of the rest of the novel concerns a series of comic misadventures involving the pedantic know-all Aristobulus Ursiclos, who has been selected by Helena's uncles as her future husband, who inadvertently conspires to prevent Helena from seeing the ray each time she determinedly tries to; the novel ends in a dramatic rescue of Helena by Oliver Sinclair in Fingal's Cave.

"THE ASCENT OF BEN LOMOND IS EASILY ACCOMPLISHED, EVEN BY LADIES"

Jules Verne no doubt had a guidebook stuffed in his luggage during his journey to Scotland. He, like all other visitors, needed to know how to travel around, where exactly to go and what to see and do. The first publisher to bring out a travel guide to the Highlands was John Murray, whose *Guide to the Highlands and Islands of Scotland* was published in 1834. Its authors, George Anderson and Peter Anderson, claimed in their introduction that it would be "descriptive of the scenery, statistics, antiquities, and natural history [of the Highlands and Islands] with numerous historical notices, with a very complete map of Scotland." The writers assured their readers that they had "purposely and personally visited almost all the scenes described by them," and that their manuscript "has, in general, been revised by friends intimately acquainted with the various districts of which it treats." The book took ten years to research and was completed by the authors, so they maintained, in their "leisure hours." Sir Walter Scott had died just two years before the guide was published, and it is likely that travelers of the day packed copies of *Waverley* and *The Lady of the Lake* into their knapsacks as well as their trusty Murray's *Handbook* as they headed north.

The book gives an extraordinary insight into what pioneering tourists in Scotland could expect from their visit in the decade that Queen Victoria ascended the throne. Just like guidebooks of today, the book opens with a section about getting to and around the Highlands, highlighting the convenience of the direct horse-drawn coach services from Perth to Inverness. These thrice-weekly services took sixteen hours to complete the journey, with a fare of £3 for an inside seat and thirty-five shillings to sit outside in the wind and the rain. Alternatively a weekly steam ship ran from Glasgow to Inverness along the Crinan and Caledonian canals, taking two days.

The book then advises travelers of the situation regarding accommodation. "The inns are very comfortable," the authors maintain, "though metropolitan elegance cannot be expected... the traveller may everywhere calculate on the luxury of tea and sugar." The guide seeks to reassure the nervous first-time traveler that he "need be under no apprehension of Highland eagles banqueting on his famished carcass," and that he would not end up staying in "chimneyless hovels surcharged with peat-reek." In some inns, however, there is "tardiness of service" and in the cheaper establishments "lamentable inattention to cleanliness... particularly around the doors." (Nowhere in the guide are specific accommodation options mentioned.)

The book was written during the height of the Highland Clearances, and its introductory section, covering the history and geography of the region, adopts a refreshingly condemnatory tone when admitting that the recent introduction of sheep farming had been completed "with an inconsiderate degree of expedition... without due respect... to the deeply rooted habits" of local populations. There are no maps beyond a fold-out map at the front of the book, and the closely-written text, which spreads over 760 pages, is mostly dust-dry in its approach, with hugely detailed digressions into history, geology, and plant life when the occasion demands. Although sights of historical interest are pointed out there is little indication of which places might be the most interesting to visit and which the traveler with limited time could easily ignore.

Occasionally, though, the authors loosen up a little and resort to poetic licence in their descriptions. Ben Nevis, for instance, is a "rocky wilderness... lifeless and silent as the grave, its only tenants the lightning and the mist of heaven, and its language the voice of the storm." The guide advises travelers that an ascent of the mountain would take three hours (which seems a little fast) and that "it is imprudent for a stranger to undertake the ascent without a guide," who can be hired in Fort William for seven or eight shillings. Furthermore, the "inexperienced traveller" should "carry with him some wine or spirits" on his ascent of the mountain—though should nonetheless "use [them] with caution."

The firm of John Murray, who produced this first guide, was (and still is) one of London's most venerable publishing houses. For just under two hundred years the firm was based at the same set of offices at 50 Albemarle Street in Mayfair, an address that appears on the title page of all its nineteenth-century *Handbooks*. Murray's guides were aimed at the educated and cultured traveler: in the *Handbook for Southern Italy*, for instance, all quotations from classical authors are given in the original, as if it would be an insult to readers to translate them into English.

Murray's great rival in guidebook publishing was the German firm of Karl Baedeker, based in Koblenz and still (unlike Murray) publishing guidebooks today. Baedeker aimed its guides (published in both German and English) at a slightly different market: their books were printed on thinner paper but they were cheaper, and the maps were easier to read. In 1887, by which time Murray's *Handbook* had gone through a number of editions, Baedeker published their first guide to Great Britain, including within it a substantial section on the Scottish Highlands and Islands. The book's author was one J. F. Muirhead MA, who "has personally visited the greater part of the districts described" according to the publisher's foreword. The pull-out map at the front of the guide indicates that Kyle of Lochalsh, Thurso, and Oban could all be reached by train, but not Fort William, which did not join the rail network until fourteen years after the book's publication.

Baedeker gives a much greater sense of the Highlands being a destination of mass tourism than Murray's book of half a century before. Hotels, the guide maintains, are good value and cater for the sophisticated rather than the intrepid; breakfast in such establishments often consisted of salmon, fresh herrings, pork chops, steak, ham, eggs, preserves, cakes, and scones. The wine on offer at dinner could often be overpriced and of poor quality, but whisky diluted with water "will be found to be a good drink for the pedestrian." Coaches are "excellently horsed" and travelers were advised to arrive early to grab the best seats. A small but exasperating annoyance for travelers on ferries was the constant demand for pier dues (2-4d) on landing or embarking, as piers often belonged to private owners. However, the book claims that fares on the ships operated by Caledonian MacBrayne were "very moderate" (interestingly a recent edition of *The Rough Guide to the Highlands and Islands* warns contemporary travelers of precisely the reverse).

After a general introduction to Scotland the guide offers descriptions of Edinburgh and Glasgow and then shepherds readers towards Loch Lomond, where the ascent of Ben Lomond from Rowardennan on its eastern shore takes two to three hours "and is easily accomplished, even by ladies." A pony with a guide costs eight to ten shillings. The view over Loch Lomond from the summit, with its "bespangling islands" and the "sinuosity of its shore… amply repays the labour of the ascent." Then it is east to Loch Katrine, where the popularity and vividness of Scott's poem *The Lady of the Lake* "renders… guide books almost superfluous for this part of Scotland." Oban itself is presented by Baedeker as "the Charing

Cross of the Highlands" and a number of tours by boat and road are suggested that use the town as a convenient base. The last part of Baedeker's chapter on Scotland covers Inverness, but stops there: travelers who wanted to press on beyond this, to Kyle of Lochalsh or the great expanses of the northwest Highlands, were on their own.

Walkers in the Highlands: "Break clear away... and climb a mountain or spend a week in the woods"

Most nineteenth-century guidebooks to Scotland included recommended walks. Precise advice on walking was often offered as something of an aside, however, and Baedeker and Murray clearly assumed that most of their readers would not stray far from a car, train, or ferry. But a new type of traveler was also beginning to make his or her presence felt in Scotland during this time. This very different type of visitor would seek a relationship with the hills that went much further than looking at heather-clad summits from a train window, and they would initiate a conflict over countryside access that would drag on for over a century.

Hiking emerged as a popular pursuit for the first time in the early nineteenth century. An interest in botany was held by many and the middle classes enjoyed seeing plants and nature up close; meanwhile workers in the burgeoning industrial cities simply enjoyed the freedom and fresh air that the open countryside provided. With its shipyards and metal industries Glasgow emerged as one of the world's great industrial cities, yet some of the world's wildest expanses of countryside spread from its doorstep (it comes as a surprise to many that the shores of Loch Lomond are only twenty miles from the bustle and noise of the city center). In 1854 Hugh MacDonald published a guide for these new walkers entitled *Rambles around Glasgow*. But the lure of the great outdoor brought walkers into conflict with Highland landowners. After Queen Victoria popularized Balmoral, aristocrats—and newly-rich industrialists who wanted to adopt the habits of the "old" rich—began to take an interest in the deer and grouse that made their home among the moors and forests of the Highlands.

Soon landowners were busily stripping the trees from their estates, converting ancient forests into the moorland favored by game birds such as grouse. But it was precisely these areas that interested ramblers and hikers. When the Duke of Atholl closed his estate in the Cairngorms to walkers he found himself involved in a dispute with John Balfour, an Edinburgh University botanist, who tried to walk up Glen Tilt with seven of his botany students but was turned back by one of the duke's ghillies (attendants). Two years later another group of botanists, this time from Cambridge University, took up the same challenge, and were again turned back. In the inevitable legal battle that followed local shepherds and drovers attested in court to the fact that the paths through the moorland had a long history of public use. Landowners were powerful people, however, and the dispute over the "right to roam" across Highland countryside soon became bitter. In response a group of working-class Glaswegians founded the West of Scotland Ramblers' Alliance, a pressure group that campaigned for greater access to the hills.

The ramblers' champion was James Bryce, a Scotsman and Liberal MP for Tower Hamlets in London, who in 1884 put forward the Access to Mountains Bill in parliament at Westminster. Bryce was a redoubtable figure—he had climbed Mount Ararat and found some timber at the top that he claimed was from Noah's Ark, and later became British Ambassador to the United States—but his bill unfortunately made no headway, and for over a century the right of "freedom to roam" over the Highlands remained a moral one rather than a legal one. It was not until 2003 that the Scottish parliament finally passed a law that fulfilled the dreams of James Bryce and the nineteenth-century ramblers, establishing statutory rights of access to land and inland water throughout Scotland for outdoor recreation.

The goals of the most serious hikers of the Victorian era were the highest peaks, and in 1891 Sir Hugh Munro, a soldier, diplomat, and founding member of the Scottish Mountaineering Club, established and published a list of all Scottish mountains over three thousand feet in height. He counted 283 in all—in fact there are 284, a figure established after Munro's death when new and more accurate ways of measuring altitude were developed. In 1901 the Rev. Robertson became the first person to climb them all and since then it is reckoned that another four thousand have followed in his footsteps; Sir Hugh Munro himself was not one of them as he died before "bagging" the summit of the Inaccessible Pinnacle on Skye. Nowadays "bagging" Munros is the hill-walking equivalent of train-spotting, with those intent on climbing them all forever anxious to head into the hills and tick another one off the list.

The highest Munro of them all, of course, is Ben Nevis, but its ascent is relatively easy compared to many others. Around 75,000 walkers reach its cloud-enshrouded summit each year, most of them following the track established in 1883 that wound its way up to the weather observatory opened the same year. The founder of this remarkable observatory was the pioneering meteorologist Clement Wragge, known as "Inclement Wragge" in Fort William. Wragge was never paid for his work but his fiery temper meant that he was not appointed keeper of the meteorological station when the post was finally advertised, and he ended up as the official government meteorologist in the Australian state of Queensland.

Those who succeeded him at the observatory used to be irritated by walkers using their path to ascend the mountain, and took to charging them a shilling for the privilege (or three shillings for those who came up by pony). But the scientists could do nothing to stop a pioneering hotelier establishing an inn at the summit, beside the observatory. The observatory closed in 1904 through lack of funds, and the hotel lasted another ten years; the scant remains of both can be seen today. The only structures at the top today are the survival shelters that can be used by walkers and climbers who get into difficulty. The mountain claims a number of lives each year, particularly in winter, and the unwary often find to their cost that the frequently arctic weather conditions at the top are nothing like those experienced at the foot of the mountain in Fort William. Snow patches remain at the summit all year round; if the mountain were another six hundred feet higher it would be permanently snow-capped.

The other variety of well-trodden path in the Highlands is the long-distance footpath, of which the West Highland Way is the most famous (and busiest). A fixed route across the mountains from Glasgow to Fort William was first mooted in the 1960s, after the visible success of the Pennine Way in England (and the growing popularity of long-distance footpaths in the United States, such as the Appalachian Trail). Endless wrangling about the precise route then followed and it was not until 1980 that the footpath was officially inaugurated. Some ninety-six miles in length, the Way starts on the high street of the small Glasgow commuter suburb of Milngavie, and skirts the entire length of Loch Lomond before following the course of the West Highland rail line through Tyndrum and Bridge of Orchy. Then come the high, exposed sections across Rannoch

Walkers crossing Rannoch Moor on the West Highland Way (Andrew Beattie)

Moor and past the entrance to Glencoe before the path finally reaches Glen Nevis and the uninspiring suburban spill of Fort William.

Much of the path makes use of disused railways and former military roads, with walkers often staying in hotels such as the Kingshouse Hotel at the entrance to Glencoe, a former drovers' hostel that now sits isolated amidst the boggy moors dwarfed by the formidable arrowhead bulk of Buachaille Etive Mor (the view from the hotel lounge was once voted as one of the best anywhere in the world). The success of the West Highland Way saw the establishment of other long-distance paths, such as the Cateran Trail, which winds through the glens of Angus, and the Great Glen trail, which runs alongside Loch Ness and Loch Lochy, linking Fort William and Inverness. Today walkers from all over the world descend on Scotland to walk these paths, which in winter can be treacherous for the inexperienced.

With rights of access established to many parts of the Highlands, preservation and protection of the scenery walkers had come to see began to assume importance. The genesis of landscape preservation in Scotland can be traced to John Muir, the greatest Scottish environmentalist of the nineteenth century, whose passion for the Scottish countryside still permeates the outdoor movement in the country. "Break clear away, once in a while, and climb a mountain or spend a week in the woods," he once wrote. "Wash your spirits clean. Nature's peace will flow into you as the sunshine flows into trees. The winds will blow their freshness into you and storms their energy, while cares will drop off like autumn leaves."

Muir played a leading role in the creation of national parks in the United States, asserting that "mountain parks and reservations are useful not only as fountains of timber and irrigating rivers, but as fountains of life." Landscape protection and preservation measures have been in force in Scotland since the 1950s. However, it was not until the early twenty-first century that Scotland finally gained two national parks—Loch Lomond and the Trossachs in 2002, and the Cairngorms in 2003. Management of the parks attempts to balance the needs of all users: the landscape is preserved for walkers and wildlife without creating an unduly negative impact on employment prospects of local residents. The creation of the national parks has meant that the great landscapes of the Highlands will be preserved for generations to come, and that access to this spectacular scenery will be maintained—fulfilling the wishes of John Muir, James Bryce, Hugh Munro, and many others who have campaigned for secure access to Scotland's wonderful countryside. The National Trust for Scotland, founded in 1931, has also preserved many valuable landscapes and buildings. Most notable among them is Glencoe, which the Trust purchased from Lord Strathcona in 1935 in an appeal organized by the mountaineer Percy Unna, president of the Scottish Mountaineering Club, who later became one of the biggest benefactors of the Trust; his rules, known as the "Unna Principles," still guide the work of the Trust today.

Taking the Waters—and Taking to the Pistes

It was not just mountain views that attracted people to the Highlands in the Victorian era. Coastal resorts developed where the hills reached the sea, chief among them Dunoon and, on the Isle of Bute, Rothesay. A hundred years ago, steamers from Glasgow would bring hundreds of trippers on a daily basis in summer "doon the watter" to enjoy some fresh air in these holiday towns, away from the grime and bustle of the British Empire's busiest industrial city. Some great models of these steamers, and other yesteryear memorabilia, can be seen in the Castle Museum in Dunoon; but at the ferry port below the museum the only boats that dock these days are pudgy little passenger ferries taking commuters and shoppers across the Clyde for the rail link to Glasgow—a far cry from the glory days of steamers and the excitement of annual family holidays.

Like many British seaside resorts Dunoon is a tired place now, its front spoilt by some thoughtless 1960s additions. Rothesay, which the 1887 Baedeker guide dubs "the Brighton of the Clyde," has fared better, with its smart fountain and its colorful palm-fringed flowerbeds and its yachting marina and its balconied winter gardens pavilion (now housing the tourist office). But many shops in Rothesay are boarded up—as are those in Dunoon—and anyway these are seaside resorts rather than Highland towns, with their crazy golf and their putting greens and their down-at-heel cafes and hotels. Further north, beaches such as the one at Arisaig, just south of Mallaig, were colonized by hardy families looking for bucket-and-spade holidays, though the weather ensured that these places did not exactly attract the crowds in their droves.

Scotland's spa towns, meanwhile, hoped to attract a more refined type of visitor than the Clydeside resorts. One of the most famous is Crieff in Perthshire, on the very edge of the mountains, whose curative waters were first championed by well-to-do Victorians in 1868. The handsome, purpose-built hydro complex still stands above the town, though nowadays it is home to some bland swimming pools and a faux-Victorian garden, and the days when Crieff was vested with the same sort of well-heeled respectability as Bath or Harrogate seem long gone. The waters at Ballater, near Braemar, were thought to cure scrofula, and during the Victorian era the town briefly became a fashionable destination, particularly as Balmoral is close by; but its wells are now dry and there is next to no evidence of Ballater's former role as a spa town.

Strathpeffer, which lies picturesquely in a fold of low hills to the west of Dingwall, is more recognizable as a formerly busy watering-hole. The town retains a genteel sense of propriety to this day, its pump room (now a visitors' center) and bandstand overlooked by a venerable hotel whose style, for a change, is Mock Tudor rather than Scots Baronial. Down the hill a little way from the center is the former railway station, which marked

Strathpeffer is one of the most venerable of Highland spas (Andrew Beattie)

the terminus of a short branch off the Inverness to Kyle of Lochalsh line. The line and the station were closed in 1951, way before all the Beeching cuts, a reflection of the changing fortunes of British spa towns after World War II. Good use has been made of the old station buildings, though, which now house a small bookshop, a shop selling fair trade products, and the cramped exhibition rooms of the Highland Museum of Childhood. The Victorian wrought ironwork of the station canopy shelters the outside seating of the museum's teashop, where tea and scones are consumed on the platform where trains that had come all the way from Euston once deposited their spa-bound passengers.

Attracting a wholly different breed of tourists is Scotland's skiing scene. The facilities and snow conditions may be vastly inferior to those in the Alps, but the influx of skiers into Aviemore, Glenshee, and Glen Nevis gives hoteliers a much-needed fillip once the walkers, birdwatchers, and water sports enthusiasts have headed home. The history of skiing in Scotland dates back to March 12, 1889, when thirty professional men—mainly solicitors, doctors, and bankers—met in Glasgow's Grand Hotel for the inaugural meeting of the Scottish Mountaineering Club. In the chair was Professor G. C. Ramsay of Glasgow University, whose brother had been a founder member of the Alpine Club.

The club intended to campaign for greater access to the mountains, the construction of bothies (shelters), and the publication of better maps. However, over the next ten years members of the club took to strapping skis to their feet as much as pulling on hiking boots. One of the most noted British skiing enthusiasts of this era was a Scot named E. C. Richardson, who in 1903 founded the Ski Club of Great Britain. "Having ascended a hill," Richardson wrote, "who can describe the feelings of the downward slide [and] the exuberant joy of swaying motion—in short the whole rippingness of a good run?" In 1904 he persuaded the club to devote their Easter Meet of that year to skiing. This they duly did, on the slopes of Ben Nevis, and the tradition of "skisters"—as Scottish skiers were known—was born. Soon the journal of the Mountaineering Club was reporting that the best skiing conditions (for a run of thirty miles per hour) came after a heavy fall of snow followed by a thaw, a sharp frost, and a fall of another three inches.

Members of the Scottish Mountaineering Club were principally climbers, and as skiing grew in popularity it became apparent that there was a need for a club devoted specifically to it. In 1907 the inaugural meeting of the Scottish Ski Club, which still exists today to promote Scottish skiing, was held at the Surgeons' Hall in Edinburgh. In the Chair this time was Dr. W. S. Brice, who had formerly been in charge of the observatory at the summit of Ben Nevis; he had skied both there and on expeditions in the Antarctic. Soon the club was publishing lists of hotels near popular *pistes* and reporting on snow conditions in the mountains, and in 1910 members of the club donated a pair of skis to the postman at Braemar to make his winter rounds easier.

The club foundered after World War I but was revived in the 1930s, by which time newly-built motorable roads allowed easier access to the slopes. In 1932 the club opened its first ski hut, above Loch Tay, while railway companies embraced a campaign promoting winter sports in Scotland and the owner of the fashionable Fife Arms Hotel in Braemar made sure his establishment was *the* place to be seen. In 1933 the first slalom race was held, at Killin, and was won by a Miss P. Raeburn; the next year a cup was donated for the race winner by a Mr. Pitman, and the Pitman Quaich

Alpine-style cable car in the Nevis Range (Andrew Beattie)

is still presented each year to this day. Two years later the snowy winter of 1936 brought serious congestion to the slopes for the first time.

The unusually snowy winter of 1945–46, coupled with limited opportunity for travel to Europe in the aftermath of World War II, meant that Scottish skiing was able to get off to a healthy post-war start. Then in 1954 a celebrated Austrian skier named Karl Fuchs married an Englishwoman and came to live in the Cairngorms, where he established a ski school at Carrbridge near Aviemore—and so ushered in a decade of rapid development. The first ski tows were built at Glencoe in 1956 and at Glenshee (near Braemar) in 1958, while the government-owned Central Council for Physical Recreation bought Glenmore Lodge near Aviemore to promote outdoor activities in the Cairngorms, with skiing high on their agenda. Soon a road was built to the lodge, funded jointly by local hoteliers and the Forestry Commission, who wanted better access to their plantations. In the late 1950s the road was extended beyond Glenmore Lodge to terminate at the base station of a new chairlift—Scotland's first—that hauled skiers to the upper slopes of Coire Cas. The lift opened for business on December 23, 1961, and new ski tows soon crisscrossed the slopes around the upper station. A second chairlift was opened the following year in Glenshee.

By now ski clubs were thriving in major Scottish cities. Buses were organized to ferry skiers to the mountains for a weekend of skiing and for a while the London Weekend Ski Club even ran an overnight coach from London to Newtonmore for skiing in the Cairngorms. Proposals for the construction of a monorail across the Cairngorms linking Braemar with Aviemore began to take shape, though in the end got no further than the drawing board. Then the bubble burst. In 1963 Mar Lodge, an elaborate palace built by Queen Victoria for her daughter the Princess Louise, was opened as a ski center, but shut down two years later due to lack of demand. Ever-decreasing air fares meant that a skiing holiday in the Alps was now affordable for many English (and Scottish) skiers and the brief heyday of Scottish skiing was over.

Developments have continued, though, financed by government grants aimed at expanding the tourism economy of the Highlands. In 1989 the UK's first gondola-style cable car was built up the lower slopes of Ben Nevis (the development is known as "Nevis Range") while in 2002 the chairlift to Coire Cas was replaced by a funicular railway. Some of these developments have been criticized for their environmental insensitivity, constructed as they are in such extraordinary landscapes. Aviemore, which emerged as Scotland's premier skiing resort in the 1960s, continues to hold that crown. Easily accessible by road and railway from Inverness and Perth, the town has its origins as a place where English aristocrats could get off the train and hunt or fish, but in the 1950s the hotels began to stay open in the winter and the town never looked back. Now it is a strange, sterile town, a mixture of faceless modern luxury hotels and the odd baronial-style pile, all strung along an anodyne strip of outdoor shops, cafés, and après-ski venues, the whole ensemble wrapped around by a gray smudge of former council estates. Only the railway station, left unchanged since the nineteenth century, retains its charm, the moreso as steam trains on a short preserved line along the River Spey use part of it.

The busiest skiing season of late at the Cairngorm Ski Centre, some ten miles away, has been the winter of 2009–10, which began on November 28 and ran through to June 21, when skiing was possible on the longest day of the year, on snow that still lay thick above the top station of the funicular railway. Between those dates the track bed of the funicular was covered in snow four times and had to be dug out, and on March 6 the conditions were put to good use when a slightly dubious world record was set for the highest number of kilted skiers sliding down a *piste*. But this season was exceptional: with rising world temperatures, snow is coming later to the Cairngorms and melting sooner, and the long-term future of Scottish skiing seems somewhat insecure.

In the early days of tourism it was the grandeur of the scenery that provided the main draw for visitors. Now the attractions are vastly more varied. Summer in the Highlands sees white water rafters careering down the River Tay, boardsailers braving the blustery seas off Tiree, boating enthusiasts catching the winds in their sails on Loch Linnhe, golfers playing the fairways on the banks of Loch Lomond, birdwatchers spying golden eagles in the Cairngorms, paragliders swooping from the slopes of Ben Nevis, and mountain bikers bumping down hillsides in the Trossachs. Fort William is the greatest tourist hub of the Highlands, if only because the tourism experience there is so diverse: holidaymakers on coach tours rub shoulders with serious hikers in summer and skiers heading for the Nevis Range in winter, while adventure tourism beckons in nearby Glen Nevis. In summer the town's guest houses and hotels are jam-packed with tourists and its roads (the busiest of which skirts the shores of Loch Linnhe, denying the town any sort of lochside promenade) groan with coaches. From Fort William tourists head west, to Mallaig and Skye, east to Glen Nevis, southwest to Glencoe—and northeast to the most famous tourist attraction in the Highlands, namely Loch Ness and its famous monster.

Loch Ness has been a popular destination since the 1930s, when a road was built along its northern shore and a London surgeon named R. K. Wilson published (in the *Daily Mail*) the most famous photograph of the monster (still widely circulated despite being revealed as a fake in the 1990s by the man who built the model that the photographer used). Today two rival "monster" museums draw the crowds at Drumnadrochit, on the lake's northern shore, and their acrimonious rivalry often excites interest from the local press. (The attraction in the former Drumnadrochit Hotel is the classier of the two—if a Nessie Museum can be classy at all—with its show, in eleven languages, spread through six rooms and its willingness to treat the whole affair with a healthy dose of cynicism.) Nessieland

Castle, a "monster adventure on the shores of Loch Ness," just a minute's walk away, has less to say (and actually repeats some of what it does have to say), though seems more willing to believe all the sonar investigations and other investigative techniques of monster hunters. Urquhart Castle, the single most popular tourist attraction in the whole of Scotland, is only five minutes away by road, and it is this tiny corner of the Highlands on the shores of Loch Ness that now claims the questionable crown as the region's ultimate tourist magnet.

THE LURE OF THE REMOTE AND THE WILD

Few of the people who throng Urquhart Castle and the Loch Ness Monster museums get anywhere near Rannoch Moor—one of Britain's most desolate expanses of emptiness. In Robert Louis Stevenson's novel *Kidnapped* the fugitives David Balfour and Alan Breck go to ground there after being accused of the murder of a British government agent, Colin Campbell of Glenure. They saw a vastness "as waste as the sea; only the moorfowl and the peewees crying upon it, and far over to the east, a herd of deer, moving like dots. Much of it was red with heather; much of the rest broken up with bogs and hags and peaty pools; some had been burned black in a heath fire and in another place there was quite a forest of dead firs, standing like skeletons. A wearier-looking desert man never saw." Balfour and Breck come off the moor alive. But away from the realms of fiction, plenty of real travelers have not been so lucky. For the moor claims lives in a myriad of ways. Travelers lose their way in its trackless interior, or become disoriented by fog, or are battered by the storms that funnel through Glencoe and then blast their way across its peat bogs, or are frozen by the snow and cold that wraps the place in frosty whiteness for much of the winter.

From a distance the Moor can appear arid and lifeless but up close it is clear how much water there is here, and how much wildlife is attracted to it: lochans (small lochs) puncture the landscape, skimmed by skeins of swans and drained by streams oily-black with peat. Yet crossing the place at night, on the West Highland Railway or by one of the winding roads that lead to the line's lonely stations, the place appears black and limitless.

The academic Robert MacFarlane is one of a number of writers who have spent time on the Moor, coming to terms with its harshness and its vastness. Describing a walk across it in his book *Wild Places,* he noted that "so extensive was the space within which we were moving that when I glanced up at the mountains west of the Moor, to try to gauge the distance we had come, it seemed as though we had not advanced at all: that, like explorers walking against the spin of pack ice, our feet fell exactly where we had lifted them." Emerging onto the A82, the main road to Fort William that crosses part of the Moor, he thought that "the angles and the straight lines of the vehicles that flashed past, and the garishness of their colours, seemed bizarre after the long hours on the moor: as strange as spaceships."

George Orwell (the pen-name of the author Eric Blair) was another writer who came to Scotland lured by the prospect of isolation. His ideal, though, was a Hebridean island rather than a tract of moorland. In his wartime diary of June 1940 Orwell admitted to "thinking always of my island in the Hebrides, which I suppose I shall never possess or see"—but in September 1945, just a few months after the war's end, he finally visited the island of Jura in the Inner Hebrides, on the recommendation of David Astor, the editor of the *Observer* newspaper for which Orwell often wrote reviews. Orwell had been recently widowed and was disillusioned with the new Labour government, which had promised so much after the war, but had failed to abolish private schools or reform the House of Lords. He came to Jura seeking the peace and quiet he needed for writing and contemplation—"somewhere where I cannot be telephoned," he wrote in a letter—and he was captivated by the challenge of leading a self-sufficient existence, living off the rabbits he shot and the fish he caught. After a few months back home in England he sold his London flat and, in May 1947, he visited Jura for the second time and began living permanently on the island.

This time Orwell was accompanied by his sister Avril and his three-year-old adopted son Richard. Their home on Jura was a remote farmhouse named Barnhill, which Orwell had seen on his first visit to the island. According to the wife of the local laird, Orwell was visibly sick with tuberculosis when he arrived at Barnhill on his second visit, "a sad and lonely man who looked as if he'd been through a great deal." When he landed on Jura he had with him only a suitcase, a kettle, a saucepan, and a typewriter. Barnhill had no electricity and poor radio reception, and its lighting was provided by flickering lamps powered by paraffin delivered in drums. The place was broken-down and desolate, which cannot have

Barnhill, the remote farmhouse on Jura where George Orwell wrote *1984*
(© Gordon Doughty/Creative Commons Licence)

helped Orwell's health, but he wrote that he was "better off living in Jura than in London" and that there was good access to wood, peat, and coal for heating.

At first he had the services of a housekeeper, a local woman named Susan Watson; but she eventually left, after a disagreement with Avril. When he was not writing, or nurturing an impractical plan to develop a commercial dairy farm on the island, Orwell spent time hunting or fishing with members of his family. On one occasion he took his son, along with his nephew and niece, out for a jaunt on his motorboat to look at the spectacular whirlpool in the Gulf of Corryvrechan, which according to local tradition was created by Hag, the Celtic sea goddess. The powerful currents in the whirlpool swept away the outboard motor and the boat was wrecked against some rocks. Orwell then had to struggle desperately to save the children from drowning, before the party was eventually rescued by a passing fisherman.

During this second stay on Jura Orwell wrote much of his masterpiece *1984,* which was originally titled *Last Man in Europe*. His study was on the ground floor of Barnhill but most of the novel was written in his upstairs bedroom; visitors regularly reported hearing him pounding away on his typewriter from the kitchen, which was situated directly below. He was still working on the novel when his worsening tuberculosis forced him to return to London, after a stay on Jura of eighteen months. The completed manuscript of *1984* was eventually sent to his publisher on December 4, 1948, and just over a year later, after a lengthy spell in a hospital in East Kilbride near Glasgow, Orwell was dead. After his death his second wife, Sonia Brownell, whom Orwell married in the last weeks of his life, came to Barnhill for the first time to look over his remaining papers, and reported being shocked and dismayed by the dilapidated state of the farmhouse. Today it is in private hands and is closed to the public, but this does not prevent a trickle of pilgrims walking to Barnhill along a track from the tiny hamlet of Lealt, some four miles away. Apparently the only item in the cottage still remaining from Orwell's time is his bath.

It is not only writers in search of isolation who have been attracted to the remote islands of the Inner Hebrides. The twentieth century saw a number of rich buyers drawn to them, in search of an unusual purchase, a long-term investment, or a remote bolt-hole that could take them away from prying eyes. In 1938 Lord Redesdale bought the tiny island of Inch Kenneth, off Mull, and two years later his daughter Unity Mitford sought sanctuary here after fleeing from Nazi Germany when World War II began. Unity, the youngest of the three notorious "Mitford sisters," was (like her older sister Diana) a fascist sympathizer and during the 1930s had lived in Germany, where she developed close personal ties with Hitler. She had even, on occasion, addressed Nazi rallies, and had used her presumed influence to try to prevent a war between Germany and Britain. When that failed, and war broke out, Unity was in Munich, where she tried to shoot herself in the head with a pistol. But she succeeded only in lodging the bullet in part of her skull. Hitler visited her in hospital and made arrangements for her to return to England via Switzerland.

On her return the press clamored for Unity's internment; her mother assumed responsibility for nursing her, first in High Wycombe and then from 1944 on the remote and isolated private island owned by her father. There, it seems, Unity steadily went mad. In the ruins of an ancient chapel on the island, which bears witness to having been home to medieval hermits, she would lead improvised religious services at which her mother would be the sole member of the congregation. Once, it was reported that they had been joined at the service by a man in a belted overcoat with a lock of hair plastered down on his forehead and a bristle of a mustache—who disappeared at the end of the service. An apparition, perhaps? Or a mischievous journalist dressed up as Hitler? The island's boatman was later adamant that no-one had crossed over to the island. The mystery was never solved and Unity Mitford finally died in 1948 in a hospital in Oban from the wounds associated with her suicide attempt some seven years earlier.

THE END: CAPE WRATH

Cape Wrath, Scotland's most northwesterly point, takes some getting to. The first part of the journey involves taking a passenger ferry across the Kyle of Durness. Then it's a bumpy forty-minute ride in a minibus, provided by an enterprising local firm, along the barely-metalled road to the lighthouse at the Cape. The road snakes its way across high moorland and over narrow valleys that are still traversed by the arched bridges built by the road's Victorian builders. Gates at either end restrict access when the military firing ranges through which the road passes are active, and here and there the ground is pockmarked by shell craters from the explosion of live ammunition.

Then, finally, the whitewashed lighthouse and its outbuildings come into view on a high ledge of rock. The grassy bank surrounding the buildings drops down to precipitous cliffs that plunge into the sea in a tangle of caves and rock arches. The eighteenth-century travel writer John Knox, who came here on a stormy day, wrote of the sea breaking "with inconceivable violence" against these cliffs, "throwing its spray sometimes over the summits." Above the slapping waves the air is alive with circling seabirds that make their homes on the cliff face. Along the coastline to the east, out of sight, are the Clo Mor cliffs, the highest in mainland Britain, home to tens of thousands of puffins, guillemots, razorbills, and fulmars.

The panorama over the ocean—covered by the sweep of the beam of Robert Stevenson's squat, sturdy lighthouse—extends a full 270 degrees. Traveling due west, the next land is Labrador on the east coast of Canada; to the north, thousands of miles of open ocean finally end at the edge of the Polar ice cap. This place, where the Highlands plunge into the sea, truly is where northwestern Europe comes to an end. Mariners have always regarded it with fear. In Neil Gunn's novel *The Silver Darlings*, the sighting of the Cape by the crew of a fishing boat "inspired [them] with awe and held them to silence." And when the sun sets over the open ocean to the west, it does so in a vast sky, occasionally calm but more often violent and torn: smudgy clouds heralding rain are constantly blown in from the Atlantic by the wind that slams incessantly against the thick walls of the lighthouse and whistles and hums through the tufts of vegetation clinging to the high cliffs.

The quality of the light here—its transparency, its openness—is one of the most remarkable features of Cape Wrath: it arises from the dustless nature of the atmosphere, and on a clear day the view out to sea can stretch for a hundred miles, while cliffs dozens of miles distant along each coast appear tantalizingly close. No wonder that, over the centuries, the place has attracted travelers who gaze with awe at its loneliness and its expansive drama. In the nineteenth century an early John Murray handbook enthused about the headland's

> stupendous granitic front, its extensive and splendid ocean scenery, and the particularly wild country by which it is approached… abrupt and threatening precipices, vast and huge fissures, caverns, and subterranean openings alternately appear in the utmost confusion, while the deep-sounding rush of the mighty waters, agitated by the tides among their resounding openings, the screams and never ceasing flight of innumerable sea-fowl, and often the spoutings of a straw whale in his unwieldy gambols in the ocean, form altogether a scene which none who has witnessed it can ever forget.

Paul Theroux was also captivated by the Cape. In *The Kingdom by the Sea* he describes it as "Unimaginable. It was one of those places where, I guessed, every traveller felt like a discoverer who was seeing it for the first time. There are not many such places in the world. I felt I had penetrated a fastness of mountains and moors." The scenery, Theroux went on to write, was "eerie… especially on a wet day… It was not picturesque and it was practically unphotographable. It was stunningly empty. It looked like the corner of another planet, and at times it seemed diabolical… I was very happy at Cape Wrath. I even liked its ambiguous name. I did not want to leave."

This is a book about the Highlands, and perhaps it is fair to leave the last word about Scotland's last place to Sir Walter Scott, the Highlands' champion, who first encountered the "dreadful Cape, so fatal to mariners" while traveling by boat around the Scottish coast in 1814. He was, at that time, at the height of his fame, and his name was associated with Scotland throughout the world. This truly remote spot—a site for the lighthouse had been selected, but as yet there was no building here—was, in Scott's words, "a striking point, both from the dignity of its own appearance, and from the mental association of its being the extreme Cape of Scotland." At the water's edge "the foam of the sea plays at long bowls with a huge collection of large stones, some of them a ton in weight, but which these fearful billows chuck up and down as a child tosses a ball," while behind the Cape the country "swells in high, sweeping elevations."

Perhaps Scott's failings—to recognize the poverty of his beloved Scotland, to properly acknowledge the cruelty of the Clearances, to pander to the prejudices about Highlanders held by his English readers—can be forgiven when his love for Scotland, and its scenery, is laid bare in descriptions such as this: for Cape Wrath is one of the few places where the magnificence of Scott's Highlands really does live up to the imagination of the Romantics—and to the imagining of Scotland in the minds of the country's hundreds of thousands of annual visitors, even if only a few are willing to put the time and energy into seeking out the exhilarating place where northwestern Europe finally plunges into the sea. Those who do get here find a landscape fashioned by fire, molded by ice and water, and pounded by the crashing waves of a sea that is as tumultuous as the country's history: to quote again the expression used by Paul Theroux to describe the scenery of the Highlands, Cape Wrath is, indeed, Highland Scotland at its most "elemental."

Bibliography & Further Reading

Geology and the Great Outdoors

Richard Fortey's book *The Earth: an Intimate History* (Harper Perennial, 2005) is a highly readable account of the geological machinations that made the earth, and includes a certain amount of information on the Scottish Highlands. E. J. Browne's two-volume biography of Charles Darwin, originally published in 1995 and republished by Pimlico in 2003, provides an excellent account of the controversy surrounding the Parallel Roads of Glen Roy.

There are numerous editions available of Gavin Maxwell's classic book *Ring of Bright Water* (1962). Little Toller Books brought out the most recent edition, in 2009, while the Penguin edition of 2001 includes *Ring of Bright Water* and its two sequels, *The Rocks Remain* (1963) and *Raven Seek Thy Brother* (1968) in one volume. Single-volume editions of these further books have not been published since the 1970s. All are masterpieces of nature writing: fluid, compelling accounts of life on the remote Highland coast. In 2013 Birlinn brought out a new edition of *Harpoon at a Venture*, Maxwell's 1952 account of his attempts to run a shark fishery on the island of Soay, off Skye. Richard Frere's 1976 biography of Maxwell, *Maxwell's Ghost,* was re-issued by Birlinn in 2011 and provides a highly readable and affectionate account of the life of this often difficult man. Regarding guides to the wildlife of Scotland, Kenny Taylor's 2002 book *Scotland's Nature and Wildlife* (Lomond Books) offers a practical, region-based guide to the country's plants and animals. Among the many other memoirs written by those who have grown up amidst Scotland's wildlife one of the most famous is *Seal Morning* by Rowenna Farre (1957, reissued by Birlinn in 2008), which is an account of a young girl's childhood in a remote Sutherland croft and the wildlife she adopted, including a talented seal, two mischievous squirrels, and a beautiful red deer.

Robert MacFarlane's book *The Wild Places* (Granta, 2008) is a personal account of the allure of Britain's last remaining wildernesses and includes much material on the Scottish Highlands. Mike Cawthorne's 2007 book *Wilderness Dreams: the Call of Scotland's Last Wild Places* (In Pinn) is a slightly more adrenaline-fueled look at some of the remotest parts of Scotland. Those who head out into the wild on Scotland's most famous long distance footpath will require Charlie Loram's book *The West Highland Way* (Trailblazer: frequently updated), which includes a history of the West Highland Way and much information about Highland geology and wildlife, in addition to practical information for walkers. *Mountain Days and Bothy Nights* by Dave Brown and Ian Mitchell (1987, reissued in 2010 by Luath Press) is a very entertaining look at modern-day hill-walking while Hamish Brown's *Hamish's Mountain Walk* (1978, reissued in 2010 by Sandstone Press) and *Three Men on the Way* (Whittles Publishing, 2013) are also excellent travel narratives concerned with walking in Scotland. *Hell of a Journey* by Mike Cawthorne (2000, reissued by Birlinn in 2012) is an account of one man's trek through Scotland (and up a number of Munros) during the depths of winter while *Gulfs of Blue Air - a Highland Journey* by Jim Crumley (Mainstream Publishing, 1997) follows one man's journey across Scotland and includes reflections on the natural landscape and the poets inspired by it. More generally, Sinclair McKay's 2012 book *Ramble On* (Fourth Estate) provides a wonderfully anecdotal history of walking in Britain, with many references made to the history of walking in Scotland. Myrtle Simpson's 1982 book *Skisters: the History of Scottish Skiing* (Landmark Press) is less well-written and rather dated but provides the only history of skiing in Scotland. Patsy Boyle and Alasdair Dawson's 1984 pamphlet *Time in his Life: George Orwell, Barnhill, Isle of Jura* offers an account of George Orwell's time on Jura, though references to Orwell's stay on the island can also be found in the numerous biographies dedicated to him. In 2011 Birlinn published the fifth edition of George Hendry's endearingly eccentric 1989 bestseller *Midges in Scotland*, an in-depth account of the Highland midge, its biology, and why it bites.

CULTURAL, SOCIAL, AND POLITICAL HISTORY

There are a number of general histories of Scotland available, such as Andrew Fisher's *Traveller's History of Scotland* (1990, most recent edition published by Interlink in 2009) but the best history of the region covered by this book is James Hunter's *Last of the Free: a History of the Highlands and Islands of Scotland*, which is dense, detailed, and opinionated, often skimming the more "popular" aspects of Highland history (there is next to nothing on Flora MacDonald, for instance) and instead focusing on the social and political history of poverty and oppression. The book was first published in 1999 and was reissued by Mainstream Publishing in 2010. The same author's *Dance Called America* (1994, reissued by Mainstream in 2010) provides an account of Scottish emigration to North America. One of the most closely documented eras of Scottish history is the Highland Clearances, and one of the most comprehensive surveys of the upheavals wrought by the Clearances is that provided by Eric Richards in his *History of the Highland Clearances,* a book originally published in the 1980s which was reissued by Birlinn as *The Highland Clearances* in 2013. This book runs to over 500 pages and provides a sober analysis of the Clearances: for a more passionate though perhaps less academically rigorous survey readers should turn to John Prebble's 1963 book *The Highland Clearances*; the 1982 Penguin re-issue is still widely available. Prebble's 1968 book *Glencoe: the Story of the Massacre* provides a compelling study of one of the most controversial events in Scottish history; it was republished by Penguin in 1973 and by the Folio society in 1996, and the author's equally compelling 1972 title *Culloden* was republished by Pimlico in 2002. Diana Henderson's *Highland Soldier: a Social History of the Highland Regiments 1820-1920* (1989, reissued in 1997 by John Donald Publishers) will be of interest to those with an enthusiasm for Scottish military history. The social history of the Highlands is encapsulated in Alasdair Maclean's *Night Falls on Ardnamurchan: the Twilight of a Crofting Community* (1984, re-published by Birlinn in 2001), which recounts the hardness of life in a remote crofting community in the west of Scotland during the course of the twentieth century.

Numerous biographies on the historical personalities with which this book is concerned can be tracked down without much difficulty—including those recounting the lives of Robert the Bruce, Mary Queen of Scots, and Bonnie Prince Charlie: in the case of the latter Fitzroy Maclean's 1989 biography (reissued by Canongate in 1998) is probably the most authoritative. Ronald Clark's 1981 book *Balmoral: Queen Victoria's Highland Home* was republished by Bloomsbury in 2012, while a heavily illustrated history of the residence was published by Heritage House Group in 1984. Roger Hutchinson's *Calum's Road*, published by Berlinn in 2006 and re-published in 2011, is one of the quirkiest and most original recent books on Highland history and recounts one man's dogged efforts to construct a road across the island of Raasay. Jill Hamilton's *Thomas Cook: the Holiday Maker* (History Press, 2005) and Piers Brendon's *Thomas Cook: One*

Hundred Years of Popular Tourism (Secker and Warburg, 1991) offer accounts of this remarkable pioneer in Highland tourism. Simon Schama's 1995 book *Landscape and Memory*, reissued by Harper Perennial in 2004, provides a fascinating survey of how Romantic sensibilities altered the perception of the Highlands and other mountain areas in the imaginations of writers and artists at the dawn of the nineteenth century.

TRAVELOGUES

Not surprisingly there are numerous modern editions of Samuel Johnson's *Journey to the Western Islands of Scotland* (1775) and James Boswell's *Journal of a Tour to the Hebrides* (1785), which can be purchased in single editions or as one volume—the latter including editions published by Penguin Classics (1984), Canongate (1996), and Birlinn (2011), each with scholarly introductions and other material. The most recent biography of Johnson is the one by Peter Martin (2009) though James Boswell's classic biography of Johnson is still in print; Yale University Press also publishes *Johnson and Boswell: a Biography of Friendship* by John B. Radner (2013) and there are numerous other writings by and about these two great eighteenth-century men of letters.

Of the other eighteenth- and nineteenth-century travelogues cited in this book, Birlinn publish a modern (1998) edition of *Burt's Letters from the North of Scotland* (originally published in 1755 as *Letters From a Gentleman in the North of Scotland to his Friend in London)* while in 2013 Rare Books Club published a new edition of Richard Pococke's *Tours in Scotland* (originally published in 1887). A number of publishers issue modern editions of Thomas Pennant's *Tour in Scotland and Voyage to the Hebrides* and John Knox's *Tour through the Highlands of Scotland* (1786), while in 2014 Birlinn published a new edition of Martin Martin's *A Description of the Western Islands of Scotland.* The Wolfenden Press publishes a modern edition (2009) of William Gilpin's essay *On Picturesque Beauty.* Walter Scott's *Voyage of the Pharos*, an account of his journey around the coast of Scotland in 1814, was republished by the School Library Association in 1998. Queen Victoria's *Leaves from a Journal of Our Life in the Highlands* (1868) was republished by Kessinger in 2010. Dorothy Wordsworth's 1803 journal *Recollections of a Tour Made in Scotland,* originally published in 1874, was republished by Bibliolife in 2009. Alexander Smith's 1865 book

A Summer in Skye, his description of a journey from Edinburgh to a rain-sodden Isle of Skye, was republished by Birlinn in 1998. *Scottish Journey,* a classic travelogue written in 1935 that takes the Orkney poet Edwin Muir across the length of the country, was republished by Mainstream Publishing in 1996.

Few modern travelogues concern themselves solely with the Highlands (or even with Scotland)—the exception being those concerned with walking, which are described in the first part of this section. Paul Theroux's 1983 book *The Kingdom by the Sea* is a masterfully wry account of a journey around the coast of Britain that Theroux completed in the early 1980s; though inevitably dated now, Theroux's portrait of the Highlands and of Highland towns such as Oban is always engaging. Bill Bryson's equally engaging 1996 book *Notes from a Small Island* has also gone through several editions, the most recent of which was published by the Folio Society in 2010. Michael Palin's first volume of diaries (*The Python Years: 1969 to 1979*) includes an amusing account of the filming in the Highlands of *Monty Python and the Holy Grail* while the second volume (*Halfway to Hollywood: 1980 to 1988*) includes a brief account of the filming of Palin's first travel program, a journey from London to Kyle of Lochalsh in the *Great Railway Journeys* BBC TV series. (Both are published by Phoenix.) The books *On the Slow Train* (2011) and *On the Slow Train Again* (2012) by the railway journalist Michael Williams (both published by Arrow) describe journeys along the rail lines in Britain that Beeching somehow never closed—including the lines from Glasgow to Fort William, Fort William to Mallaig, and Inverness to Thurso and Kyle of Lochalsh. Miles Kington's *Steaming through Britain* (1990) is more photo-based in approach but includes an account of a journey by train to Mallaig. John Thomas' 1965 book *The West Highland Railway* was reissued by House of Lochar in 1998 and is one of numerous books that recount the history of the rail lines that were built across the region.

The nineteenth-century travel guides mentioned in Part Three of this book, such as the 1834 John Murray *Guide to the Highlands and Islands* and the 1887 Baedeker *Guide to Great Britain* occasionally turn up for sale on internet auction and antiquarian bookselling sites. The best of (many) contemporary travel guides is the *Rough Guide to the Scottish Highlands and Islands*, which is updated every three years.

Fiction

The most prolific writer of Highland-set fiction is Neil Gunn, most of whose books have been re-issued in modern editions by the Edinburgh-based publishers Canongate (through their imprint Canongate Classics) and Birlinn (through their imprint Polygon). The most widely-read these days is the lyrical and reflective *Highland River* (1937, reissued by Canongate in 1997), which concerns the quest of a young boy named Kenn to catch a salmon in a Highland stream; *Butcher's Broom* (1934, reissued by Polygon in 2006) is set during the Highland Clearances, while *Sun Circle* (1933, reissued by Canongate in 2001) is set among a tribe of Christianized Picts facing a Viking invasion in ninth-century northern Scotland. Other works include *The Silver Darlings,* Gunn's 1941 novel recounting the life of herring fishermen on the Scottish coast who had been displaced by the Clearances, which was re-issued by Faber in 1978, while in 1993 Souvenir Press reissued Gunn's 1931 novel *Morning Tide*, which tells the story of a young boy growing up in a tiny fishing community on Scotland's east coast.

The novels of Sir Walter Scott, through which a semi-mythical historic Scotland was created in the nineteenth century, are all readily available in modern editions, published by Penguin Classics, Wordsworth Classics, and Oxford World Classics, among others. The most famous of Scott's Highland-set novels are *Waverley* (1814, reissued in 2011 by Penguin Classics), which is set during the 1745 Jacobite rebellion and features a brief appearance from Bonnie Prince Charlie himself, and *Rob Roy* (1817, republished by Wordsworth Editions in 1997) which recounts the colorful adventures of an English aristocrat and his involvement with the notorious Highland outlaw, Rob Roy MacGregor, during the 1715 Jacobite rising.

Later novels from this era include Jules Verne's *The Green Ray* (1882, reissued by the Luath Press in 2009), which follows the journey of a young woman along the coast of the Highlands as she seeks to witness the elusive "green ray" that appears over the sea at sunset, and *John Splendid,* the 1898 novel by Neil Munro (reissued in 1994 by Black and White Publishing) that is set during the military upheavals in Scotland caused by the English Civil War and in particular the Duke of Montrose's attack on Inveraray. Munro's tales of Captain Para Handy, who sails his Clyde puffer *Vital*

Spark between Glasgow and west coast islands and ports, have proved far more enduring than this little-known novel, and a new complete edition of the tales was published by Birlinn in 2001. Then there is Robert Louis Stevenson's *Kidnapped* (1886, reissued in 2012 by Vintage Children's Classics), an adventure yarn of derring-do that is set during the Jacobite uprising. *Kidnapped* was written as a children's story, though may be a bit hard-going for today's young readers; Kathleen Fidler's children's books *The Desperate Journey* (1964, reissued in 2012 by Kelpies), which tells the story of a family uprooted by the Clearances, and *The Droving Lad* (1955, reissued by Floris Books in 2003), which is set in the world of Highland cattle drovers, may be more accessible. Dick King-Smith's 1990 children's novel *The Water Horse*, about a boy who finds an egg on the shores of a Scottish loch that hatches into a monster, was reissued by Puffin in 2013.

Contemporary fiction with a Highland setting includes *Salmon Fishing in the Yemen* by Paul Torday (2006), which tells the story through interview transcripts, emails, and diary entries of an engineer who assists an Arab sheikh in his quest to bring salmon to the parched wastes of Arabia; and the very different *Morvern Callar* (Vintage, 1996) and *These Demented Lands* (Vintage, 1998), both by Alan Warner, which are the best works of the most important living Scottish author of literary fiction. Ian Crichton Smith's *Consider the Lilies* (1987, reissued by Phoenix in 2001) is probably the best-known contemporary novel set amidst the Highland Clearances.

Poetry

Birlinn's imprint Polygon publishes *The Poems of Norman MacCaig* (2009), edited and collected by his son Ewen, and *Sorley MacLean: Collected Poems* (2011). Hugh MacDiarmid's best poems were published by Fyfield in its 2004 *Hugh MacDiarmid: Selected Poetry.* In 2007 Forgotten Books published a new edition of James MacPherson's *The Poems of Ossian.* Duncan Ban MacIntyre's poems appear only in various anthologies. There are several recent editions of Walter Scott's poem *The Lady of the Lake*—the most recent was published by CreateSpace in 2013—while Forgotten Books published *Selections from the Poems of Sir Walter Scott* in 2012.

Index of Literary, Mythical, Scientific, & Historical Names & Themes

Index of Places & Landmarks